The Mind Under Siege:
Mechanisms of War Propaganda

Alexandra Kitty

The Mind Under Siege:
Mechanisms of War Propaganda

Alexandra Kitty

Academica Press
Washington - London

Library of Congress Cataloging-in-Publication Data

Names: Kitty, Alexandra, author.
Title: The mind under siege : mechanisms of war propaganda /
Alexandra
Kitty.
Description: Washington : Academica Press, 2020. | Includes
bibliographical
references and index. | Summary: "Alexandra Kitty's vital new book is a
guide to the stratagems and techniques of war propaganda. When nations
go to war, governments need reliable and effective methods of rallying
public opinion to support their actions, regardless of the political
leanings or educational background of citizens. The Mind Under Siege
explores real life case studies and research in human motivation to show
why propaganda is more powerful, potent, and effective than other types
of persuasive messages. Reliance on primal phobias, and the threat to
reproduction, well-being, and life itself make propaganda a reliable and
powerful tool. For journalists and other news producers, Kitty's book
shows how to ask the right questions and avoid spreading misinformation
and propaganda and how to see more insidious forms of manipulation
and
narrative through psychological research and case studies"-- Provided by
publisher.
Identifiers: LCCN 2019055314 | ISBN 9781680531169 (hardcover) |
ISBN
9781680531190 (paperback)
Subjects: LCSH: Propaganda. | War--Public opinion. | Press and
propaganda.
| War--Press coverage.
Classification: LCC HM1231 .K57 2020 | DDC 303.3/75--dc23
LC record available at https://lccn.loc.gov/2019055314

To my grandmother

Contents

Author's Note

War propaganda has been defined in numerous ways over the years. Technology has made those old definitions obsolete, incomplete and problematic to studying its impact on individuals and groups. Social media has not just changed our thinking and habits; it has also pushed the boundaries of what war propaganda can now be considered. I strive to have a complete and current term, and have taken the past, present, and future to heart when operationalizing the phrase *war propaganda.*

For the purposes of this book, I define war propaganda as the deliberate, choreographed and strategic deep psychological manipulation of individuals and groups in order to gain mass compliance and uniformity of thought to rig beliefs in order for a targeted in-group to draw the conclusion that prejudice against an out-group is necessary and the proper action to involve violence, and war. The impact of the manipulation must be immediate, severe, and assured. The goal is to gain acceptance for troop deployment, bombing, torture, confinement, and to see those actions as necessary, just, and noble for the survival of the in-group.

It must also involve dividing people into a binary of in-group and out-group with the in-group seen as superior than the designated out-group.

Preface
The War Project

*If there's a book that you want to read, but it hasn't been
written yet, then you must write it.*

Toni Morrison.

War propaganda has interested me ever since I was a teenager.
The first time I realized how devious it could be was the revelation that
the first Gulf War's showcase atrocity of Iraqi soldiers storming a hospital
to kill newborns was a lie. That a weeping teenaged girl made up a yarn as
she hid her identity floored me. That a war could be *sold* by public
relations despite there being countless media outlets defied all logic. By
the time the Civil War in the former Yugoslavia broke out, I was still a
teenager and a university student, but I began to look whether this war was
also being *sold,* and the answer was sadly, yes. I was hardly the only one
who knew about it, but it inspired me enough to *study* war propaganda as
a psychology student, writing numerous essays as an undergraduate, and
then as a graduate student studying journalism. War propaganda was how
living nightmares were manufactured to destroy collectives, and I refused
to play along.

What I found most frustrating was the lack of resources on the
subject from the perspective a journalist: experimental psychology and
law enforcement had their own manuals and body of research to separate
truth from lies in their profession, journalism did not. There was no DSM
or CCM, even if there was a treasure trove of empirical studies that, if
brought together, could do precisely that for the war correspondent or
those taking wire copy and presenting it to a mass audience.

Yet I was left to my own devises to find the answers I sought. I
wanted to know why we believed those lies, and more so than true cases
of inhumanity. As a journalist, I did not want to infect the information
stream with those lies that could hurt people or forever alter and ruin lives

for no good reason at all. When I became an author, separating truth from lies became my quest and my calling.

So much had it become part of my identity that I always looked for propaganda by default. It can be a depressing enterprise as the powerful lie to maintain dominance over others at any cost, but there are times when what you see uplifts you. The Shaw Festival in Niagara-on-the-Lake has "Secret Theatres" where the audience has no hint or clue what the show will be about until they arrive. It is one of my indulgences, and in 2018, after a horrific personal year for me, I went to their final one of the season, as I refused to give in and was determined to live my life to the fullest.

The play was simply entitled *War Project*. It was out in a lush park in a beautiful and welcoming town that, as charming and peaceful as it is, has war and battle firmly ingrained in its identity. To my surprise, there were no actors delivering lines, just a single actor sitting off and singing songs on an acoustic guitar. There was no stage save the park with empty black boots strewn with scrolls inside each one. The audience was to walk in the field, go from boot to boot, take out those scrolls, and read stories from other members of the audience about the war stories they were told by their families, with plenty of paper and pens to include your own to a boot.

It was a profoundly moving experience, and one I noted that had not a single propagandistic yarn in them. They were personal, and real. These were stories of sorrow, regret, sadness, trauma, and despite all the stories, ones where people did not see enemies: only the suffering and triumphs of others as they marvelled at their resilience, kindness, and resolve to restore peace once more. Far from there being Us Versus Them, these were stories about survival, shock, despair, and hope, all woven together, even in the fewest of words.

Those were the stories that have lasted in families across time and space. Not the lies used to create disharmony among us. It is those kinds of stories we need to hear. They are the reminder that we are far better a people than what war propagandists want us to become. We must never give in to those games, and it is the reason I am driven to write this book. When we are driven to hate and to fear, we need to remember the stories of tearing down the barriers and looking at those on the other side as people, not beasts.

We can restore our humanity, but we should never drag ourselves into war in order to do it. This book is your guide to looking beyond the feints and ruses in order to find the most constructive solutions.

A note about the studies used in this book: where possible, I kept with literature which focussed on human behaviour. While there were studies showing the various animals had similar responses to our own, I selected studies dealing with human behaviour to simplify reading and make equal comparisons easier.

Alexandra Kitty

SECTION ONE
A Propaganda Primer

Chapter One
It's in the marrow

When the winds of war speak to us, it often reflects collective rage and fear that has been left unchallenged for too long in the minds of too many. The culmination of both hate and terror begin to blind us and we begin to justify our worst tendencies as being self-preserving ones.

We see destruction as creation. We justify evil as morality. We see war as peace.

Worst of all, we see lies as truth. Those winds have the ability to confuse the collective with a single blow, and then we can no longer orient ourselves: what is down is up and what is up is down. Inside is outside, and outside is inside. Light and dark are interchangeable to us. Our sense of right and wrong becomes displaced, we confuse sophistry with logic, and we are no longer rational or logical citizens of peace. We become feral animals primed to see our survival in the destruction of our designated enemies.

We become gullible to lies as we turn skeptical of the truth. As Sun Tzu warned us centuries ago in his classic text *The Art of War,* war is deception, and its deception of choice is propaganda.

Most of us would laugh at the mere suggestion that we could be taken in and be incited to cheer destruction, torture, oppression, and mass murder, but history has shown us to fall for the same ruses time and again even when we have everything to lose and nothing to gain. How else do we explain mass compliance and support for the First Gulf War when the seeming testimony of one teenaged girl who claimed Iraqi soldiers stormed a Kuwaiti hospital to steal infant incubators, and left infants on the floor to die. It was just on one girl's say so that citizens are the world demanded action without questioning the logical inconsistencies that proved her story was a hoax.

As we will see in later chapters, it was not just a ridiculous canard that sparked the first Gulf War. It took civilian lives in the bargain, but it was hardly the last time the press would turn to engage in questionable reportage. The CBC in Canada convinced viewers that their camera crew and reporter were in peril in Syria when they walked in the darkness, shushing each other as their lighting was turned on as their cameras rolled.

Are we to believe Syrian soldiers possess super-hearing, but are blind to bright lights? How do we believe a report when the theatrics are filled with blatant inconsistencies?

We cannot count on any source for rationality during times of violence: social media has been a breeding ground for propaganda recruiting those in peaceful nations to come and spread violence, but so has the traditional press and governments themselves.

It is critical for citizens to evaluate information from every information outlet, from word of mouth to the Internet, as political operatives, vested interests, PR firms, and propagandists have developed sophisticated techniques to make the case for war from the grassroots forums posting to the nightly newscasts. Often, these are inter-related and coordinated affairs, as we will see in later chapters.

What happens when there is a collective breakdown, and rationality is scarce? Within the last few years, various media outlets have fallen for war propaganda, only to be revealed as vectors who polluted the information stream with deadly and destructive misinformation as dangerous as a plague.

It is not as if every war correspondent falls for propaganda, yet there are red flags which hint at a troubling tendency to do so. When there are complex and nuanced reports that sees human nature as it is, we can be secure that what we are getting is information, yet to do so imperils the chronicler. Daniel Pearl was kidnapped, tortured, and murdered for it. War photographer Dickey Chapelle died in the battlefield for it. Their work was not one-sided or jingoistic with melodrama with simplistic narratives which suggest someone provided a prepackaged yarn. Here, things are not what they purport to be, and images and anecdotes must be vigorously questioned with a high degree of skepticism as false stories are polluting the information stream with a false presentation of due diligence and vetting.

But what is more troubling is that those same false stories have been effective for *hundreds* of years, despite advances in information technology and the mass education of the public. Many people who read news or Internet reports (from wire stories to social media posts) do not think critically about the information they receive.

They believe lies as their xenophobic tendencies convince them that it is Us Versus Them, and not Us Versus Us.

We have seen what believing war propaganda does: it compels us to fight in wars, while ignoring more peaceful solutions that do not require death and destruction. We need to look no further than the second Gulf War of that had *New York Times* journalist Judith Miller convince the world that Iraq was a hotbed of Weapons of Mass Destruction. Her work was cited time and again without question, leading to war.

Yet Miller's *Weapons of Mass Destruction* did not exist, yet a single journalist's insistence brought bipartisan support for war, not collective skepticism nor asking where was the *evidence* of such claims. The social nets and cohesion of a single nation was destroyed as justifications began to ring increasingly hollow. Only after it was too late and it became obvious that those *WMDs* were never found did cooler heads prevail. The damage was already done and lives were needlessly lost.

Big threats to frighten average citizens is nothing new. False stories of rival soldiers cannibalizing innocents was used in the Second World War, and then again during the civil war in the former Yugoslavia, with no evidence, but few had the presence of mind to demand it. With so many wars sparked by lies, and real threats repeatedly ignored, we are rushed to make life-altering decisions while being dragged away from genuine atrocities. We choose governments based on misinformation, and support causes that can provide no solution to us or others.

How can propaganda – a system based on deception – be repeatedly successful for hundreds of years, despite advances in education and technology?

The answer is simple: it is in the marrow. Propaganda targets our evolutionary drives and our basest instincts, striking at our most primitive of fears and prejudices, often without our knowing that our deepest xenophobic terrors are being used to prime us toward destruction as our biochemistry is altered by the primal images that are paired with stressors.

Our very lives are threatened, and while we may see ourselves as educated and refined, propaganda is not successful because it appeals to our sophisticated sense, but the slumbering primitive drives that keep us alive as we hunt for our survival. It is in our spiritual shadows where propaganda lurks, and it goes into our deepest layers to prime, groom, and lure us to believe a swarm of psychopathic brutes are about to destroy us. We fall for our most basic patriarchal narrative structures that once served as our childhood bedtime stories. We deify our in-group and personalize each member as we demonize the enemy as erase their faces so that we no longer see them as human. Like science fiction novels that treat entire planets of foreigners as monolithic threats, we quickly turn neighbors into monsters as we forget they once were our allies and friends. Civil wars have torn people apart in a heartbeat, and propaganda becomes a force more powerful than an army with bombs.

Nazi propaganda was racist in nature, mutating images of African-American soldiers into simian-like brutes and rapists, while US propaganda did the same of the Japanese enemies. Nothing changed by the time the first Gulf War broke. All enemies are portrayed as rapists and murderers, turning average citizens into monsters to be destroyed.

How do we go against what infects our psychological marrow? How do we find the antidote that inoculates the public from falling for the traps of misinformation in the first place? Is it even possible?

The answer is yes.

We can study the structures and content of war propaganda and see how they function, how and why they are believed, and find methods of not falling for the rigs in the first place. So much of war propaganda is childish and illogical in nature that by learning to shift our focus, we can immediately override its brute force and dismantle its effects.

And we may be shocked when out-groups do not hold the same lofty views of our in-group as we do, and do not see our role in conflict as heroic or righteous. For example, when one US resident living in South Africa complained about the *New African*'s negative coverage of her homeland's coverage of the Iraq war, the response was a *cover story* in the magazine entitled *The 'hoax-masters' who have seized America* in response to her letter that the magazine had "overtly negative reports." Author Cameron Duodo began the piece in this way:

> I was amused by Ms Katie Phelps' complaint, for Africa is often maligned by the Western media. Now, I am not saying that just because they publish what we consider "overtly negative reports" about our continent, we too must do the same. What I would tell Ms Phelps is that if she had taken the trouble to read the articles she complained about, she might have found that they are all based in fact, not perceptions and prejudices, as Western reports on Africa tend to be.

We take for granted that our in-group are the good guys and cannot perceive otherwise, and yet out-groups take for granted that we are the *bad guys* and also cannot perceive otherwise. When we venture into the world of out-groups, we suddenly find ourselves in hostile territory where our actions are viewed with suspicion, and we have no idea why the mindset are the *opposite* of what we have taken as normal reality. Few of us can see the structures and mechanisms that always rig perceptions in favor of the in-group, or see that the reality of the situation is rarely what an in-group or out-group has decreed it is.

This book is your guide to understanding the mechanisms of war propaganda: from how it spreads to why it is believed in the first place. We will examine real life case studies of war propaganda over the decades straight though the modern age.

War propaganda is a special kind of communication: while it is deceptive and manipulative in nature, it also follows its own scripts and rules. It does not appeal to our intellectual functioning, even if it seems to at first glance. It is *primal* form of communication, and as we will see throughout this book, the kinds of horrors it presents are of the most brutal variety. In other words, it suppresses reason to provoke our basest fears and instincts.

Before we begin, let us orient our thinking by determining whether what report or article we are examining has the potential of spreading war propaganda:

1. **Is this story about two collectives with tensions, unrest, and violence between them?**: As there will almost always be a *narrative,* and one with patriarchal structures of a hero and villain, one of these groups will be seen as a hero, while the other will be seen as a villain by default. While this dynamic may be the case, it is also a red flag that information may be skewed, enhanced, downplayed, or omitted to make the hero and villain roles fit better.
2. **Is the story emotionally triggering?** If you feel compelled to take one side over another, it is another sign that there is more to the story than mere emotion.
3. **Are the heroes personalized or the villains seen as a faceless collective?** It is a sign that one side has made their case to the public without the journalists or chronicler looking at verifying information from the other side.
4. **Is violence implied as the only possible solution to the conflict?** If so, there is a good probability that one side is considering using war as a solution.

As we will see throughout the book, there are many other red flags to look out for and the reasons why they are red flags signalling manipulation and deception. These four questions should be the *first* ones to consider before making any judgements as war propaganda is a higher persuasive form of communications that is meant to stifle debate and critical thinking. But why is war propaganda so potent and effective? There are many reasons, but perhaps its greatest power rests in its swiftness of strength. Let us begin by examining the reason why propaganda is the most deadly and destructive of persuasion communications.

Chapter Two
Immediate is the message

Propaganda is a predatory, patriarchal, and antagonistic form of communications that is meant to create a mental siege where there can be no debate. There is a goal, usually for an institution or collective to grab power and control the terms of debate as it filters our view of reality. The longer it takes to persuade, the more likely alternative voices can begin to present counter-arguments and support for extreme measures is lost.

The message must be *immediate* and instantly effective.

In modern warfare, two instances of such ploys became apparent: during the First Gulf War and during the civil war in the former Yugoslavia. Let us take a look at the latter case first.

The civil war of the 1990s had a clear patriarchal narrative: the Serbs were the sole villains, yet the region itself was not a high-profile one, and of all the warring factions, the Serbs would be the least likely to be seen as villains given their participation in both World Wars. The First World War the Serbs were allies and their losses were proportionally the heaviest in Europe: one third of their population were killed in the conflict. By the the Second World War, they were marked for extermination by both the Croatian fascist regime, the *Ustashi* as well as their higher-profile allies the Nazis. The Croats made no secret of their campaign, photographing their brutality of beheading Serbs and running a concentration camp to exterminate Serb, Jewish, and Roma children in Sisak. The atrocities committed by the Croatian regime were savage, and not just against the ethnic Serbs: one Jewish man was sent to a Croatian concentration camp for the mere reason that he had a more enviable stamp collection than the region's leader. In another instance, thousands of Jews were sent on a train to be killed so that Ustashi soldiers could make use of their beds. While Serbs were the primary targets, they were not the only religious and ethnic group who had been killed.

Just as the Nazis recorded their atrocities, the Ustashi did the same, but unlike the Nazis, who were captured and were sent on trials for their crimes, the Ustahi were smaller, and many received safe passage to go to other countries to start again, or became part of Josip Broz's Yugoslavia, becoming one nation with the very group they tried to exterminate. For the rest of the world, particularly North America, there were no Serbs or Croats, only Yugoslavs.

It is important to understand that tensions in the region were neither addressed nor resolved, yet the nation saw ethnic intermarriages that seemed to show everything resolved itself, even if there were quiet signs over the decades that the situation was far more complex than Tito's regime implied, particularly as various regions and their ex-pats lobbied various politicians for their interests outside of Yugoslavia proper since the mid-1960s.

Yet when the civil war began, the narrative was completely different from the very beginning, but why when the region had not been on Western media's – or general public's – radar for any length of time? The quagmire of contradictory narratives delving into centuries' old feuds would not have been noteworthy to Western sensibilities. Most people outside the country would not have known the difference between a Croat and a Serb, yet were absolutely certain that "the Serbs" (who were treated as a monolithic entity throughout the conflict) were entirely the sole aggressors of the conflict, even if they did not know how the nation fell apart or why.

It was more than obvious that it was not historical record guiding their answer. It was not cultural or religious literacy as many media reports, including one ABC News "special report" erroneously labeled Serbs as "Greek Orthodox" (they are *Eastern Orthodox,* which differs significantly and follows a different calendar). Often, news reports were mislabelling groups, even if their uniforms unequivocally identified which side they were fighting for. Most who covered the war were not fluent in Serbo-Croat, nor knew anything of the history, politics, religion, geography, or culture of the warring sides, yet from the very start, said with absolute confidence that the Serbs were the villains of the war.

How did the press be able to come to such a confident decision so quickly?

The answer would lie in the preparedness of the various provinces in obtaining Western public relations who were prepared from the start, but unlike many other firms who usually do not speak of their ways in public, one of the firms – Ruder Finn – did, and the singular interview with a French journalist provided a tiny, but pivotal look inside the workings of effective war propaganda.

When Ruder Finn's Jim Harff boasted to Jacques Merlino in 1993 that his firm "managed to put Jewish opinion on our side. This was a sensitive matter, as the dossier was dangerous looked at from this angle" because then Croatian President Franjo Tudjman "was very careless in his book, *Wastelands of Historical Reality*. Reading his writings one could accuse him of anti-Semitism," as his book asserted that 'only 900,000 Jews were killed in the Holocaust, not six million.'"

Harff told Merlino that "the Croatian and Bosnian past was marked by real and cruel anti-Semitism. Tens of thousands of Jews perished in Croatian camps…[o]ur challenge was to reverse this attitude and we succeeded masterfully" as they "outwitted three big Jewish organizations — the B'nai B'rith Anti-Defamation League, the American Jewish Committee, and the American Jewish Congress." He also went on to boast that:

> …when the Jewish organizations entered the game on the side of the [Muslim] Bosnians, we could promptly equate the Serbs with the Nazis in the public mind. Nobody understood what was happening in Yugoslavia. The great majority of Americans were probably asking themselves in which African country Bosnia was situated.

The admission was a breathless one. Harff assured Merlino that it was the first message that counted as denials and restrictions had no effect, meaning that:

> …by a single move we were able to present a simple story of good guys and bad guys which would hereafter play itself. We won by targeting the Jewish audience. Almost immediately there was a clear change of language in the press, with use of words with high emotional content such as ethnic cleansing, concentration camps, etc., which evoke images of Nazi

Germany and the gas chamber of Auschwitz. No one could go against it without being accused of revisionism. We really batted a thousand.

Foreign agents who hire US lobby, public relations, or law firms must register with the US Justice Department through the Foreign Agents Registration Act, or FARA (their searchable database in available on Fara.gov). It has been in effect since 1938 as then government at the time wished to keep enemy propaganda out of mainstream circulation. Ruder Finn was hired by the Croatian regime to manage their image to the West during the conflict.

So successful was this campaign that Serbs became villainized in Western media regardless if they possessed evidence or mere anecdote. Cokie Roberts of ABC News compared Serbs to Nazis in an August 5, 1992 report, while one day later, both the *Orlando Sentinel* and *USA Today* published an editorial cartoon by Dana Summers of Adolf Hitler with the word "Serbia" as he infamous mustache.

Time magazine had in their August 17, 1992 edition, a cover story *Must It Go On?* a long and factually dodgy piece solely condemning the Serbs for the war, while using "proof" of their culpability a photograph of a mass grave showing those who were slaughtered in the war with the clear implication it was Serbs who killed their various enemies. The cover for the issue proved to be a gross misrepresentation, but it was not the only one. The problem was that the markers were crosses, not diamond-shaped as the Muslim markers in the area would have been, meaning the buried could either be Serbian (who are Orthodox Christian) or Croatian (who are Roman Catholic), but as they were all marked with *Cyrillic* writing, they could only be Serbian as the Croats use the *Latin* alphabet. The very article used a variety of propagandistic antidotes, such as recounting a small Muslim boy who had a wish of peace for Santa Claus.

An interesting story given that Saint Nicolaus is a *Christian* tradition, not an Islamic one. Whether the canard was true or fiction was never determined, but more likely it was a piece provided by one of several firms hired by the Bosnian or Croatian governments to manage their global image during the conflict. Not surprisingly, the only side not to have a PR firm during the war was the Serbs, explaining the peculiar and over-the-top lopsided coverage. Retired Canadian Major-General Lewis Mackenzie who was deployed in the region during the war, noted that the main reason the Serbs were seen as the sole aggressors was that they were the only side that had no PR front battling their public image.

Many Serbs assumed their history in two World Wars would vindicate them, yet that was not the case for several reasons, with the most important reason being that their rivals planned ahead, and gave their message *first*. Each side had their share of victims and villains, but once the prepackaged narrative was set, everyone stuck to the script, regardless if the narratives defied all logic, and as we will see in Chapter 15, some of the stories during the war defied basic common sense, yet were still believed in the mainstream press and other governmental institutions due to cultural ignorance and prejudice.

The stories became increasingly nonsensical, as *Le Monde Diplomatique* noted about the skewed coverage in hindsight in this April 2019 article:

> [Serbs] play football with severed heads, depose corpses, tear off fetuses of pregnant women killed and grill them," said the German defense minister, the Social Democrat Rudolf Scharping, whose words were repeated by the media…

Yet Ruder Finn was not the first US-based public relations firm to sell a war to peace-time public through journalists, and hardly the first to use speed to sell false narratives. Perhaps one of the most infamous modern cases came from the firm of Hill and Knowlton, who was hired by the Kuwaiti government to sell the idea of foreign military intervention against Iraq, who had, as John McArthur recounted in the book *Second Front,* the stories of Iraqi soldiers killing infants circulated through anonymous sources for days, yet US support for invention was low. The Kuwaiti elite had a reputation for decadence, and those citizens from other countries were not swayed to send their nation's troops to liberate them.

The idea that militaristic alliances and government policy could be marketed and sold by public relations the same way movies are sold to audiences is a stunning one. Military support can be bought, or at least rented with the right advertising campaign, yet Hill and Knowlton had done so, not with facts, reason, logic, evidence, research, or even pragmatism, but through primitive and *nonsensical* war propaganda delivered by a fifteen-year-old girl who falsely claimed during an unofficial US Congressional hearing that she witnessed a logical impossible atrocity in Iraqi. Her true identity was not disclosed, as it would have tipped off the public that her testimony was not as genuine as it first appeared. Chapter Seventeen will give more details of the hoax, but it is worth noting that the first wave of baby atrocities were reported as fact within the first couple of weeks after the invasion.

When it became clear the message did resonate with Western citizens, a second offensive came by means of a sympathetic teenaged girl weeping to the world using the same propagandistic tale; this time, instead of a faceless rumor, there was a young eyewitness who seemingly had no reason to lie or possessed any media training. As journalists received press releases and video news releases (VNRs) from the firm regarding Kuwait, they were well aware of the connection, but never disclosed it to news consumers who assumed that journalists received primary sources and raw information and did not use PR firms for their information. By the time *Harper's* publisher MacArthur revealed Nayriah's identity in a *New York Times'* op-ed piece, the war was over and the firm's job was done.

Hill and Knowlton had very little time to act; after all, had some other outlet reported on the PR firm's involvement or divulged the identity of Nayirah, the gambit would have failed. The invasion was still fresh in the Western public's mind, and with a fickle press always shifting their news pegs, striking with a powerful message must be done before the next potential scandal or celebrity stunt usurps attention and nullifies the impact.

Speed of the message is essential in communications is simple: there must be no room for a counterattack. In the case of Kuwait, they country was small and unknown to the Western Middle Class in the early 1990s: their value as a newsworthy entity was limited. The same held true for the former Yugoslavia, an Eastern European nation who at least held the 1984 Winter Olympics in Sarajevo, but had little else to distinguish itself from any other Eastern European nation at the time. There could be no room to orient and think, let alone think about something *else.*

Facts must not emerge in order for a narrative to be believed. Judith Miller's fantastical narrative about Iraq's *Weapons of Mass Destruction* hinged on the public feeling terror in *anticipation* of what weapons Saddam Hussein's regime *may* have been hiding, giving doomsday scenarios if citizens took the time to ask for definitive proof. Like the television special *The Mystery of Al Capone's Vaults,* of 1986 where journalist Geraldo Rivera built up suspense only to reveal an anti-climatic *empty room,* the WMD proved to be of the same barren outcome. There was public pressure to enter a war without any facts – but mere speculation that no one had time to debate.

Miller had a long history covering Iraq for *The Times.* Her 1990 book covered the first Gulf War; her own employer reviewed it with the primitive headline: "The Bad Man of Baghdad." By the time the second calls came in 2003, her work clearly questioned those who could not find those WMD by appealing to authority on January 24, 2003:

> In a speech in New York yesterday, Deputy Secretary of Defense Paul D. Wolfowitz made a rare public acknowledgment of the administration's reliance on defectors. He said, for instance, that defectors had told the United States government about Iraq's construction of mobile units to produce biological weapons.

> "Today, we know from multiple sources that Saddam has ordered that any scientist who cooperates during interviews will be killed, as well as their families," Mr. Wolfowitz said. "Furthermore, we know that scientists are being tutored on what to say to the U.N. inspectors and that Iraqi intelligence officers are posing as scientists to be interviewed by the inspectors." This was the first time the administration had accused Iraq of specific acts of intimidation against its scientists.

Her April 10, 2003, also presented a push to find the weapons at any cost:

> "Of course, we're disappointed that we didn't find a chemical agent," said Chief Warrant Officer Richard L. Gonzales of the 75th Exploitation Task Force who leads the mobile team. "But if we keep up this momentum, we will find it."

> At the same time, the site visits revealed weaknesses in the military's methods of reporting sites where chemical, biological and other unconventional weapons might be hidden. The visits also provided hints of how the political power vacuum in Najaf and other Shiite Muslim towns in southern Iraq was being filled.

The sense of urgency is meant to explain away why WMDs weren't found. So powerful was the first narrative that finding no weapons was ignored and the war went on as planned. Plot holes in a propagandist's tale must not be seen or else, the spell is broken. The longer the narrative goes on, the more likely someone will ask the question that exposes the flaws of the narrative.

But speed require simple stories or else confusion demands extra time to sort out the tale. The sides of Hero and Villain must be simple to spot. Victims must be pitiable as well as sympathetic. We cannot entertain the notion that both sides may be in conflict, but have both positive and negative qualities to them *both*. We are given a false choice in a world of Us Versus Them, never being allowed to see that it is really just Us Versus Us.

The Nazis had that idea in mind when they began to isolate their targets in the 1930s. There was a *problem,* according to the narrative, and one that infamous proffered needed a *Final Solution.* The very concept demanded *immediate* attention, and roused enough ordinary German citizens to take a horrendously murderous turn in order to be part of that dark solution. As we will see in later chapters, fascist propaganda may have been the most successful in terms of gaining prolonged mass compliance, but its methods have been used in modern propaganda campaigns as well.

The over-the-top stories are illogical: *they are forcing us to be cannibals! There are Weapons of Mass Destruction! The soldiers are killing babies!* And yet, we are so unbalanced and stunned that we dare not ask if any of it could be a lie. Who would possibly go out and deliberately lie when there are *experts* out there, actively vetting information? We do not consider that there are stories that do not lend themselves so easily to that kind of scrutiny or that our deeper biological drives blind us to certain kinds of deceit.

It is the reason why propaganda's most important task is of being the first to deliver a message. The messenger must control the rules of engagement and prevent democratic debate. Ruder Finn knew its clients had a fascist past that they did not disavow: had it been brought in to play *first,* their campaign would not have succeeded. So powerful was their message that mislabelled graves could be presented in an international newsmagazine and almost no one thought to point out the obvious flaw.

Being first also means that memories of events can be better controlled and manipulated through loaded language. Eyewitness testimony can be manipulated by a variety of means, and many times, even if the witness is aware of memories being implanted by an outside source, the damage is done. For example, Lindsay and Johnson's 1989 experiments found that subjects still believed outside factors that impaired their original recollections were still their own *memories*.

In 2005, Garry and Gerrie showed that false memories could be implanted in subjects by presenting them with *doctored* pictures of them during childhood (in this case, a fabricated picture of a childhood balloon ride), and though images served as a viable tool for it, *narrative* was still the most powerful method of achieving the same ends. In a separate 2005 study Garry and Wade showed it took as little as *forty-five words* to implant a false memory in a subject.

From vivid false recollections of committing crimes to false childhood memories, our memories are not accurate representations of events, particularly if a third party decides to intervene in the formation of those memories. They can prime us, focus our attention on the wrong things, and then write the script for us to believe.

When we are *bombarded* with stressful images and stories about outside threats, our memories will align to prime us to believe, even in the short term. The war propagandist usually does not a long-term commitment.

More fascinating is the ability to create false memories of fabricated political events. Frenda, Knowles, Saletan, and Loftus, E. F. presented subjects a variety of doctored photographs and asked subjects whether they recalled the event. The results were surprising, yet telling: conservative subjects were more like to falsely recalled former US Democratic President Barak Obama shaking hands with the leaders of Barack Obama shaking hands with the president of Iran, while liberals were more likely to remember US Republican President George Bush "vacationing with a baseball celebrity during the Hurricane Katrina disaster."

Neither scenario ever happened, yet when we look at the flaws of out-groups, we are suggestible to remember negative things about them, but not the false negative fabrications of our in-group. A war propagandist has the odds stacked in his or her favour: we are primed to believe the worst of our rivals, and should the manipulator strike first, we will recall whatever we are told to believe.

If law enforcement and prosecutors are grappling with the quality of memories of witnesses in a legal setting, we would expect others to grapple with it as well, yet questioning the veracity of sources – and the *audience's* memories after propaganda has been disseminated, has not been a priority in most communications fields.

We often believe that journalists will see the ruses, and yet there are troubling problems with the profession: it does not use academia to conduct empirical studies on how to better to their jobs, while those in crisis communications, public relations, and propaganda spend billions of dollars in research in how to improve their messages. It is an uneven fight on every level. While Big Tech companies such as Microsoft offer supposed "verification" tags such as NewsGuard, they have neither the expertise nor tools to make determinations, and have been proven wrong repeatedly in times of peace; what would get past the censors during war is a troubling reality to face.

Journalism is a peculiar profession without empirical rigors or attention to the mechanics of their discipline. Psychology has their *Diagnostic Manual of Mental Disorders*, where those in the profession have a guide differentiating various disorders in order narrow down the possibilities of affliction – including if the individual is *malingering.* Law enforcement has the *Crime Classification Manual* that gives guidance of the signs of various felony crimes and how to investigate each crime to find the perpetrator and the evidence to convict. We have no such manual for journalism or how to spot war propaganda.

Which is peculiar given that the global toll over the centuries because chauvinistic lies were believed are staggering. Our ability to reflect is suppressed and the consequences are death, destruction, and never-ending vendettas.

Yet propaganda remains effective precisely as it concentrates on reaction, not reflection in delivering propagandistic messages. Because the first message is the most important one (as Harff noted, retractions have little or no effect), the terms of debate are set quickly – too quickly, in order for an audience to weigh evidence and options to make an informed decision. The speed of propaganda is necessary to stifle debate and alternative options and explanations. How many could truly dare to challenge Miller on WMD? What if their skepticism was wrong? When lives are at stake, people will err on the side of saving lives, even if they are, in fact, causing more death in the bargain.

When we are evaluating messages to determine if they are, in fact, war propaganda, there are many questions we need to have answered:

1. **Is the message too simplistic?:** If it a story of conflict, what is the history between the two warring sides? What are their economic interests and what do they have to gain should they be completely victorious at the other side's expense?

2. **What public relations firms have been hired to spread their narrative?:** This may be the most important question to have answered. Finding out if one, both, or all sides have hired outside firms, lobby groups, and operatives to spread their messages will help you determine what much spin is involved. While many activist groups are legitimate and objective, others are manufactured entities conjured for the express purpose of spreading propaganda. To avoid a confirmation bias, it is important to look at every side in a conflict, and then confirm or refute whether they have employed professional help in spreading their narratives.

3. **Is there a sense of urgency and shaming of skeptics or those who wish for more proof?** Asking for facts and verification is essential to finding realistic and construction solutions that last. If reflection is being discouraged, it is a dangerous sign that there is a propagandistic whose narrative would fall apart on closer inspection.

4. **Have lines been drawn implying two sides are separate entities who are polar opposites of one another?:** In times of peace and prosperity, we are encouraged to see people as people. In times of peace, but discontent, we are encouraged to look for an "other" to blame as we begin to see phantom differences. When it is unrest or war, we are to believe that another group of human beings come from a vastly different planet. Whenever a collective is isolated and ostracized, we

know there is a war propagandist at play, working hard to build barriers to isolate a group in order to destroy it.

While the race to be first is crucial for war propaganda to work, it must also be effective in gaining sympathy of those considered part of the in-group as the following chapter shows.

Chapter Three
Mass compliance

During the First World War, Britain had its own singular revelation. The UK discovered that Germany had a propaganda bureau and was actively using it to win the perception battleground. The Brits decided what was good for the goose was good for the gander and struck back.

Wellington House was the UK's own war propaganda bureau and its mission was twofold: to cut-off German's communication lines preventing them from spreading their own propaganda, and ensuring British propaganda replaced the old guard. It was effective, and accomplished as much as did troops with lethal weapons.

However, in each case, *both* sides first worked on censoring the other side. Monolithic patriarchal structures do not allow for debate. One side controls the narrative of how the other is to be perceived and interpreted. Censorship is justified on moral grounds. The populace must be "protected" from alternative points of view. If citizens are not presented with facts that refute the propagandist's narrative, then they are less likely to question what they are told.

For example, the Nazis were keenly aware of the necessity of mass compliance and created the Reich Ministry of Public Enlightenment and Propaganda in 1933 to ensure their message was the only one Germans heard and heard *first*. As Joseph Goebbels, a former political journalist himself, assured Adolph Hitler after their 1932 victory, "The national education of the German people will be placed in my hands." It was not just news products that were targets of propaganda, but also their films, and the entire educational system as well from grade school to university. When those who were not born during that era wonder how could a nation turn irrationally xenophobic, they do not see that a propagandist creates artificial environments that are deliberately stifling and anxiety-producing, even if *they* are undergoing a version of it themselves. The Nazis were careful who could be at the helm of any communications outlet: only those who were deemed "pure" by their standards could remain. This ensured a single perspective would consistently be disseminated at all times. Nothing was left to chance.

The Second World War saw no shortage of propaganda posters and films: all with authoritative and definitive messages. The Nazis were not the only ones who used horror movie-like images to frighten their collectives into obedience, but they used it to incite their people to agree to increasingly disturbing state policies that confined them and ultimately impoverished and endangered them. Jews were the villains that were the sole cause of society's woe, making blacklisting, discrimination, and abuse normalized before rounding up an entire group – including *children* into concentration camps before the notion of mass murder became seen as *moral.*

Homosexuality was reviled as the Nazi regime required more potential workers and soldiers and breeding directives became normalized. By December 1935, Gestapo head Heinrich Himmler began a national program named *Lebensborn* (Fountain of Life) that encourage young "Aryan" women to reproduce and replenish their *breed.* The births were in secret and many women were unmarried. The goal was to boost the population of "pure" citizens to 120 million. When that did not happen, as many as 100, 000 children, many of them from Poland, were kidnapped and brought over to be *Germanized* instead.

In the span of less than a decade, an entire nation found itself supporting murder, kidnapping, racism, forced breeding, and torture. They agreed to their freedoms being revoked, and then agreeing to enter a war in which they could not win, perishing themselves as they were torn from their own families. The shame and global outraged after the war destroyed families as well as lives.

And yet, instead of a nation rejecting everything that harmed them and forever altered their lives, went along willingly, seemingly oblivious to the obvious flaws in the master plan.

Where was the voices of reason? How could so many people willingly go along with such horrific policies in the name of morality?

The mystery of mass compliance is one we still do not completely understand. We are primed to believe *first* messages. Our memories can be altered in short order. In one classic study, subjects all watched a film of the same car accident, yet the group who were asked about the collision reported *lower* speed estimates than the one who were asked about the *crash.* In another experiment, subjects watched one of two films of a bank robbery. Subjects who watched the film without a gun were more likely to remember seeing one if asked about *the gun,* rather than *a gun.*

If our memories can be easily altered, then so too can our tolerance for atrocity. We can be primed to accept it, and even *demand* it, if we are not exposed to multiple perspectives.

Debate and diversity of opinions works against war propaganda, and it is the reason why hateful messages must get mass agreement and reaction. If we begin to seek to murder those we are told stand in our way, but those we admire and respect snap us out of our delusions, those who gain by exploiting us no longer hold power, and they seek to cut off lines of alternative communications. Cults isolate members from loved ones who point out the ludicrousness of the cult's purported "beliefs" and rituals. Abusive spouses isolate their partners from their friends and family for the same reason. When the environment is artificially *rigged* to a forced outcome, we may begin to believe that is the only option available to us. Hitler understood this dilemma, and was strategic in his orchestration of shutting off opposing viewpoints.

But how does propaganda demonize naysayers, while suppressing individuality and necessary disagreement? There are several ways to do it. War propaganda targets the young. Mao Tse-Tung understood it as his campaigns were specific to young men in schools who were frustrated, and on the cusp of adulthood. Hitler targeted the educational system in order to reorient the population. The dreams and fantasies of youth have not yet had a chance to be disproven or humbled in reality. The lack of life experience prevents the psychographic from understanding its dreams for massive adulation and success have no chance of succeeding. The propagandist assures them that they *can* have all that they want, if only they rid themselves of the old guard who are "holding them back." Hitler appealed to youth, as did the fascists in Italy whose own manifesto, as we will see in Chapter 4, seemed to be the blueprint to paradise. It was merely a lure to sucker the young into subservient and expendable pawns on their quest for absolute power and control.

Youth have energy. They also lack life experience. They are strong and fully developed *physically,* even if their brains do not fully form until their early twenties, meaning that young adults have a differently wired brain that is ripe for psychological exploitation, particularly as they also have little life experience (known in some experimental psychology circles as "pseudo-stupidity"), making them psychologically the most vulnerable to such messages.

Youth are the prime target for "new" political ideologies, even if they are anything but new. Fascism was geared specifically for youth and their demands, but mass compliance is predicated on a *greed* scam: followers are promised rewards with minimal effort. You will be *given* things.

Contrast the false promises of fascism to a short-lived by iconic European art movement at the turn of the twentieth century: *Jugendstil* or Art Nouveau saw young artists in Austria and Germany write *manifestos* demanding change and access to the markets their more established elders enjoyed. However, though some of those manifestos seem to declare *war* on the old guard, most simply demanded the right to have a chance to *work* to succeed. As aggressive as the Secessionists were, they merely wished for opportunity. Those peddling war promise utopia without risk, but then ask their followers to gamble away their lives with violence.

It game of false promises to secure mass compliance is a complicated one. Islamic terrorist groups of the early aughts recruited their new followers not by threat, but by *promise* of utopia and adventure. Their social media campaigns praised their target's bravery and implored them to join something bigger than themselves. It was only after they arrived in their clutches of their exploiters that threats, isolation, and severe censorship kept them in place in a dystopia as they were instructed to kill and risk their lives doing so.

Mass compliance involves cultivating an in-group to be deemed as the only correct, and hence, superior groups. All else are inferior villains of the out-groups. Youth are the prime targets as they are naïve, healthy, exploitable, and of breeding age. They have the energy to seek adventure, and are idealists whose reasoning skills have not fully developed. Their hormones often still overwhelm them, and their behaviour is easier to predict and control. They often have not been exposed to different ways of life. They are the war propagandist's most malleable and credulous prey, and as we will see in later chapters, war propaganda targets every fear unique to that psychographic.

But rounding up the flock is not an easy task or one that can last more than a decade. Sooner or later, reality itself becomes the voice of reason when every promise has proved to be an empty one, but by then, there is a body count and destruction all around the collective psychic implosions. Despite the cunning of many dictators and their resources (from Saddam Hussein, Muammar Gaddafi, Mobutu Sese Seko to Nicolae Ceausescu), their regimes ultimately lost and were humiliated. From fascist regimes to terrorist organizations, despite the infusion of monetary resources from wealthy benefactors to their military might, often to try resurrect their fortunes, but ultimately fail in the long term.

And yet, we have no shortage of graves that were created needlessly as young lives that had promise were degraded and destroyed as there were no voices of reason, just the winds of war spreading its deceitful messages all around them.

Whenever you are analyzing information about the goings on in a war zone or after a terrorist strike, there are questions to ask in order to know where to begin verifying that information:

1. **Is the target audience in danger of being isolated and ostracized if they wish for more evidence?:** If response to questions is to shame or malign, it is an logical fallacy known as the personal attack and it is a red flag that there is a narrative used to bolster scant information. If accusations of treason are lobbed at those merely looking for deeper intelligence, it is a troubling sign that the narrative given is war propaganda.

2. **Are racist or bigoted stereotypes being used to describe an out-group?:** If the in-group begins to describe an out-group with the definite pronoun *the,* it is a red flag that the argument will hinge on an appeal to bigotry. When a mosaic of people are described in monolithic terms, it is done so in order to

make the real or perceived threat larger and more dangerous than it is.

3. **Is there other logical fallacies such as Sink or Swim, the Strawman Fallacy, Appeal to Authority, or the Confirmation Bias being presented as fact?:** If the threat is genuine, then the facts alone will be enough to inform an in-group of dangers. If there is over-reach by using an argument fallacy, it is a sign that either information is incorrect, fabricated, or an in-group institution sees an opportunity to gain mass compliance for other purposes.

Chapter Four
Special messages

It is not as if the structure of war propaganda is strictly confined to mass indoctrination. In fact, much of the same elements can be found in narrative "choose your own adventure" type video games where the same kind of forced choices and narrative weaknesses are frequent. For example, *Until Dawn* is a popular 2015 horror survival game that mimics the tone, primal threats, and even archetype of "survival" cannibalism that leads to the evil transmutation. The demonic monster in the game – the human-consuming *wendigo* is of the same facial structure as many Second World War propaganda posters, not surprising as the fabled creatures have been in Native North American lore for centuries, indicating that the monsters have a deeper and more primal base in our psyches; however, in the game, the central wendigo villainess is targeting a small in-group of friends who turned on her when she was in her original human form.

In fact, the game's central theme of the *Butterfly Effect* is the quiet threat that the tiniest misstep or immoral slip will absolutely result in the death in one or all of the central protagonists. The survival cannibalism tales have been used in war propaganda, including unsubstantiated reports during the Yugoslav conflict and were common in both World Wars. Once the central antagonist succumbs to being forced to feast on human flesh (her deceased twin sister, no less), she becomes possessed and primed to kill, even though she still retains *feelings* for her surviving brother, and unrequited love – but the monstrosity that she has become overrides her humanity and she alone can track down and slaughter her former friends with ease unless they try to stick together and build stronger ties with one another. The game's base is parallel to classic war propaganda using much of the same psychological drives and fears, with the difference it is mere disposable entertainment, but it is interesting to note that replaying the game is encouraged through multiple endings: we can see what happens to a group when we *fail* to follow the rules of the game.

What is also interesting to note is while the villainess is the butt of a cruel retaliatory prank by her and her sibling's dislikable friends as a punishment of her scheming to steal the boyfriend of one of the group of friends and has some sympathetic qualities at the preface, she is ultimately *deceitful* and premeditated in her scheme to snag a boy who is already spoken for and puts her plan into action once her emotionally-troubled older brother is passed out drunk in another room. She has taken quizzes to see how to best take him. She gets a tattoo to appeal to his bad boy disposition. She is ready to bed him at the first opportunity. If her scheme occurred at the *end* of the game rather than the beginning, she would be a reviled villain as her companions would be lauded for exposing her by means of a ruse.

When she and her sister vanish for good that night after she calculatedly runs away in hopes of still snagging the boy she covets, her brother feels helpless and concocts a plan of non-lethal revenge that goes horribly awry. If he survives to the end of the game (*Until Dawn*, naturally), his now monster sister recognizes him, and takes him away to the same cave to meet her fate, knowing he will be forced to commit the same sin and be trapped in a fate worse than death. Though he is also sympathetic, he is nevertheless *duplicitous* and calculating by nature, targeting both those who were involved in the fateful prank, but also those who were innocent, and is the only protagonist character who can be turned into the same monster as his younger sister. None of the other seven playable in-group characters are ever placed in such a situation, and the villain's moral twin dies instantly, and is never made to be a monster. In fact, every character that turns into the beast did not just perform cannibalism – they were deceitful prior to the ultimate sin (one of the earlier ones, Billy Bates, was a trapped miner who had an affair as he cheated on his wife. He and the other surviving miners kept the charade of being "miracle" men in the press. Even in the game's prequel *The Inpatient,* the player's roommate in the sanitorium is a doctor *feigning* to be a patient to observe the journalist who was caught looking for the truth. Eventually, if the player does not become the wendigo, the doctor does. It is a *prerequisite* that to turn into the lethal and feral enraged beast, one must already have been *untrustworthy* to begin with).

The other characters in *Until Dawn* can either live or die, but not be turned into a beast, even if bitten by one. In the end, it is Us Versus Them, with Them being the *beasts* that must be defeated by Us, the player. We have the same mechanisms at play, just a different venue or purpose. Games are to entertain, while propaganda is to manipulate; however, the line between both is a narrow one that can vanish should social or geopolitical circumstances take a turn for the worse.

But even with other sort of video games, there are propagandistic assumptions. Another popular game *Life is Strange* has a female protagonist who has the ability to go back in time to alter her actions to change an outcome; in this case, she tries to prevent her town from being decimated in a storm where everyone perishes. Again, this is a game with the Butterfly Effect in full play, and she discovers, quite inexplicably, that the only way to save the town is to allow her close friend to be shot to death. She reveals this dilemma to her friend who seems *supportive* if she chooses to let her die, yet the player is not offered other methods of phoning in a false threat of mass violence in order to evacuate the town right before catastrophe hits.

In both cases, the message is clear: our personal feelings or ideas of morality do not matter or serve as any internal barometer of what is just, even though the narrative has too many flaws to be credible, and the forced choices ignore countless other solutions that can balance the needs of individuals and collectives as well as competing collectives. The structure of games are innately competitive and antagonistic. So, too, is war propaganda. Our drive to compete and be victors are constant factors that we often ignore as we fail to question how those drives can be exploited by others to serve their own ends at our expense.

So much in common games have with the structure of war, that even the video game *This War of Mine* was based on accepted narratives of the Yugoslav conflict: civilians must survive and make grim choices that seem logical if we do not ask questions. While many "shoot 'em ups" have militaristic elements, it is the survival horror genre that is more closely aligned with war propaganda, while shooter games merely hone techniques of aiming and firing.

Why does war propaganda messages differ from other, more mundane forms of communications? What is so special about it than other forms of advertising or mundane reportage?

The one-way nature of propaganda encourages false and forced choices, for one. We must either slaughter a threat or the threat will slaughter and confine us. We have no other alternatives. The enemy is a disease that destroys, not unlike a fictional zombie outbreak. If anyone should question an authority's decreed militaristic-based solution, the skeptic will automatically face unwanted accusations of disloyalty to the in-group. Sometimes the skeptic will be accused of psychopathic selfishness that enables the helpless in-group to be vilely slaughtered by the out-group. Or the skeptic will be accused of gross naïveté.

When the 9/11 attacks shocked Americans, then US President George Bush had a simple answer to any potential voice of caution: "Every nation, in every region, now has a decision to make. Either you are with us, or you are with the terrorists." It is classic sink or swim, and makes certain that those not in a position within the sanctioned authority have no ability to ask questions about what course of action could be taken that does not involve war. We are bound to a single solution, and to suggest otherwise is seen as treasonous.

Yet argument fallacies are the back-bone of war propaganda. We must deploy troops are be taken prisoner (the aforementioned sink or swim), our government has intelligence that must be true (appeal to authority), or the enemy is evil and we are not (confirmation bias). We are encouraged not question what we are told, and go along with solutions that can potentially kill us. Propagandists do not seek opposition to their decrees: they require conformity. As they rile up the masses to be afraid and hateful, they control the optics as they manipulate their targets. Al Qaeda and ISIS both concentrated on inciting their recruits into killing in the name of morality and heroism. None of the young men who left the comforts of their home questioned their forced choices as they believed they were recusing others and were guided by spiritual reasons. Many perished, while others were captured, and taken back home to be tried and sentenced to prison. None of these young men saw the refuting evidence that bombing and confinement is not a sign of a peaceful or moral intent. They were encouraged to leave home and sever all ties with those who would have provided a counterpoint to the heroic narratives that lured them in the first place.

The primal nature of propaganda also has much in common with the horror genre, whether it be films or games. Both show how vulnerable we cane be. Freddy Krueger invaded our sleep. Jason Voorhees slaughtered naughty teens in the wilderness. All it takes is a single misstep and everything is lost. To be free is a sin that is punishable by death, and the stern warnings of authority must be adhered to as those without experience have made a mess of things with their ways and must now submit and do their penance by becoming as violent as the threat. The horror genre is geared to the young – those old enough to fight in wars, and presents threats to their lives as it serves as a morality tale to keep them equal parts frightened, violent, and sexually aroused.

Because traditional press were also gate-keepers, their one-way communications structure prevented skeptical and dissenting voices from speaking or from having any sort of control of the message. When Hill and Knowlton presented a teenaged girl making her bogus claims, we did not see her before or after her performance. What we saw on television was all we were given. Print, radio, and television did not allow from opposition. If an out-group was labeled an enemy, they had no means to correct a record or challenge the narrative. Propaganda could flourish and falsely equate authority and ubiquity with reality. Traditional media prevents two-way communication, but that would seemingly change with the introduction of the Internet and more importantly, social media.

It has changed the dynamic to a more back and forth dynamic, and yet, even its confines have shown the sturdiness of propaganda. With the ability to bypass the legacy media as the middleman, political operatives can disseminate through social media, freely recruiting new flocks into their in-groups, use shaming and abuse to silence opposing voices, and give the appearance of natural and organic grassroots reactions. As author Ginger Gorman recounted in her book *Troll Hunting*, abusive misogynistic online behaviour was well co-ordinated and targeted dissenting voices as a *campaign.* These were not average people who were going after dissenting voices: these were operatives who were issued decrees and followed orders.

Because there are no empirical verification standards for social media, propaganda can flourish by giving the appearance of numbers. Fictitious followers are purchased. Ghostwriters and publicists craft social media replies. Photos can be doctored. Operatives can target and abuse opposing voices as they shame and ridicule in a public forum. While traditional media thrived in presenting a false narrative of the One, social media has been exploited to present a false narrative of aligned Infinite. As neither have ever taken war propaganda – or any sort of potential deception and manipulation – into consideration, media has always been vulnerable to war games.

Technology not only does not prevent such messages from being questioned, in fact, greatly helps those messages to control free thought. Governments in 2019 have made calls for regulation and control, yet have not proposed any empirically-based measures to ensure that facts are verified, paid interests cannot rig narratives, or that propaganda of any origin be exposed immediately.

The measures are not based in research, but reaction and folksy logic as those making demands do not seem to know what separates these types of exploitative communications from other types of communications. If we do not know the differences, then how can we trust *any* government or corporate measure? Not even journalists know the difference, and yet those who study it have provided roadmaps into those differences, even if they, too, are not entirely aware the significance of what they have discovered.

Take Herbert Paul Grice's theory of personal communications, for instance. His theory on conversation implicature is elegant, yet not fully explored. At its most basic level, he offered four qualities for good conversation:

> **Quality:** What the speaker says is the truth.
>
> **Quantity:** What the speaker says is informative, but is no more informative than is needed.
>
> **Manner:** What the speaker says is clear.

Relation: What the speaker says is relevant.

We know that useful conversation requires simplicity, but how does war propaganda also take advantage of it?

By *reversing* the roles of speaker and listener. The base implicit assumption of Grice is that the speaker is taking the listener's needs in mind, not his own. Grice assumes the message is you-centred. Propaganda's goals are me-centred: the point is not to tell, but to sell. Propaganda is not about *Quality.* It deceives. Its *Quantity* is not about being informative, but manipulative. Its *Manner* is about creating confusion, not clarity.

But it is about *Relation:* it is relevant, but only to the goals of the propagandist.

Yet it must *appear* to be about the other three. It must appear truthful, informative, clear, and relevant to the audience, meaning these are qualities can be *mimicked.* We can make a propagandistic message seem superior to one that genuinely follows the rules of Grice. A speaker needs to be able to discern the genuine artifact from its imitations.

It is this precise point where our exploration of war propaganda must begin. If we do not know the difference between the real and the fake, then we are stuck in a vortex. If we can see the difference, then the vortex ceases to exist. As with many past cases of war propaganda, what seemed real was anything but reality. History has repeatedly shown us that deception is chosen over veracity to our destruction.

The Second World War is a frightening testament to it. The Fascist Manifesto was not a large document when it was first published in Italy in 1919, but a substantial portion of it seemed to offer youth very progressive ideals:

> *Italians! Here is the program of a genuinely Italian movement. It is revolutionary because it is anti-dogmatic, strongly innovative and against prejudice.*
>
> *For the political problem: We demand:*
>
> *(a) Universal suffrage polled on a regional basis, with proportional representation and voting and electoral office eligibility for women.*
>
> *(b) A minimum age for the voting electorate of 18 years; that for the office holders at 25 years.*

(c) The abolition of the Senate.

(d) The convocation of a National Assembly for a three-years duration, for which its primary responsibility will be to form a constitution of the State.

(e) The formation of a National Council of experts for labor, for industry, for transportation, for the public health, for communications, etc. Selections to be made from the collective professionals or of tradesmen with legislative powers, and elected directly to a General Commission with ministerial powers.

It did not advocate oppression. It seemed to do the opposite:

For the social problems: We demand:

(a) The quick enactment of a law of the State that sanctions an eight-hour workday for all workers.

(b) A minimum wage.

(c) The participation of workers' representatives in the functions of industry commissions.

(d) To show the same confidence in the labor unions (that prove to be technically and morally worthy) as is given to industry executives or public servants.

(e) The rapid and complete systemization of the railways and of all the transport industries.

(f) A necessary modification of the insurance laws to invalidate the minimum retirement age; we propose to lower it from 65 to 55 years of age.

It also seemed to demand equitable redistribution, yet it is here where the "demands" seem to get murky:

For the financial problem: We demand:

(a) A strong progressive tax on capital that will truly expropriate a portion of all wealth.

(b) The seizure of all the possessions of the religious congregations and the abolition of all the bishoprics, which constitute an enormous liability on the Nation and on the privileges of the poor.

(c) The revision of all military contracts and the seizure of 85 percent of the profits therein.

We can see a clear Us Versus Them divide. The manifesto is not about how *we* as a society can negotiate or improve: there are demands, and there are enemies who must capitulate to those demands as if they were some sort of out-group. There is no introspection, and no consideration of whether those making the demands may have contributed to the problems that plagued their nation. Yet still, it is difficult to imagine that such a beginning would result in censorship, oppression, submission, and slaughter, yet the lure is to appeal to youth and promise their in-group paradise if they are willing to add their number to the list of demands. Cults offer divine salvation, but politics offers the pragmatic means to obtain some version of it.

But that is not the only manifesto to offer the same promises. In 1848, *The Communist Manifesto* played the same gambit: it targeted the young. It presented a narrative of Us Versus Them, dividing people by their socioeconomic status where the in-group of one group were to go against those in the out-group. It is patriarchal and does not consider alternative ways of ending poverty, for instance. It identifies as it demonizes certain groups.

The in-group is special: it is being denied as it is moral and worthy. The out-group are villains who keep what is owed to the in-group. We plant the seeds of destruction when we begin to separate groups with one deemed superior to the other.

It is at this second point where we must follow another line of inquiry: if our first task is to learn how to separate truth from lies, then the second is to stop seeing collectives as *Them,* but as *Us.* Propaganda exploits by creating false *Thems* to fear and hate: if we cease looking at others as *Others,* then we can begin our journey into learning what is truth and what is a lie – and how and why we confuse them too often.

We can often start to see a set-up or preface to war propaganda, or a "foot in the door" message used to bait an audience into becoming credulous and trusting pawns. Whenever we are presented with information about unrest, we must ask the following questions in order to determine whether the message has propagandistic intent:

1. **Does the message divide people into a binary paradigm?:**
   If the groups are being divided, is the designation arbitrary? Does it create a pecking order whereby one group is deemed superior to another? Sometimes the division is based on beliefs or values, and other times, it is based on geography or

nationality. If the purpose is to pit two groups against one another, the reports will stick to strictly *contrasting* mechanisms to show differences, and not *comparing* ones to show similarities.

2. **Are stereotypes and generalizations being used to describe the groups?:** Unless there is real and verified empirical or historical evidence to show differences among groups, most accounts may be an attempt to isolate or malign one group at the expense of another.

3. **Is one group being blamed for a problem for another group?:** If there is a set-up of Us versus Them, there will be accusations of the targeted group being completely at fault for the other group's troubles. If the solution hinge on abusing another group with the assumption that all wrongs will be righted with a happy ending, it is red flag that darker intent is behind the campaign. Most problems are complex and involve multiple groups, and even if all parties should make changes, there will be new problems that arise as the world changes. A simplistic narrative of blame is the backbone of war propaganda.

Propaganda is a special kind of message that wants us to see the world in a false binary as we believe false narratives. Once we reject propaganda's demands and decrees, we can finally begin to explore it without being beguiled by its manipulative messages, because its power can fool us with one strike, as the following chapter explores.

Chapter Five
One strike

There is a peculiar quote many journalists have employed when confronted with a lie they have disseminated during war. They will cite US Senator Hiram Johnson when he allegedly said that the first casualty of war is truth. There is even book entitled *The First Casualty: The War Correspondent as Hero and Myth-Maker from the Crimea to Iraq*, directly citing the quote.

Except Johnson may not have said it, or even said it that way. It is an apocryphal-based excuse, and it is strange that a profession, whose mandate is to find truths to give an accurate and reliable account of reality no matter what the circumstances (particularly when it counts the *most,* as is the case of *war*), see truth as a *casualty*, not a hostage that journalists must find and *liberate.* Why do we settle for the lies of propaganda instead of the truths of reality?

For one, finding the state of reality takes risk. If war is deception as the *Art of War* told us, then the keys to peace is finding the truth, making journalists professionally obligated to ensure what they have presented is truth in order to bring a lasting peace. Otherwise, spreading lies is an act of violence that prolongs the deception, but those who are deception-mongers (and that is what a war-monger is), will do anything to prevent the truth from coming out, yet will seeks ways of amassing as much truth as they can on others to keep their fortress from crumbling. *Wall Street Journal* reporter Daniel Pearl was one who sought truths in dangerous areas, and was kidnapped and then executed on February 1, 2002 for it by terrorists in Pakistan. War photographer Dickey Chapelle was killed in the line of fire in Vietnam on November 4, 1965. What is the most valuable of information is hidden and the means to keep it hidden is by misdirection or psychological sleight of hand known as propaganda. Often, the truth of deceptions is on the battlefields, but other times, it is in the offices of corporations and governments that keep those secrets hidden in times of peace, but also war. French journalist Jacques Merlino did not have to venture on the battlefields in the former Yugoslavia to see the truth – he saw it in a Washington, DC PR firm office. *Harper's Magazine* publisher John MacArthur merely made a phone call.

For another, it takes training to spot deceptions and expose them. While PR firms and political strategists spend millions on honing and perfecting their campaigns, journalists do not. They do not have empirical methods to counter those ruses. Forensic psychiatrists, police, and experimental psychologists do, but they are not geared to a mass or general audience, and during times of war, they are not the ones the public looks to for information.

Finally, more times than not, it takes a willingness to even the battleground with information, and not appeal to authority who are the ones who gather intelligence and create the campaigns, even in times of peace. WikiLeaks founder Julian Assange, exposed global governments through computer hacking, exposing many important and shocking campaigns and information that ran counter to sanctioned narrative, but found himself running counter to the law. After spending seven years in Ecuador's London embassy, he was arrested for hacking, but his woes were exploited by some in the press who used his plight to argue the press is at risk (implying the press was also risking their freedom by hacking into the servers of elites), with AFP making curious assumptions in an April 12, 2019 article entitle "WikiLeaks set 21st century model for cyber-leak journalism":

> Using cryptography and virtual drop boxes, Julian Assange's WikiLeaks created a revolutionary new model for media to lure massive digitized leaks from whistleblowers, exposing everything from US military secrets to wealthy tax-dodgers' illicit offshore accounts.

However, WikiLeaks' methods were nothing like their own – nor has the established narrative in the legacy press been altered since, making the claim dubious at least. The article suffers from a convenient *confirmation bias* as well, never considering how cryptography can be used by governments to leak favourable or slanderous propaganda without leaving a trace, or worse, having political operatives and PR firms also manipulate the system in order to hide their own involvement and bypass laws such as the US's *FARA*. The false assurances merely draw attention to how little the press uses critical thinking in their own simplistic theories of reality.

On the other hand, pro-Establishment journalists placed themselves higher up on a non-existent pecking order to hackers, as one Canadian columnist did in an April 12, 2019 edition of the *National Post*:

> That's the thing about journalism: We too may seek to shine the light, but we have to be careful, and there are rules — laws that should be obeyed, conventions that good practitioners follow. We may still be hacks, but we're better than hackers.

Journalists have spread war propaganda that has cost millions of people their lives, demonized the innocent, sparked and prolonged wars, and then shrug their shoulders claiming the first casualty of war is truth, nor do they question authorities or wonder why they are told certain narratives that are antagonistic rather than cooperative.

Yet the charges against Assange seem laughable against what corporations, particularly Big Tech and governments regularly do: quietly gather and sell "big data" on their customers without their knowledge or consent, follow them through their smartphones, and tailor-make their advertising based on their private and personal information. Amazon's virtual assistant Alexa have live employees listen to personal conversations. Smartphones track movements, and then present owners with targeted ads based on their movements, search engine requests, and even email content and conversations. Assange merely made the mirror a two-way one, and then was demonized for it.

The narrative was one that Assange was a "spoiled brat" who needed to be punished, never mind that the organization provided a rare window to see how governments and large corporations operated and saw the world.

But why is that of any importance to regular citizens?

When it comes to those same entities calling for violence and war, citizens need to be given more than narrative: they need to be given facts, and when it comes to war propaganda, citizens need to understand precisely why they are being asked to give up their rights, livelihoods, homes, peace, reputation, health, sanity, and lives. Yet we are rarely given a reason other than *you are either with the government or against it the way the enemy is against it.*

It is war propaganda that strong arms the skeptic into forced credulity.

Propaganda serves several important functions in the political, social, and psychological spheres. Politically, it stifles opposing parties. The regime in charge can make accusations of rivals being in bed with foreign enemies. It eliminates the need for arguments, debate, or proof. If there is a declared victory, it all but guarantees re-election, though there are notable exceptions, such as George Bush's victory in the First Gulf War did not translate in a second term for him, though the second Gulf War did do more than its trick for his son: in fact, it allowed his party to retain control of the House and the Senate during mid-terms, a rare event in American politics. War may tear people apart, but politically, it can bring internal rivals together, albeit temporarily.

There are social functions to propaganda. It gives many youths a *heroic purpose.* Propaganda *romanticizes* a soldier's life as we will see in Chapter 9, and translates military engagement with virility. It defines in-groups and uses symbols and rituals to strengthen cohesion. It simplifies what is acceptable and what is not. Rules do more than bind: they form predictable and unnatural habits. Citizens are easier to control and predict. The Nazis took a nation and gave them simply rules to follow. ISIS followed the same templates.

Propaganda reinforces the rules and guides collective behaviour to allow more social efficiency. In the US during the Second World War, there were not enough young men to work in factories to produce munitions; the solution was to encourage *women* to take up those posts through propagandistic icons, such as Rosie the Riveter flexing her muscle declaring that *We can do it.* What that "it" was had not been stated outright nor defined, but a young, comely woman with full make-up who was immaculately dressed seemed to imply the "it" was working grueling hours in a physically-demanding job and still be refreshed for a night on the town. So powerful is the conflicting image that even today, she is seen as a feminist icon rather than a propagandistic one who message was not of female empowerment, but forced female obligation to produce the weapons of war. Women were actively discouraged from pursuing careers unless it suited the male Establishment's purpose – and only then were they *permitted* to work.

Finally, the psychological importance of war propaganda is direct: it is to alter thoughts, values, opinion, perceptions, interpretations, and beliefs with a single strike. Free will must be relinquished, and it must be done so quickly. The in-group must be forced to weigh the options and decide the most prudent course of action is to comply. Rosie inspired women as did Uncle Sam. Brute force is used as both a threat and a fantasy: we submit, but feel that our individual submission will bring collective strength. We change our focus from the individual to the collective.

Why? Because war is not about individuals. That is the realm of crime and law enforcement. War is about violence against collectives, not one or a few citizens. It is larger in scope, and hence, shifts its focus. To go against a collective requires another collective. Our survival is dependent on the group. In survival horror fiction, the group is picked off one by one by supernatural forces. The threat is real, and when the group splits up, the carnage becomes worse. Fiction, however, is prepackaged fantasy for individuals, and eventually the Final Girl goes up against the evil force alone. That is what separates the horror genre from genuine war propaganda: with war propaganda, we are not allowing the individual to daydream about being The One who saves the day; we are demanding they sacrifice for the survival of their nation or in-group.

The focus is on the group's survival. It is not about the self. We must forget about our egos and worry whether we will be killed, maimed, or enslaved, and we are to not rely on our own thoughts, we need a substitute – the government or regulating authority.

Rosie the Riveter represents the effectiveness of war propaganda: in order for the pretty young thing to live, she must toil for the collective. She is a young woman of child-bearing years, and she is comely enough and fit enough to catch the eye of young men. She is not a feminist icon. She is not concerned with her rights, but worried about her freedoms should the enemy win. She is taking a risk by working a hard and physical job, but the collective need her to survive. She represents a biological argument that supports the collective, not an intellectual or individualistic one.

Propaganda allows a narrative that gives *reasons* to trust the authority – who must gain trust. Image is key. The ways of successful leaders was the focus of the theories of Niccolo Machiavelli, who argued that leaders were not to be beloved, but be feared. Hatred is reserved for the enemy, but the in-group leader must be stronger, smarter, and more powerful than the collective. The in-group must not only fear what is on the outside, but also on the inside. The leader must have an endgame, and victory must come at any cost – or, the end justifies the means.

Propaganda is one of the most powerful means available to a leader.

Sun Tzu, on the other hand, was writing about war, yet he might as well have written the manual for successful war *propaganda.* The most successful victories, he argued, were the ones achieved without fighting, meaning propaganda is not just targeted to the in-group, but more importantly, aimed squarely at the out-group. Appear weak when you are strong, and strong when you are weak, he cautioned, meaning you are never to tell your enemy the truth. Deception is an act of psychological aggression and violence. Fool the enemy into surrendering – or worse, embolden them before luring them for slaughter. These feints can be achieved by a single method, propaganda.

Not everyone who mused about war and propaganda were trying to game it to secure authoritative power, however. Noam Chomsky and Edward Herman's Propaganda Model, focussed on the mass media's influence on collective thought. It manufactures collective consent that would otherwise not occur through organic means. Propaganda is to come up with a strategy, and then force a collective to draw the same conclusion. Original or critical solutions are to be buried or ridiculed, meaning there must always be some form of propaganda disseminated in the public to keep them compliant – but war propaganda is the extreme version of it.

Jacques Elul noted in his complex works that propaganda set in stone and formed mass opinion. It altered the filter on our view of reality and rigged our perceptions and interpretations on a mass scale, but he was more concerned with the mundane formation of our collective beliefs to keep us in check. We are exposed to propaganda from cradle to grave and we do not see when it happens or how. We accept it as normal, and think what we belief is organic when it is cultivated carefully from the earliest onset. War propaganda is an extreme form, and is not of the same variety, but takes much of it as collectives are primed to accept certain truisms without question.

Brett Silverstein, a psychologist whose experiments were geared to discover a "science of propaganda" showed in studies that it took very little to create in-groups and out-groups. In one of his most well-known and powerful studies, random subjects were assigned groups and then asked to measure themselves to various out-groups on looks, intelligence, and the like. Regardless of the group, in-groups consistently rated themselves higher on positive traits than out-groups. The implication is clear: it does not matter who is in the in-group or how they came to be together, there are instinctually predisposed to see themselves as *superior* to others.

Garth Jowett and Victoria O'Donnell see propaganda as a more powerful form of persuasion – in the First World War, Hollywood's films were a concerted effort to present a propagandistic narrative to mass audiences. Propaganda nudges as it pushes the collective into reaching the conclusion the propaganda wants.

Finally, Sam Keen examined war propaganda in his classic book *Faces of the Enemy,* and also noted common threads in various propaganda, regardless of nationality, race, or era. We see out-groups as dangerous and homely brutes, not humans we can reason with or find common ground.

Keen's theory seems to be on solid footing: in one of the most peculiar non-wartime examples in the modern age, the 2016 US Presidential election did not just result in a hard divide between Republicans and Democrats: it was their mutual blindness to their own xenophobia that was shocking: the Right campaigned on "building a wall" as they demonized Mexican immigrants and claimed they were dangerous for the nation, while the Democrats accused Russians of political interference and claimed they were the ones dangerous for the nation. Neither side saw the irony or how their own prejudices sounded to other nations. Each side saw their chauvinism as just, not a weakness ripe for psychological manipulation for political gain.

Propaganda is no different than a magician or huckster's card trick of forced choice: it is far better to deceive your audience into believing they had a say over their choice than feel helpless and dejected when they need to feel confident and assured enough to go into battle and face weapons and armies. The appearance of choice builds confidence as the authorities nod their heads in approval and praise the intelligence and morality of their marks. Rosie can do it even if she has very little say over it.

She is not cowering in the corner feeling as if she has no say over her destiny, even if that is the truth of her circumstances. As we still have celebrities pose in the same way in the modern age, the ruse is still an effective one.

Each of the above theories has much to contribute, but we can delve deeper to find the atom of truth that can serve as an antidote to propaganda's insidious influences – after all, how is it possible for propaganda to be powerful – and often *more* effective as time goes on? Why haven't we progressed in recognizing propaganda that appeals to our ideals and ideology, for instance? We may notice the propaganda of out-groups, but when it comes to our own in-groups, we become defensive, and can accuse neutral parties of being in bed with our ideological or political rivals.

The psychological is tied to the biological, after all. Propaganda may appeal to our instincts and our subconscious far more than our intellect. We may come up with sophistry why we have agreed to risk our lives to fight rather than negotiate a more effective solution that does not create grudges and vendettas, but those arguments are never right, and rarely convincing.

The case that war propaganda may be a biologically driven rather than a psychologically driven form of communication can be made. Abraham Maslow's classic hierarchy of needs showed that our drives for survival come first and are far stronger than our need for self-esteem: we can only think about the latter if we have met the former. When propaganda tells us that an enemy will take our food and safety away, a different set of mechanisms come into play.

Propaganda must rely on both societal cohesion and self-preservation to be effective. If we are to survive (self-preservation), we must stick together. There are too many of Them for a simple I – it must be an Us, and a more primitive version of use. It is the scale-back, minimalistic version that is subservient to the collective, but to stand out in a propagandistic environment can be deadly.

As we begin to look more critically at messages about conflicts, we have many factors we need to consider before deciding if the message is factual or propagandistic in purpose:

1. **Do those who rely the message qualify it?:** Should the messenger make excuses about the "first casuality" or that a reporter's knowledge is thirty miles wide, but only one inch deep, you are being told that no one can stand by the information with any confidence. Whenever information has exceptions, justifications, and excuses, the credibility of the report is in doubt.

2. **Are symbols, color, or triggers being used as a form of misdirection?:** Whenever there is a lack of factual information, a war propagandistic will divert attention away the lack of data by using filler. Symbols of strength is one form. Emotional triggers are another. Color with vague anecdotes is still another. When looking at reports, begin to circle hard information and compare it to the number of irrelevant details: the more filler there is, the more likely the report is a form of propaganda.

All it takes is a single strike, and the enemy wins. The Rosies must make the bombs and the tanks to prevent that fateful strike from coming to fruition. War propaganda taunts the in-group, and gives them a face-saving *out* to justify their circumstances. It is not *You Must Do It!*, but *We Can Do It!,* after all, even if the audience knows they have very little say in the matter. The consequences if they don't are too terrifying to imagine, even if propaganda draws the diagram of the worst-case scenarios as the next sections illustrates.

SECTION TWO
The Psychology of Survival and Instinct

Chapter Six
The animal in all of us

Hasna Ait Boulahcen looked like any other young and comely woman in her early twenties. She had a penchant to wear a cowboy hat, wore revealing clothing, and spent a good deal of time on her smartphone focussed on her social media accounts. She had a troubled childhood in foster homes, and she was dubbed a "wild child" by those who knew her.

If anyone seemed to be an independent free spirit, it was Miss Ait Boulahcen.

When she died at 26 during a police raid in Saint-Denis, she was radicalized, and involved in 2015 Paris attacks. She her swapped her cowboy hat and flattering t-shirts for religious garb, and the free spirit turned into an ardent support of ISIS with a trail of pro-terrorist postings on social media. She was under direct investigation for drug trafficking by police when they discovered she was harboring a cousin who was involved in the plot through a phone tap that was already been in place. A police raid left her dead – and though the initial reports claimed she was a suicide bomber, her cause of death was labelled asphyxiation, though her family believed she was shot by police.

The Guardian took the initial report of her last act of violence as fact on November 20, 2015:

> French forensic and medical experts are examining what remains of the woman who blew herself up during a police shootout after the Paris terrorist attacks, believed to be Islamic State supporter Hasna Aitboulahcen.
>
> The Frenchwoman, aged 26, was heard engaging in an almost hysterical exchange with police shortly before she triggered a suicide belt, killing herself instantly.

She was described as someone who "always complained" and "refused to take advice", but the article emphasized her devotion to a terrorist group:

Her contact with the terror cell was of little surprise to those who had been following her...

She also expressed her admiration for Hayat Boumeddiene, the widow of Amédy Coulibaly, who carried out the attack on the the Hyper Casher supermarket in Paris three days after the Charlie Hebdo attack in January, killing four people.

BFMTV said she was "obsessed by jihad", but had never made it to either Syria or Iraq.

The *Independent* also used a moralizing narrative to paint a gory portrait of her:

It was an inglorious end for Europe's first woman suicide bomber. She failed to hurt any of her enemies, instead killing just herself and injuring her cousin, Abdelhamid Abaaoud.

And it was through intercepting her telephone calls that the security agencies were able to track the Isis commander and six other terror suspects to their last hiding place.

The last moments of Hasna Ait Boulahcen were truly terrible. "Help me, help me, I am on fire," she screamed before the explosion. Her body parts were strewn across the road.

But by a day later, the newspaper corrected itself, and by January 21, 2016, completely altered their narrative:

The family of the woman prosecutors wrongly accused of being a suicide bomber have filed a murder complaint after claiming she was a "victim of terrorism".

The *New York Times* also used heavy narrative in the November 20, 2015 piece on her death:

When about 100 heavily armed police officers and soldiers took position shortly after 4 a.m. Wednesday outside the building in the Paris suburb of St.-Denis where the presumed ringleader of the Paris attacks was holed up, a young woman appeared in a window.

"Help!" she shouted, according to the reports of witnesses. "Help me!"

But Hasna Aitboulahcen, a cousin of Abdelhamid Abaaoud, the Islamic State jihadist believed to have orchestrated France's deadliest terrorist attacks to date, did not fool the officers, who suspected a trap.

What is interesting to note is the updated article corrected the assertion that she was not a suicide bomber, but still made a reference that it "did not matter" as she would still be seen as a martyr.

The web of propaganda in this case comes from every side: Ait Boulahcen was radicalized and her illegal activities all collided together to seal her fate. She was a vector of propaganda herself only to be used as a symbol of propaganda by both the police and the press through villainization – and then some in the press went further, using the propagandization of her to push their own meta-propaganda to turn her into a symbol of victimization. Her truth may never be known. She had become a symbol co-opted by various conflicting factions, and mostly forgotten when it there was no more use for her.

But the Paris Attacks frightened the West. There were 130 dead in multi-stage attacks, and they were well coordinated: the terrorists struck during a soccer match, cafés, restaurants, and took hostages at the Bataclan Theatre where an Eagles of Death Metal concert was taking place. These venues targeted the young during their most leisurely and social pursuits. The message was clear: while Parisians are lax and leisurely, they are not paying attention to the signs of dangers, and can be destroyed with ease. The perpetrators of the attack, Islamic State of Iraq and the Levant, did not target hospitals, nursing homes, or any place where those who are older or sicker would more likely be found. There was a primal message to those in the West: our youth are more prepared than your own. The very attack was the most basic form of theater, and itself was war propaganda. While we often think of posters, songs, or movies as war propaganda, or even news reports, propaganda goes beyond the medium to deliver its message, and while Marshal McLuhan postulated that the *medium is the message,* war propaganda is not dependent on the medium to shape that message because its messages speak to our basest awareness.

The basics of human instinct and evolutionary psychology drive war propaganda. Without them, we cannot survive. Progressive nations focus on education, science, technology, economics, and politics, believing these are the keys to survival, but they are luxuries human kind has created to improve our lives, but any and all can be destroyed in a split second, and we are forced to rely on ourselves for our very survival. The

Islamic State of Iraq and the Levant proved it out in the open in Paris as they had very little resources and manpower compared to an entire city with police, surveillance cameras, and numerous other pricey safeguards, and in a blink of an eye, 130 were dead. Rhetoric cannot hide the fact that when there is an enemy determined to devise a powerful message, they will write it with the blood spilled of others.

Yet war propaganda need not be so gruesome or deadly to have the same impact. It targets our drive to live as it shows us our greatest fears, and we begin to lose our focus and scramble to find safety at all costs.

To begin our journey into creating an inner anecdote to war propaganda, we need to look deep inside our psyches. This examination is no simple feat. We are not dealing with a person in the inner core of our being: we are dealing with an animal, and a feral one we have neglected as we fear its violent and irrational behaviour. It often seeks food when we are not hungry, as it convinces us it is starving. It wishes to relieve its urges on anyone we find desirable, whether or not they are willing. When it is angry or feels threatened, it has drawn pictures in its cave, showing us how it wishes to unleash its violence until the person who is making us angry has been torn to shreds. When it is envious of the greater success of someone in an out-group, it wishes to take away their territory and their resources and enslave them as punishment.

If even for a briefest flash, the animal within lets its presence known. Society shames such behaviour and does not sanction it during times of peace, but there are times when states or individuals see the *benefits* of speaking directly to that frustrated animal, promising it to be unleashed and free to roam – so long as it does the bidding of its masters, and offers the moral or pragmatic reasons for it so the animal within doesn't feel afraid to come out and roam out in the wild. Those who protest the opportunity are seen as traitors to the animal within, wishing to confine it, and even destroy it. Peace becomes the enemy. War becomes the friend.

War propaganda is an insidious form of communications as it infects more than just the information stream: it creates a topsy-turvy world with its own primal logic that rhetoric cannot persuade. It has its own moral code. It has its own reasoning. It is not human logic, but animal logic. Those who do not wish to fight become an out-group – another enemy to battle. Intellectualism becomes deceptive lunacy and a plot to sabotage the in-group. Those who do not know the logic and language of the animal within merely succeed in bringing out the animal within and prime it to destroy all opposition. Virtue-signalling, conversational narcissism, and intellectual pecking orders – genuine weaknesses in a person's character – are exposed and become apparent, and the as the animal within is not an intellectual or social creature, sees the flaws over the well-intended pleas for calm, and rebels against the messenger, whose own animal within begins to stir and wish to dominate, creating a hypocritical rival in the process, and the antagonism grows.

Basic human evolutionary survival mechanisms gave our ancestors an advantage. If they built fires in the cold, they kept warm enough to survive. They could cook meat and ensure they would not as easily be felled by contamination. If they formed tools and weapons, they could improve their chances of survival. If they understood how to overtake a predatory threat, such as an animal or a warring tribe, they could expand and increase their chances of reproducing.

They had their own concerns to contend with at every waking moment. Our evolutionary ancestors were nomads who did not attend school nor had technology at its disposal. They had limited resources, and fought for their territory. From survival to reproduction, they had a minimalistic existence, but with illness, violence, and dangers all around them, they had much to fear. They had to hunt for their food, and there was no refrigeration. They had the crudest of medication, all of it from the plants and roots they had at their disposal, which could not cure most of their ills. Infection was deadly. Weakness could result in being sacrificed or expelled from the tribe. There was violence and domination. They were vulnerable to the elements. There were plagues and diseases. They were exposed to animals with venomous bite that could paralyze and kill them. Terrain was not cultivated, and they were at the mercy of insects and larger predatory animals.

There were numerous death traps, from child birth (still, in many parts of the world, a real threat to a woman's life, including the United States where mother mortality rates have risen for minorities) to violence to starvation and disease. Death was a way of life, and women reproduced early and often with many losing children to sickness and predators. Today, we have countless organizations demanding funding for children with disabilities, yet there was a time where children's fates were determined by their health and robustness, and those who could not keep up were *culled* directly, or indirectly. We often forget that modern views of children's value have radically altered even in the last century. We still have factories with child labor, and children are trafficked globally. The animal within still roams free, we have still progressed.

Primitive and magical thinking was part of that world. Human remains in Oxfordshire, UK were recently discovered, and even three thousand years ago, people were killed as sacrifice, with hands bound and feet removed. If humans were not slaughtering each other, they were fighting for their lives against the weather, predatory animals, and disease. To survive to reproduce and expand the in-group was no easy task. There were no social safety nets, governments, or charitable organizations. All the modern inventions we take for granted did not exist. You either survived on your own abilities and attributes, or you perished. There was no third option.

The animal within still thinks in those terms. Shouting "fire!" in a crowded building with still cause people to run over one another in panic. It would be safer and more rational to form a plan and walk single file to safety, yet at the first shout of danger, people die in stampedes as they claw at one another. For example, in December 2018, six people were killed in a stampede during a concert in Italy when the crowd began to panic when someone used pepper spray. Dozens were injured, and yet there was no need to for the *mass* over-reaction, but when the animal within panics, only frenzied heads prevail.

And war propaganda does its best to unlock and free those frenzied heads to control and manipulate them. The animal within must be kept off balance and over-stimulated with no chance to accurately assess the situation or question what it is being told. It is inexperienced, and in a world where we do not have to fight for territory or our next meal, it is has little training or experience, yet needs it to be able to keep the individual and the collective out of a manipulator's clutches.

When fear and anxiety levels increase with too many messages to process, less sophisticated behaviour and thinking emerges. Sensory overload turns into a threat. Hebbian theory accurately postulated that repeated firing of neurons leaves a trace, meaning new and stronger connections are made, creating a change in the brain. When we are taxed and overstimulated, our neurons are firing rapidly, decreasing our ability to make informed decisions. It is the reason why many people and animals cannot move out of the way when a car races toward them: the danger overwhelms their mind and they can no longer think from the internal lighting of their over-fired brain. When propaganda begins to fire externally to achieve the same ends, we are vulnerable as our attention is focussed on the danger, and we have fewer mental resources to begin to think skeptically or rationally.

British psychology Alan Baddeley's experiments on working memory showed our ability to think and remember becomes diminished if we have too much stimuli. When the stimuli are the threat of death or harm, we are being burdened. If a war propagandist adds to the mix, we may no longer be able to function and begin to stampede or become violent. The Paris Attacks were very different the Italian Stampede, yet if one concert-goer's use of pepper spray caused panic, then what did the attacks do to the psyche of survivors?

The animal within is not necessarily a brave beast. It has phobias, and many take little sense from a modern perspective. The fear of spiders or small animals, such as mice or snakes seems ridiculous in many regards, yet Hugdahl and Öhman's 1977 experiment showed that subjects who were paired with an electric shock viewing pictures of fear-irrelevant stimuli showed less anxiety and faster acquisition of a phobia than those who were given shocks viewing pictures of fear-relevant stimuli, such as spiders. Irrational phobias are not irrational to the animal within us – it was those animals whose infected bite could bring our demise, and it still feels the threats, even if antibiotics and sanitation have made those fears less relevant. Martin Seligman's 1971 concept of phobia *preparedness* theorized that we are born primed fear certain stimuli over others.

That may explain why we fear snakes and heights, but what causes xenophobia and mob mentality? Why are we willing to join on collective to destroy another?

Stranger anxiety is innate and begins to form during infancy, at approximately seven months to one year. Social Anxiety Disorder – and extreme form of stranger anxiety – affects almost seven percent of the US population. Xenophobia – or bigotry is still prevalent globally. While the FBI data has consistently shown that intra-racial murders account for 87% to 97% of all homicides in the US (depending on the race), there idea that it is more likely to be murdered by someone of a different race than your own.

In fact, we are more likely to be murdered by some in our immediate in-group (i.e., a relative) than a stranger, whether it is South Africa or the US (both nations independently studied had the rate at an overwhelming 80%).

Why do people distrust strangers or believe logically improbable hate-mongering? In terms of our ancestors, strangers guaranteed death. With scarce food and land, an invasion meant subjugation or enslavement, or war. The in-group may have exiled or killed their own, but to waste a human resource at the expense of expanding the group or having enough females to reproduce or young men to fight and hunt would could cause a group's extinction.

Even in modern history, we have seen attempts of the annihilation of smaller groups. The Kurds, Armenians, and the Tutsi have all been targets of genocidal policies. We have not gotten away from those who have decided the best way to expand one's territory is to rid it of other out-groups. They are presented as *threats,* even when their numbers are too small to justify the accusations, and blood is spilled for irrational reasons.

Our drive to stick "to our own" is also ingrained. The Propinquity Hypothesis indicates that we prefer those who are physically closer to us than those who are at a greater physical distance. It was safer for our ancestors to stay with those who are at a shorter distance than venture out in the unknown and darkness looking for better company.

Our drive to stick to those who are physically similar to us is another strong drive. In one 2016 study by Richter, Over, and Dunham, preschool children showed preference to their in-groups, even as young as three, while previous research placed the age somewhat higher at five or six. In 1965, Byne and Nelson's experiments indicated that similar attitudes were seen as more attractive in test subjects than those who held different ones. In one 2008 meta-analysis of 460 experiments, Montoya, Horton, and Kirchner revealed that similarity made a significant and large determinant of how attractive and likable a subject perceived others.

In the most basic level, Us seeks Us. We do not like They, and we define They as those who look and think differently than we do. We do not question ourselves. We seek to expand the pool of Us as we try to shut out the They. Opposites do not attract. They repel.

It explains why war and genocide still happen in modern times. It will keep happening, and it can occur in any nation at any time. Where there are tensions, there is a vulnerability where a propagandist can strike, and make mass murder seem noble and the only option available for survival. The animal within will be all too happy to believe it, yet if we begin to educate that animal, and show it love, respect, guidance, and strength, it will unleash itself without the need to destroy, taking away the propagandist's advantage to control and manipulate us. But how do we begin the process of taming a wild and primitive beast inside us?

By taking a closer looking at how we process information and see the world around us when we are afraid for us lives and feel threatened, we can begin to see the mechanisms of how war propaganda appeals to our baser human desires and needs, regardless of our educational level or political and ideological leanings. In other words, why no one is immune to war propaganda, not the professor, not the libertarian, not the atheist, and not the journalist or politician. War propaganda humbles us all as it shows that at the base of our brains, we are not individuals who are any different than our enemies. We will both fall for the lies our in-groups tell us when we believe it is our lives on the line. We may deceive ourselves into thinking that we rebel against authority in our own nations, but if we suddenly have a political affiliation with the *opposition* party and see them as our new in-group, then they become our authority and we are vulnerable to their narrative manipulations just the same, and when we are disenfranchised from them, we may assume our old enemies or rivals must be correct by default. In either case, we are making decisions by panic and not rationality, and we continue to be vulnerable to propagandistic messages unless we begin to learn how to train our basest instincts to use emotional logic to navigate where we fear the most, but where manipulators know how to control our behaviour.

Yet we do not know how to control our own thinking. We are not deliberate or skeptical. We do not ask questions or bother to listen to responses. In order to break old habits of credulous panic, we need to assess information to determine if our primitive evolutionary reactions are being primed to prevent critical thinking:

1. **Is the narrative structure set up to be an Us Versus Them Narrative?:** If so, we need to consider that at the very least, we are dealing with political propaganda, but in times of violence, we can add war propaganda to our checklist.

2. **Does the narrative imply that the safest course of action is to stick to the in-group for safety?:** Crime statistics repeatedly and consistently show that the greater danger lies with the in-group far more than the out-group. If the opposite is implied, we need to find what are the statistics of violence between the groups – and *within* them. We must compare and contrast these numbers in order to see how common it is to be harmed by a member of the out-group.

3. **Are primitive phobias being invoked to "sell" a narrative?:** Phobia is irrational and debilitating fear that impedes normal functioning and social interactions. If we are being whipped up to an irrational frenzy, this is a glaring red flag: the point of disseminating facts is to bring rationality and useful information, not fear to the point of dysfunction. This question may be one of the most important ones to answers if you are determining whether or not a story is war propaganda.

4. **Is a single person or event being used in conflicting ways by various groups to bolster their cause?:** A contradiction in narrative roles (hero, villain, or victim) is a sign that a person has become a tool to sell a policy or action. Information that is unflattering to the image will be distorted or ignored, and it is critical to look for evidence that confirms, but more importantly *refutes* the theory to give a more accurate account of the individual. In the case of events, we will often see the same group of players be called "freedom

fighters" by their in-group, but "terrorists" by the out-group. Look at the circumstances leading up to the event, and assume that all sides have done both good and bad in the situation. Keeping a balanced and open mind prevents a propagandist from luring you into believing a false narrative.

5. **Is the person or event being presented as a milestone for extraordinary evil?:** While it is possible someone is doing something wicked on a grand scale, it is also possible that the actions are being exploited to further an oppressive and violent agenda by one or both sides. Other times, the "milestone" is a hoax. It is crucial to confirm and refute information to obtain an accurate and reliable picture of reality.

6. **Is the subtext of a narrative that evil from an out-group is surrounding us?:** Like a game of Go, the object is to surround an opponent with enough stones in order to prevent them from advancing. Often, during military campaigns, this is the goal, but when that is not possible, the war propagandist will create the *illusion* of being surrounded. It is important to determine if you are being beguiled into thinking you are being surrounded by an out-group who has no intention or even resources to do so.

7. **Are the basest of human instincts being invoked in the narrative?:** If the narrative is that of a horde of feral enemies will come to starve and destroy, this is a sign of inciting a group to fear. It can be done by an out-group to psyche out a target, or by an in-group to, in fact, strike first and provoke violence and war.

8. **Does the story or information spark instant panic?:** If you are discouraged from thinking, analyzing, or questioning, you may very well be manipulated to panic and not scrutinize information for logical flaws.

We can begin to identify war propaganda by breaking down the narratives right away, but other times the information is inflammatory enough to alter our brain chemistry as the following chapter explains.

Chapter Seven
At the base of the brain

As author George Orwell wrote, "All the war-propaganda, all the screaming and lies and hatred, comes invariably from people who are not fighting." It is the ways of war propaganda: the point is to incite *others* to risk their lives in order to obtain something of value that is too large to obtain through mere strategy alone. When we deal with violence on a smaller scale during times of peace, police will search for suspects who have the means, motive, and opportunity to commit violence. With war, we do not look at the act in the same way. The weapons are those who are forced or persuaded to fight. It is not a normal act as it takes extraordinary circumstances to compel millions of people to sanction mass violence as a feasible solution.

Often people leave the comfort of their homes to spend years in horrific conditions without food or shelter. They must submit themselves to the orders and decrees of people of authority who do not see the dangers that those on the front line see, but expect obedience regardless. Supplies will be lacking, intelligence dodgy, and there may be cultural and language barriers making the situation worse. From air strikes to landmines, there are dangers and threats, and this does not factor in disease or psychological trauma that may induce a soldier or veteran into ending his or her own life. In 2018, fifteen Canadian soldiers took their own lives, despite that government's implementation of a prevention strategy. In 2017, it was sixteen soldiers who ended their lives. War veterans, on average have a higher suicide rate than the civilian population: in Canada it is almost two and a half times higher than the average population, for instance. In a nation with a population of almost thirty-seven million, and an army of 68,000 active personnel and 27,000 reservists, the numbers are unsettling.

In the US, the rates have been called a "national emergency", with troubling statistics, according to a September 26, 2018 article in the *Guardian*:

> More than 6,000 veterans have killed themselves each year since 2008, according to the VA data. Veteran suicide rates increased 25.9% between 2005 and 2016, as suicide rates in the overall US population also increased. But between 2015 and 2016, the rate for veterans decreased slightly, from 30.5 per 100,000 population to 30.1.
>
> The suicide rate was 1.5 times greater for veterans than for adults who never served in the military, even after adjusting for age and gender.

The data is more troubling in lieu of the fact that we are incited to go to war in order to *prevent* our deaths. We fight to survive, and yet even if we achieve our ends, the dangers of war do not end at the cease fire. Often, the worst is yet to come. Homelessness and mental health issues also plague those veterans who return home, though the call to arms was to stop the destruction of the in-group in the first place.

These facts are not to disparage those who fight, nor do we need to ignore those veterans who have done well and accomplished great things; however, when there a significant percentage of those who do battle to prevent the very things that befall them once the war propagandist no longer has use for them, we must begin to examine the troubles and question how it is that death and trauma harmed the soldier long after the wat has ended. The war propagandist's manipulations linger on.

Yet the plight of veterans of wars past does not deter future soldiers from enlisting in the war, or the public to support it. The jingoism to rally support can often be *childish* in its logic as it is aggressive, even if the circumstances are grim. Often, the call for war comes from journalists first, not overtly from the government or military, and the practice is modern as it is global. For example, the March 1, 2019 edition of *Foreign Policy* draws attention to India's media with regards to a terrorist attack:

> Ever since a suicide attack in Pulwama, Kashmir, killed more than 40 paramilitary Indian soldiers on Feb. 14, India's television news networks have been baying for blood, as have ordinary citizens on social media. The attack was carried out by a suicide bomber from the Jaish-e-Mohammed terrorist group, which India blames Pakistan for harboring and sponsoring.

It also noted how its message seemed misaligned with its own institutions:

> Yet the retired generals and diplomats commenting on the issue have been nowhere near as bellicose—proving that it's usually those with no experience of war who are most enthusiastic about it. It's been a long time since India actually fought a full-on war, instead of dealing with insurgencies and terrorist strikes, and the lack of experience seems to have left a generation of Indians with dangerously misplaced ideas about the glories of battle and victory.

All it takes is a single attack to begin the process to prime citizens into war despite the consequences of those extreme actions. But violence is a powerful icon that triggers fear on multiple levels: it can kill us, but should we survive, it can disfigure us, cripple us, cause us chronic pain, bankrupt us, traumatize us, and even stigmatize us. When the violence comes by means of a bomb, for instance, we have little chance to escape. Convoys have been bombed where some family members survive while others do not. The notion of brute force often offers brute force as a solution.

The notions of violence can manipulate us, and in unscrupulous hands can be used to cover dishonesty. For example, Jack Kelley, a *USA Today* star journalist, wrote an August 9, 2001 article about a harrowing account of a suicide bombing inside a pizzeria in Jerusalem, which he claimed to have witnessed himself. Kelley claimed to have seen three men decapitated:

> Three men, who had been eating pizza inside, were catapulted out of the chairs they had been sitting on. When they hit the ground, their heads separated from their bodies and rolled down the street.

Kelley also wrote that one Rabbi Moshe Aaron found the hand of a little girl "splattered against a white Subaru parked outside the restaurant," and that the dead girl "was probably 5 or 6, the same age as my daughter."

However, the rabbi in the article did not exist. Neither did the girl. Kelley did not witness the actual bombing. The bomber was not the way he described, and neither were the victims of the attack. Kelley fabricated numerous stories, often in places where there was civil unrest and English was not the standard language of the region, yet the unilingual Kelley repeatedly seemed to have found those with pithy quotes to offer in the middle of the danger. His downfall came when he reported he saw a book with proof of Serbian genocide; however, like a disturbing number of his stories, it was a fabrication. Yet he was shortlisted for a Pulitzer prize in beat reporting in 2002 for his seemingly solid international coverage. He got away with his deceptions for years precisely because he picked a beat where we do not judge information through objective, rational, or empirical means.

The animal within doesn't scour information for facts: it seeks to *feel* its surroundings. In-groups try to protect themselves by paying attention to the threats of violence. Out-groups, on the other hand, instil fear to others by making physical threats. Predatory attacks will be prominent news, often in nations not in the crosshairs of the danger, and when the threat has a symbolic significance, it will get prominent play as it did via the CBC in Canada on September 11, 2004, three years after the 9/11 terrorist attacks:

> Another voice on the tape, attributed to al-Zawahri, calls on Iraqi guerrillas to "bury" American troops in Iraq. "Devour the Americans just like the lions devour their prey. Bury them in the Iraqi graveyard."

We do not want to be reduced to prey. We want to survive and destroy the predator permanently. We want to be victorious and show the out-group what happens when they prey upon our in-group. As is often the case with war propaganda, however, each side will spin the narrative to accuse the other side of being the aggressor, while the other side does the same. The tensions mount as the factions threaten as they feel threatened.

In one June 3, 2009 *Canadian Press* article Osama bin Laden used a narrative of retribution in order to justify – as well as frighten the out-group US:

> Osama bin Laden threatened Americans in a new audio recording aired Wednesday, saying President Barack Obama inflamed hatred toward the United States by ordering Pakistan to crack down on militants in Swat Valley and block Islamic law there.
>
> The al-Qaida leader claimed U.S. pressure led to a campaign of "killing, fighting, bombing and destruction" that prompted the

exodus of a million people from Swat Valley in northwest Pakistan.

…"Elderly people, children and women fled their homes and lived in tents as refugees after they have lived in dignity in their homes," bin Laden said. "Let the American people be ready to reap what the White House leaders have sown," he added.

"Obama and his administration have sown new seeds to increase hatred and revenge on America," bin Laden said. "The number of these seeds is equal to the number of displaced people from Swat Valley."

Yet, over a decade before bin Laden's words, then US Secretary of State Madeleine Albright used the same structure of thought in an August 20, 1998 speech:

Yesterday, in a brazen public statement, Osama bin Laden's terrorist network informed the world that more Americans would be targeted for murder.

At the time of the latest tragedies, we said that our memory is long and our reach is far. Today, we reached into two locations on the far side of the word; today we acted to pre-empt future terrorist acts and disrupt the activities of those planning for them. While our actions are not perfect insurance, inaction would be an invitation to further horror. While we did not seek this confrontation, we must meet our responsibilities.

Bin Laden and his network were repeatedly warned to cease their terrorist activities. In response, they declared war on the United States and struck first, and we have suffered deeply. But we will not be intimidated. We will work hard to identify future threats and thwart them. As today's strikes illustrate, there will be no sanctuary or safe haven for terrorists.

Had we masked the geographical locations and identities, it would be difficult to know which side was which. The base of the brain doesn't know, either: it hears a threat from an out-group, and then it becomes primed to find the simplest and fastest method of survival. The same words that threaten an out-group reassure the in-group. Yet how we interpret those messages differs greatly depending on who is the in-group and who is the out-group: the in-group see retribution and assurance of authority, while the out-group hears a threat of brutality and vengeance.

What neither side usually hears the parallel nature of the contents of the message. The animal within does not compare and note similarities, but see differences. Propaganda primes the audience to hear the content of the message as it prepares them to *dismiss* the enemy. We are not alike; ergo, our messages cannot the same.

How do we not see the similarities between groups?

The in-group will not see itself as an aggressor, regardless if it is or isn't. War propaganda will always provide a *reason* why a first strike was necessary, and why continued strikes are needed. Whatever the reasons for the conflict, the war propagandist will make a serious of requests that are to us, unnatural habits. We live our lives as we go to work or school and spend time with our families. The request is one that will increasingly alter our routine as we receive threats from the out-group to harm us – or by the in-group should there be resistance to the idea of violence. As the acts become more unnatural, we will begin to justify why we are agreeing to more sacrifice and behaviour that places us at a high risk for harm.

Our cognitive dissonance begins to justify our actions: we cannot possibly hear similar gambit by the warring sides: it would mean our actions may not be reasonable, just, or correct.

And cognitive dissonance leaves its imprint on our brains. In 2009, Van Veen, Krug, Schooler, and Carter scanned subject's brains with an MRI as they were under conditions spurring cognitive dissonance within them. The results showed that subjects:

> [E]ngaged the dorsal anterior cingulate cortex and anterior insula; furthermore, we found that the activation of these regions tightly predicted participants' subsequent attitude change.

Furthermore, "These regions might therefore be responsible for representing or triggering the negative affect and related autonomic arousal associated with the dissonance." The anterior cingulate cortex regulates our heartbeat and blood pressure. But it is also the area of the brain that is involved with morality, impulse control, rewards and *decision-making.* The anterior insula, on the other hand, deals with emotional reactions. When war propaganda modifies our behaviors in unnatural ways, it begins to *tax* the mind, provoking our emotions as well as influence our decisions and our feelings over them.

If war propaganda provokes us as it impacts our mind, then hat are the primary motivators, needs, and desires of people it wishes to exploit? What are the fundamental elements that can cause us to begin to bend our own personal rules and moral codes?

It does not seem to invoke modern considerations in its campaigns, for instance. We do not see threats to our theatre-going habits. It doesn't make threats about our social standing or the chances of us getting a job promotion or a socially-acceptable prom dress. Unlike advertising propaganda that second-guesses our choices in tooth paste and music streaming service or advices us that we will look awkward to our peers if we do not know the latest offerings of video games, war propaganda does not bother the frivolous trivialities of middle-class life. It doesn't provoke anxiety over yellow teeth or body odor, which may make us outcasts of our peace-time in-group; it ups the ante by speaking to the animal within us – not the mundane human, but to reach the primal animal, it must strike at the base of the brain with dire threats that can harm us permanently. It speaks to our evolutionary ancestors, by reminding the primal about the threats that *it* needs to contend with, and provokes it into action.

War propaganda plays upon primitive "icons" that cab still affect our modern-day behaviour. We must eat to survive. We must find shelter. We must find allies. We must make weapons. We must engage in combat. Our needs are down to the absolute essentials for bare survival.

When it comes to suspect interrogation techniques, much has been chronicled about optimal conditions to induce information or confessions. Hinkle (1961) noted that extreme conditions, such as heat, cold, starvation, and the like, had profound and multiple effects on the brain, from the lack of vitamins to trauma to sleep deprivation. The brain alters when there is a lack of food, sleep, or peace, and when there are tensions, rations, and war propaganda, we begin to alter our basic *biology* as our thinking changes as a result. The biological and neurological foundation and workings for our instincts begins to shift from sophisticated to primal.

The endocrine system is impacted in times of great stress. Pico-Alfonso, Garcia-Linares, Celda-Navarro, Herbert, and Martinez, M. demonstrated in a 2004 experiment that women in physically abusive relationships had significantly different cortisol levels as well DHEA levels (which regulates human hormones) as well as higher instances of PTSD and depression. When we are under threat, our bodies and more importantly brains begin to make the appropriate adjustments based on the environment. The war propagandist knows they must induce stress and anxiety through psychological sieges: we are then primed to feel trapped and helpless, and begin to look for the simplest and quickest answers, which the propagandist is more than willing to supply.

While we may be more varied in our thoughts and actions during peace as we indulge in personal individuality, but when disaster hits, homogeny sets in quickly as "first-world" affiliations prove to be worthless in terms of survival, and trivial in comparison to the threats of death. We worry about having enough to eat. We worry about whether a bomb will kill us or merely make us homeless. We worry whether we will have a future with a mate and offspring. Ensuring that our genes are passed on to the next generation becomes a priority. We begin to look at mate selection in a different way. In times of peace, we can celebrate all sorts of body shapes and sizes. But when it is times of war, we shift to looking at who is strong and healthy. Propaganda posters have heavily exploited this inner chauvinism by presenting both male soldiers and females at home as attractive, powerful, and with a robust and rosy complexion, regardless whether they are out in the battlefields with tanks and guns, or back home farming or building weaponry.

We are suddenly in competition with the enemy as we wonder if the out-group will attack us with illness, pain, or threats to our well-being and life. We no longer worry about having an environmentally-friendly lip balm or plant-based meat substitutes: we worry about living until tomorrow. We have been turned into prey, yet, in nature, prey are low-quality, but high-quantity. Prey have eyes on either side of their heads, are usually herbivorous, and are not built to hunt. Predators, are high-quality but low-quality. Their eyes are closer together in front, are carnivorous, or omnivorous, and are stronger and sturdier as they are born to hunt.

However, war propaganda presents the in-group and out-group as a peculiar combination of the two: we are prey who have the enviable qualities of predators, but the out-group are predators who have the unfortunate traits of prey. This mix is has a highly offensive subtext, but it is a sleight of hand maneuver, where the in-group will be primed and groomed to become *predators* to attack the out-group *prey*. It implies the out-group do not know their place in the natural pecking order, and must be punished for their insolence toward the superior group, yet the message is a primal one that begins to target our basest survival instincts.

We are built up as our adrenaline levels rise, and should be find ourselves in combat, they rise further. Our hormone levels increase as does our aggression. We play the role that the war propagandist assures us will bring us peace and freedom, and it is not unlike undercover police officers who go in deep cover to deal with dangerous individuals and groups.

But like the officers who break away from the role and its unnatural habits, they experience a *crash:* so too does those who were immersed in a world carefully crafted by the war propagandist. Once the danger is over, we no longer react, but *reflect.*

And far too often, once the danger has past, self-assessment takes its toll on us as we begin to question whether our decision was the only option available to us – or was there some superior method to handle the problem. Speeches may provoke us into action, but speeches are not facts, but tools of persuasion.

When we begin to take a deeper look at a series of stories and images barraging us and imploring us into action, we must begin to break down each piece of information to ask more clarifying questions:

1. **Are we being presented with a predator-prey dynamic?:** If we are presented as the hunted, we are being provided with a narrative of initial helplessness. Prey are of low-quality, high quantity who are in essence, nature's lunchmeat. If that is the opening salvo, we must take care not to panic, as the second part of the message will be to propose we take a more predatory approach to our enemies, as they will now be portrayed as low-quality, high quantity. These conflicting predator-prey messages are illogical and, in most cases, highly offensive and bigoted, but will be spun in such a way as to seem noble and logical.
2. **Is there an implication of a physical threat?:** If so, it doesn't automatically mean the threat is nonexistent; however, if it is used to imply that we have a single course of action, we must

resist the propagandist's solution to find less destructive alternatives.

3. **Are you feeling emotional or psychological changes after hearing the narratives?:** If you feel your heart race, or an adrenaline rush, the outcome may be deliberate on the part of the propagandists. Many advertisers and PR firms test run their campaigns on focus groups, literally hooking up them up to machines or scans to note the physiological changes and revising their messages for maximum impact. Neuroscience tools are real (for example, in 2010, Gozzi et al's experiment showed that interest in politics "modulates neural activity in the amygdala and ventral striatum." If you are becoming distressed, it may be your greatest clue that the message was carefully constructed to provoke you in a certain way to rig an outcome.

Persuasion works best in fear and creating an environment where it haunts our choices as the next chapter shows.

Chapter Eight
Primal fears

Human beings may fancy themselves for their bravery and have countless narratives on the glories of courage, yet it is their primal fears that drive their behavior more profoundly more often. Our fears, when they become pathological in nature, can be debilitating and life-altering, particularly if we have fear of open spaces (agoraphobia), medical procedures such as needles (trypanophobia), germs (mysophobia), food (cibophobia), foreigners (xenophobia), or everything (pantophobia). Phobias are not just most common anxiety disorders in the US; they are also the most common psychiatric disorder in general, trumping even depression. We are a species primed to be fearful.

For a very good reason: fear brings avoidance of dangers. If we fear touching a hot stove, we avoid burning our flesh and making permanent damage. If we fear diseases, we will seek ways to avoid illness. When we do not fear the dangerous, we find ourselves in greater peril.

Yet our fears can also endanger us. Those with trypanophobia – fear of medical treatment – often dubbed "anti-vaccers" fear vaccinations, and have endangered their children and those with weakened immune systems, such as cancer patients undergoing chemotherapy. In one 1998 study, researchers compared the rates of pertussis (whooping cough) in nations where there were higher rates of anti-vaccination movements to those with low rates. Those nations where the majority of citizens took the diphtheria-tetanus-pertussis vaccines (DTP) ten to 100 times *lower* than those whose anti-vaccination rates were higher. Those who feared the disease were far *healthier* than those who feared the antidote. There are similar studies for the efficacy of vaccines for deadly diseases, such as smallpox.

If we are to hedge our bets where we should place our fear, it is wiser to fear what our evolutionary ancestors did than what our modern ones do. It is not a foolproof plan as guns were not around back then; however, there were primitive *weapons* and even then, avoiding the danger proactively was the shrewder survival strategy than taunting the one holding the weapon. Those who were wise survived to reproduce. The ones without the sense of fear did not live long, and their genes did not move on to the next generation. It was survival of the fittest with no social safety net nor government regulation to step in to help those without adequate survival skills of their own.

As Öhman and Mineka (2001) noted, phobias are more likely to occur with stimuli that are fear relevant in an evolutionary perspective, its activation is automatic, it bypasses cognitive control, and it "originates in a dedicated neural circuitry, centered on the amygdala." In other words, it is *emotional*-based learning rather than cognitive or intellectually-based. We are *prepared* to fear snakes, for instance; however, we are also primed to fear other kinds of threats as well. In 2007, Fox, Griggs, and Mouchlianitis demonstrated in their study that subjects were equally able to spot dangerous threats whether they were evolutionary-based, such as snakes, as well as modern threats, such as guns, supporting that a threat superiority effect was firmly in place as other stimuli, such as flowers and other non-threatening objects were not as noticeable as quickly. Furthermore, in 1989 Hugdahl and Johnsen's experiment showed that fear conditioning for guns was not as powerful when an image of a gun shown from a side view than when it was shown pointing directly at the subject. Our fears are simple to condition – just showing a *photograph* while giving a mild shock is often enough to show physiological distress in subjects even though there is no imminent danger present.

Psychology studies have found that primary phobias are not of modern-day dangers so much as evolutionary ones. Acarophobia (the fear of small insects) is far more prevalent than other types of fears in the general population. We are primed to fear and our fears still align with our evolutionary ancestors, despite the advancement of both medicine and technology. While we fear weapons, such as guns, those weapons are no less lethal than a spear or an arrow. Nor do we have to see an image of a snake ready pounce toward us for us to develop a phobia to them: a side image will be as potential, while weapons take more for us to begin to fear them. It is still the case that the most of the most common fears we have are those which have little modern-day relevance to us.

The types of phobias common in modern society are also the most primitive, yet they have debilitating consequences for those who suffer from it, and it takes very little to spark a phobia. While direct trauma (stimuli-response learning) is still the most common way, often, it is merely *reading* about a trauma or seeing an image of it that will spark it.

Both the mind and body react to fear: panic attacks alter respiratory functioning. Hypocapnia (the decrease in carbon dioxide in the blood) is present. In 1987, Cameron, Lee, Curtis, and McCann found those who had panic attacks had their plasma prolactin elevated at the peak the attacks and it correlated with the attack's severity. Plasma cortisol, growth hormone, and their heart rates were also elevated during the attacks, while plasma norepinephrine showed some increases as well.

And it is here where the war propagandist interjects to take control of emotions. Even watching stories of stressful events increases stress in the viewer. In 2019, Thompson, Jones, Holman, and Silver found the Post Traumatic Stress Disorder could occur a year after watching news stories of traumatic events such as the Boston Marathon Bombing and the Orlando pulse nightclub massacre:

> Unfortunately, coverage of these and other large-scale collective traumas (e.g., terrorist attacks and disasters) appears in traditional and social media with increasing frequency; this extensive media coverage is often repetitive and regularly includes graphic images and videos, as well as sensationalized descriptions of the events. Repeated exposure to news coverage of these events has been linked to poor mental health outcomes (e.g., acute stress) in the immediate aftermath and posttraumatic stress responses and physical health problems over time. The 24-hour news cycle and the proliferation of mobile technologies mean that much of the viewing public is regularly plugged into news updates. Thus, media coverage of collective, community-based traumas may transmit distress by broadcasting an event to whole populations, extending the reach of an event that would otherwise have been restricted to local communities.

If ubiquitous coverage through traditional media and social media begins to bring out PTSD in audiences, then war propaganda takes those emotions to extreme levels. War is an *ongoing* saga with new reported deaths every day. We are threatened with rape, torture, starvation, and subjugation. Then what of the coverage of the reports of the Burmese genocide of the Rohingya Muslims in the October 11, 2017 edition of the *New York Times*:

> In the next violent blur of moments, the soldiers clubbed Rajuma in the face, tore her screaming child out of her arms and hurled him into a fire. She was then dragged into a house and gang-raped.
>
> By the time the day was over, she was running through a field naked and covered in blood. Alone, she had lost her son, her mother, her two sisters and her younger brother, all wiped out in front of her eyes, she says...
>
> Survivors said they saw government soldiers stabbing babies, cutting off boys' heads, gang-raping girls, shooting 40-millimetre grenades into houses, burning entire families to death and rounding up dozens of unarmed male villagers and summarily executing them.
>
> Much of the violence was flamboyantly brutal, intimate and personal – the kind that is detonated by a long, bitter history of ethnic hatred.

And what fear did this February 20, 2001 column in the *London Times* spark when it was made clear if the UK did not bomb Iraq, atrocities would come to their own turf:

> The real reason why Saddam deserves to be a target for British bombs, and much more, is not "humanitarianism" but self-interest. We should fight him, not to protect "his" people, but our own. There is nothing singular in Saddam's willingness to terrorise his own subjects to maintain his hold on power, it is the stock in trade of regimes from Zimbabwe to Burma, against whom we heft no swords. What is exceptional about Saddam, and left unsaid by our Government, is the threat he poses to us by his development of weapons of mass destruction (WMDs).

As Iraq was rich in oil, the thought of what havoc it could cause would bring much panic, but it was not the only panic-inducing work. The *Washington Post* used a different sort of gambit in their May 23, 2016 critique of then president Barak Obama:

> If [President Barak Obama] had attacked the Islamic State cancer early, Obama could have stopped it from spreading in the first place. But instead, he dismissed the terrorist group as the "JV team" that was "engaged in various local power

struggles and disputes" and did not have "the capacity and reach of a bin Laden" and did not pose "a direct threat to us." He did nothing, while the cancer grew in Syria and then spread in Iraq.

Now the cancer has spread and metastasized across the world.

It *metastasized.* It is now too late and then terror has completely taken over the entire planet, according to the column. Of course, it is a gross exaggeration, but the point is not accuracy, but triggering primal fear.

But fear is a common element in war propaganda, and readers could feel reporter's Christopher Jones' fear in the December 20, 1981 edition of the *New York Times* magazine as he recounted his investigative piece on the Khmer Rouge:

> I was awakened by gunfire. It was 3:45 A.M. I had been in the camp for two days. From very close, a prolonged burst of pom-poms lighted up the night, and I could see yotheas scurrying amid the trees. Above the crackling of machine guns I could hear orders being screamed.

However, it was later discovered that Jones *fabricated* his story, relying on propagandistic methods to make his piece seem authentic. Jones is not the only journalist who was caught fabricating war stories. *USA Today's* Jack Kelley had a penchant of doing it in various global hot spots, but was discovered years after he made a name for himself. He, too, invoked color that encouraged *fear.* So powerful is fear-mongering that war propaganda is a trade in encouraging fear over rationality.

Because it is effective. When we are afraid, we react, not reflect, too afraid of stepping back and wasting moments instead of facing our fears and finding the facts. We are primed to survive, not realizing our survival depends on not giving in to anxiety, but finding our way to rationality and skepticism.

In fact, when we are afraid, our cognitive performances *improve,* making us more oriented to learn what a war propagandist wants us to learn. In one 2007 study, Chen, Katdare, and Lucas found that female participants "performed a word-association task while smelling one of the three types of olfactory stimuli: fear sweat, neutral sweat, and control odor carrier" and "found that the participants exposed to the fear condition performed more accurately and yet with no sacrifice for speed on meaningful word conditions than those under either the neutral or the control condition."

When we fear, we are primed to look for connections and then find a way to survive, and *quickly*. We believe we do not have time; hence, we learn with accuracy and more importantly to the war propagandist, we learn with *speed*. The animal within never had to contend with overt propaganda and psychological manipulation with artificial constructs of a manufactured environment, however. It could trust its senses, but when those dangers are presented on our television screens, laptops, and smartphones, that environment is an *artificial* one, yet the animal within does not know the difference, yet it is not excuse for the human in us to recognize the feints and ruses and begin to think critically.

When we are given stories and anecdotes that are filled with color and imagery of various horrors, it is then that we must look for evidence over narrative. It is not as if atrocities and violence do not happen, but often the proposed solution of the war propagandist is for the in-group to cause more violence and atrocities that are counterproductive, dangerous, and often illegal, even in times of war. There may be arguments to steal and plunder what is not ours to take. Proposals to murder children to prevent "the cancer" from spreading often are used in indirect or even direct ways. We are asked to suspend more than just our rationality, but also our morality, and once the war propagandist has no more use for us and discards us, both our humanity and rationality return to demand to know why we abandoned them when it counted the most. When it is a siege of fear, we must take extra care to verify and ask questions before agreeing to extreme measures when rational ones would be preferable and ensure future vendettas are less likely to cause future generations grief later on.

When we are dealing with a narrative that encourages reaction and panic over rationality and calm, we must begin to ask questions in order to see how much of the narrative aligns with reality:

1. **Are primal fears being used to frighten a target audience?:**
   The in-group or out-group may be the ones invoking the fears, but it is important to question how much of the fear is justified, and how much of it is misdirection in order to focus attention away from logical holes in the arguments. Out-groups may be weaker and wish to seem more ominous. In-

groups may wish to oppress their members. In either case, it is important to question why such primitive fears are being used.

2.   **Are emotions being manipulated?:** The point of information is to inform with facts and logic. If there are scant facts, but too many emotional triggers with vague first names, it is a sign that real information is nonexistent.

3.   **Is there an analogy of terminal illness used to describe the chances of survival?:** Is the danger a cancer that has spread too far? Are the out-groups plagues who have already overtaken us? In these cases, it is important to look for refuting evidence: if your life has not changed, and yet you are told all of your freedoms have been lost, it is a sign of melodrama for more deceptive purposes.

Fear is one provocation to stymie rationality, but sex is also another as the following chapter shows.

Chapter Nine
Sex sells

The *Boston Globe* seemed to have scored a coup in May 2004 when it published graphic photographs of what appeared to be images of US soldiers raping Iraqi women. The pictures were circulated elsewhere on the Internet, and the images seemed to be shocking proof of depravity.

However, the photographs came from pornography sites and were staged. They were not evidence of torture, but commercial fantasy play.

The *Globe* was forced to explain itself in a May 4, 2004 column:

> It is an understatement to say that the Globe erred when it ran a photo that, if you look closely, showed images of men dressed as soldiers having sex with unidentified women. It's also an understatement to say the paper regrets the error – as was evident in the apology published yesterday as an editor's note. There's no excuse for what happened – but, for the many readers who asked how the Globe could publish a photo that included sexually explicit and unauthenticated images, there is this explanation:

> First, the context. On Tuesday Boston City Councilor Chuck Turner held a press conference to display photos he said showed Iraqi women being raped by US soldiers. Some news outlets didn't report on the press conference because the photos were unverified – and there was reason to doubt them – but the Globe Metro staff decided it was better to write the story, raise questions within it, and let voters judge Turner's actions.

> Tuesday afternoon a photo staffer reviewed photos taken at the press conference. They showed Turner next to a display of four sexually explicit photos that he said were from Iraq. Picture editor Thea Breite – failing, she says, to realize that the sexual images were recognizable – asked the photography director, Catie Aldrich, if she had a problem with the photo running. Aldrich, who was on deadline and says she had no idea that Breite was asking about the photo's appropriateness, gave a routine OK.

At that point the question of taste, says Aldrich, should have been raised more explicitly. Says Breite, "I would have . . . if I had thought you could see something [inappropriate] in the photo."

The red flags were more than obvious that the photographs, while disturbing and racist, were not what the *Globe* claimed they were, and even then, there were those in the newsroom who has their doubts, but published the images without verification or skepticism.

However, the narrative and the shock value had overridden any notion of common sense as they were provocative, and the newspaper published fraudulent images as if they were real, and then were left to explain their credulous actions.

But times of war and catastrophe differ from times of peace and prosperity. Abraham Maslow's theory of motivation had elegantly spelled out what drives would ensure our survival: at the base came physiological needs such as food, water, heat, and sleep. Safety came next. In the center of the pyramid came intimacy and belongingness. Then came self-esteem, and at the crown self-actualization, such as creativity reaching one's full potential.

In times of peace and largess, the drive is the reach the top needs, and use rhetoric and narrative to justify the fixation on them. We can easily forget how the pyramid of needs can come crashing down on us should a cataclysm overpower the collective. Winning Miss Small Potatoes at the county fair is meaningless when suddenly the enemy has bombed your farmers out of existence and food becomes scarce as the chance of death becomes increasingly certain. When there is death and danger, suddenly, the revelation that those paper crowns are meaningless and offer no salvation hits us, and we begin to wonder how truly essential the top "need" was all along. Then when peace returns, we begin to creep back to the top level once again, scheming for the paper crowns once again.

But nestled in the center of the hierarchy of needs is intimacy. We seek members of our in-group, such as friends, but also seek a mate. To our evolutionary ancestors, it was safer to be with at least one other than to be completely alone. Pooling resources was advantageous, and a mate for reproduction completed our biological mandate of propagation.

Parental confidence ensured the male was more likely to look after the offspring and not kill them.

Yet intimacy needs are in the center of the hierarchy as it a special kind of need: it is the fusion of basic biological need, and of more psychological one seeking meaning and worth. It is one of the most powerful needs we have precisely because it is the place where one foot is in the world of mere survival, and the other begins to explore the world of the emotional – the reason we fight for survival in the first place.

It is also the place where a war propagandist has firm control of our thoughts and behaviors: we can be shamed, isolated, ostracized, and even exiled if we do not comply with the collective's beliefs. To have companionship we must connect with others within the in-group. We must be able to relate to them as they to us. In times of peace, we can be liberal and lax with intra-group differences, but during times of war and chaos, we narrow the range as we lower the bar, and behavior and beliefs are scrutinized in order to weed out any secret out-group members wishing to sow the seeds of discord in the group.

When it is times of civil unrest and war, the in-group seeks tight inventory and control over who is a desirable mate. It is not just fellow members of the in-group, but the *ideal* mate will be presented as comely, fit, young, and sexually willing. Second World War propaganda posters did not show in-group soldiers or their unwed females as overweight, cross-eyed, short, or sulky with a double chin and an overbite. The goal was in replenish the stocks with young and healthy children to ensure as many members of the in-group would survive given the scarcity of resources. In a land of plenty, more can achieve their lower needs and strive for the highest one. When there is danger and uncertainty, it becomes a competition for resources against out-groups – but also within the in-group. When we have plenty, we can afford to stand in line politely and wait our turn. When there is nothing but wisps of rations, it is no-hold's-barred free-for-all without whoever is the strongest and fastest getting the most first.

While North American advertisers now represent different shapes and sizes of product endorsers in an effort not to "body shame" their own citizens of whom they wish to spend their money on their products as they have the disposable income to do so, the imagery would be very different should a recognizable outgroup invade. Needs of self-esteem and self-actualization would be removed from the hierarchy, and the top tier would be our need for relationships and intimacy.

The "ideal" has *nothing* to do with ability or worth: in fact, the ideal body images are *propagandistic* ones which represent hyper-strength, stamina, and health on outward appearance. These body types are difficult, if not impossible to obtain or maintain; that is the *point* of propaganda: to ensure that the marks can never reach the desired goal and have enough internal insecurity and doubt (i.e., *away* from the top two tiers of needs) to continue to depend on the authority message for guidance.

Human sexual behaviour from its most basic – and base – origins isn't about romance, but ensuring the survival of the in-group to the next generation. Regardless of religion, its mandate has been to cultivate in-groups, devise the rules to which they abide, and then ensure plentiful procreation. As science and technology made it possible to reproduce through artificial methods and medicine gave hope to fragile births, the shift went beyond liberation from religion: it allowed traditionally marginalized demographics to have children, and altered what rules we break, yet when disaster strikes and those supports are knocked away, the animal within resorts to the old methods for its survival, and we revert to default heuristics to get us out of danger.

War propaganda pushes us toward those defaults: the instinctual is more uniformed than the divergent opinions and ideas of intellectualism. Attractiveness is often a product of our current trends and environment and what is considered modern and successful, yet there are reliable habits a propagandist can exploit, such as our attraction to nonverbal cues. In 1988, for instance, Friedman, Riggio, and Casella had students rate others on attractiveness and those who were emotionally expressive, extroverted, and physically attractive had been evaluated more favorably in these initial encounters than those low-scoring ones. We see war propaganda explicitly exploit these elements, particularly the posters and movies of the Second World War. Both attractive male soldiers and the scantily-clad women they are saving exhibit all of these non-verbal traits. They are bold and *expressive.* They are fit and do not have a hair out of place. *I want you –*

to join the army is a classic propaganda poster used to recruit make soldiers, and the female expresses emotions, attractiveness, and is focused on the audience.

In another study in 1989, Sprecher found that university students – the precise demographic most vulnerable to propaganda – rated physical attractiveness as their most important factor for initial attractiveness, but they also rated potential earnings and expressiveness as also important. A physically healthy and capable mate who can ensure offspring survival is never far from our minds. Mate selection is about shoring up resources. It is about investment. Modern romantic notions began to be an acceptable narrative in the Victorian Era when women began their battle not to be seen as their husband's property, but as individuals due rights and freedoms. When we see revolutions and wars take hold, women's rights are often the first to go. We have seen during the rise of ISIS that focus on the subjugation of women. Women in Mozambique during the war in the 1970s and 1980s also found their well-being under threat in similar ways. Perhaps most chilling was the 2014 Chibok schoolgirls kidnapping when Boko Haram, an extremist Nigerian group, took almost 300 girls without warning to be used as bargaining chips and a show of force and terror.

It was also a firm warning of what the group felt entitled to taking. For these young girls, they no longer had rights or a basic say. When there is unrest, there is regression before oppression. Women revert to becoming men's property as those men are fed propaganda that encourages their feelings of entitlement and incites them to cause harm to women.

But during times of peace, people react to and behave different around sexual matters. People wish to put their best foot forward to find an optimal mate. Our notions of attractive clothes and hairstyle wax and wane according to modern fashion, but youth, attractiveness, emotional openness, health, and success remain constant. While society often tries to engineer inclusivity and enlightenment in this regard, drawing from Maslow's top two needs, but when it is war, the top erodes away, and we become increasingly vulnerable to manipulation of our animal within.

When war takes away our resources, we find reasons to deny others those resources, rigging the outcome for our strongest and shrewdest to have them. We then spend decades rebuilding after the carnage, and then cycle begins again. War propaganda's success depends on making the covert case that we can no longer selfishly demand our right to self-esteem or self-actualization, and we must do the math and sacrifice for the survival of our in-group. The point of choosing a mate is to create an environment where resources are pooled together, and basic needs are met as both work toward higher-end of needs. We speak of youth *settling down* when they are married. Wedding showers pool familial resources, often with the notion of raising money for a down payment on a home. Marriage is the union based on more than just love and attraction, but also ensuring a future realistically.

From flirting to mate selection to even sexual jealousy, the point of relationships is to ensure that the *other* needs are met below it – as well as above it. The need for human intimacy is strong. We seek those who we feel are *similar* to us, sometimes physically, other times psychologically. We are forming an in-group of our own. When young men are targeted by war propaganda, he is sold the notion of female sex and devotion as both his right and his reward. The female is sexualized as she is dehumanized.

But enemies are presented as potential sexual rivals. Rape is repeatedly used as a war propagandist's tool. Nazi soldiers were repeatedly depicted as rapists, but Nazis depicted US soldiers as rapists as well, with the racist twist of presenting *African-American* soldiers as rapists – enhancing the *differences* in order to present a narrative of an emergency to young German men that they would be losing out on Aryan women unless they got themselves in uniform and went to the front lines to stop it. During the Civil War in the former Yugoslavia, the stories of rape *camps* were used to encourage global intervention in a small region with few strategic reasons for such massive resources to be employed. The term was not been in play until that conflict. While the term *ethnic cleansing* was also coined by Western journalists during this war, it was not used to trigger fear of losing potential sexual mates, but the horror stories of the former were.

It was hardly the only time the image was used and seen as a legitimate method of reportage. When journalist Edward Behr died in 2007, praise for the tactic was given in the August 6, 2007 article in the *Guardian*:

[Behr's] often hilarious experiences gathered when covering dozens of conflicts provided fodder for arguably the funniest book on war reporting since Evelyn Waugh's Scoop.

"Anyone here been raped and speak English?" was the war reporter's irreverent but eminently practical question, and became the title of his book. The question was shouted out to hundreds of just rescued European survivors of a siege at Stanleyville in eastern Congo in November 1964 as they disembarked from US Air Force C-130s landing.

War propaganda serves as a reminder that the pool of women can run dry. Women can be isolated from their in-group men to be at their enemy's mercy. It becomes urgent with no time to question what can happen, especially if there are threats to lower level needs such as safety and sustenance. The point of reproduction is to ensure the in-group lives on and enjoys those internal resources, and if the enemy has taken away "the women," paternity confidence is diminished.

Yet it is not just times of war where paternity confidence alters the behaviour of men. In times of peace in developed nations, men's behaviour had radical shifts depending on how confident he is that the children he is raising are his own. For instance, in their 2007 study, Anderson, Kaplan, and Lancaster showed that men from Albuquerque, New Mexico spent far less time and financial resources after divorce if they had low paternity confidence, but it is not just humans. Animals often kill the offspring of their female mate if her brood were sired by another male.

Filicide is complex during peacetime, and there are contradictory studies, and many whose methodology, at best, is questionable; however, there is an increase in filicide at the hands at a stepparent over a parent, given other factors such as the offspring's health and economic health of the family. When one or more of these factors bring stress (i.e., lower level needs are wanting), children become more vulnerable to filicide.

From a biological and evolutionary standpoint, humans have little tolerance for scarcity of their more primal needs, as do animals. When we are under financial stress, our ability to meet our primal needs are in jeopardy, and its impact begins to spread to our needs for intimacy. War propaganda offers solutions to preserve a mid-level need, but at a cost of sacrificing our top-level needs. We must bring in the army in order to keep the enemy away from us.

Rape is invoked as often as is murder, and is usually the number on the list of feared outcomes. Take one *Toronto Star* editorial from July 9, 1986:

> In contempt of the World Court and world opinion, the American Congress has bowed to the pressure of President Reagan. The Contra leaders, with no political or social program but that of self-aggrandizement, have been given a new lease on life, now better able to kill, rape, pillage and mutilate the people of Nicaragua.
>
> …The Canadian government can no longer sit by and ignore the irrational, illegal and immoral actions of our American allies. A strong and early response is required to stem the tide of bloodshed and tragedy which afflicts the people of Nicaragua.

Threats to life and threats to the gene pool come first: these are the most basic needs on Maslow's list. These directly impact all but the top two needs on the list. As we will see later on, during the First World War, German soldiers were not just accused of raping young Belgium girls, but *cannibalizing* them. When it comes to the notions of sexual oppression and enslavement, it is not enough for the propagandist to use a rape icon, but also one of the more primal needs on the hierarchy. Rape during war is a crime of opportunity. Rape propaganda is, in fact, the real weapon of war, but is usually an auxiliary used to frighten men into enlisting, or at least sanctioning their nation's intervention in foreign conflicts.

War propaganda exploits young men and shamelessly so. It is conflict of messages: the enemy is raping our women, but our women will find their in-group soldier more attractive. The messages conflict, and provoke aggression, both physical and sexual. Men are exploited and reconditioned through images of their in-group females being harmed, and then again as they are presented with comely in-group females who want them to join the army to save the collective. The aggressive masculinity is revered and rewarded, and many notions of what makes a man desirable have been based on the narratives of war propaganda.

Yet the longer we have peace, the less desirable male sexual aggression is viewed. During times of peace and prosperity, those traits become demonized. When the #MeToo movement took root, few imagined how many rich and powerful men would be taken down so quickly, and many did not understand why they were suddenly were turned from Great Men to monsters. For decades, male prowess and success was predicated on being desirable to as many women as possible, when there was no strategic use for it, it was shunned, and there suddenly became a difference between masculinity and *toxic* masculinity, with many men unable to see the difference and accusing others of trying to "end" masculinity outright as if women had complete control of power and narrative in times of peace and war. While the origins of it were a response to political rivalries and anger toward an unexpected outcome in the 2016 presidential election, much of the movement was disjointed.

#MeToo's origins were not propagandistic: it lacked a leader or "face", a coherent voice, nor any doe-eyed innocent ingenues claiming abuse by a single group of powerful men as those from both political leanings were accused. The women were seen as successful and powerful before their confessions. They were not waifs who had a clean slate. It netted an odd assortment of men, most of whom weren't actual "gets" in terms of political power, and some of these men, while powerful within circles, would have needed a name tag to be identified by the public. #MeToo was a force in spite of its amateur flaws.

Regardless, war propaganda does not strictly target men. On the contrary, it targets women and has done so for a variety of reasons. During the Second World War, it was to encourage young women to enter factories to partake in gruelling and dangerous work building the weapons and vehicles of war. Women who weren't working were reminded of the importance of food rations and the consequences of being reckless with a grain of sugar.

Yet there are other forms of war propaganda aimed squarely at women's third step of needs. Many so-called ISIS Brides were lured via social media using a variety of means. Some women were fleeing poverty. Others were already radicalized, and wished to join the cause. Some were thought they were idealists.

And some were lured by romantic notions to join. Sex sells for women as well, but the research here is very scarce and timid. We understand how war propaganda manipulates young, childless men, but for young women, the research is threadbare and there are reasons – not all of them sexist – for the scant attention.

The problems in studying women's victimization in war propaganda are numerous. First, much of feminist scholarship believes it cannot reconcile with evolutionary psychology, committing several conformation biases. Evolutionary psychology defies narrative or deals with the upper echelons of Maslow's hierarchy. It is base, primitive, and feral. Neither men nor women can reach the higher levels of self-esteem and self-actualization unless the previous three baser conditions are met. Otherwise, women are as base as men, no better, no worse. During times of war, people are expected to kill strangers on the demand of an authority they will never see, an act that would horrify us during times of peace. Women have no better fate and must come to grips that they are as base as their male counterparts when it comes to bare survival. Experimental psychology, that examines the flaws in human thinking regardless of self-identity with evolutionary psychology being one small subset of the discipline.

The second problem is that we often neglect the reality of women, particularly in times of upheaval. They may be cannon fodder or damsels in distress in various narratives, but how they may be targeted for manipulation is not a consideration for even feminist scholars. Yet women are targeted, and had their own animal within exploited to their devastation, even in times of peace. Like cults that have traditionally lured women to see themselves as subservient units to be exploited, war propaganda is meant to orient our thinking to see ourselves as deficient and innately so, form unnatural habits, isolate the targets, and then use cognitive dissonance to spin a narrative that the only salvation is to surrender free will and partake in degrading rituals.

We can be victims of horrendous abuse and be blind to our indoctrination because are too far away removed from the base of Maslow's pyramid that it is our blind spot. When we have resources and are prosperous, but have not reached the top level of self-actualization, we begin to look to others to show us the way, and the unscrupulous find a vulnerable mark to recruit. Cults often use the lure of promising to help us reach the top level of needs, while quietly removing the levels we have already reached: we begin to lose our self-confidence and esteem before we are alienated from our family and friends, and soon, we are dependent on the cult for our safety, shelter, and food, while being assured we will reach the top from the very bottom.

And this method is still more than viable, even in 2019. NXIVM, a cult that primed, lured, and groomed wealthy heiresses such as Clare Brofman, as well as actresses, such as Alison Mack to agree to being a part of the toxic machinations of an abusive cult. Female members funded the leader, as they allowed themselves to be physically branded, and were willing "sex slaves" in a scheme where they gained nothing, but lost all sense of self with criminal charges as their reward. None of the women gained anything in joining the farce: they were rich, successful, powerful, and had supports and even a staff to advise them, yet all fell for a low-level grifter's scam that degraded them at every turn in their quest to reach the top level of needs. War propaganda functions much the same way, but insists the top two are selfish pursuits that must be abandoned for survival.

The third and perhaps largest problem with scholarship is its filters on reality are in the top two hierarchy of needs. Academia is in ivory towers, not war zones or impoverished areas with marked civil unrest and violence. The mindset is a troublesome obstacle, and more so when modern scholarship is compared with the Post-War scholarship in the late 1940s where many scholars experienced war first-hand, having fought as soldiers, or having survived the horrors of concentration camps. The more realistic and humble perceptions of the basest and most primal of human behaviour and reaction are more readily found here where punches were not pulled or mired in posh Middle-Class self-assessments that have been sterilized and shaped by other forms of propaganda, namely advertising.

We have a wealth of research of the various ways men – particularly young child soldiers existed. The void is about how women were manipulated and psychologically conditioned to behave in ways that went against their baseline behaviors during peacetime.

These real constraints and misperceptions must be acknowledged in order to be removed, and here, there is a profound lack of empirical data; however, what we do have is some understanding of how female have been recruited from other nations to join ISIS as *jihadi brides*.

Varvara Karaulova was such a bride, though her background made her a seemingly unlikely candidate:

Philosophy major Karaulova, from a middle-class, non-Muslim Moscow family, was unusual among Russian IS recruits who typically hailed from impoverished provincial backgrounds in the North Caucasus.

Karaulova, a convert to Islam, insists that she fell in love with a man she met online and wanted to marry him in Syria but did not share the radical ideology of the IS. Her father had pleaded with the court to acquit Karaulova, saying that he was seeking help from Russian authorities by filing a missing person's report, not vengeance against his daughter.

Karaulova, who was expelled from university shortly after her arrest, told the court on Tuesday that her trip to Turkey was "the most foolish thing I have ever done in my life and the one I'm still punishing myself for."

The primary bait may be romantic and adventurous – just as male soldiers are lured to enlist, but it is not the only motivator. There are, just as primal attraction during peace, hints of empowerment, and prosperity. The promised land is there, all it takes is to come with notion that the need for intimacy will be met. ISIS successfully appealed to very primal motives that drive initial physical attraction to women, the same as with men with gender-specific roles in mind.

Propaganda manipulates the animal within us, and the animal is on the hunt to satisfy its needs. It is a process without end as our needs are never permanently fulfilled. We always need food and water. We always need shelter for our long-term survival prospects. We always need interaction with another human being to stay sane. There is always a threat, however slight, that it can all be taken away from us in a single strike. War propaganda takes full advantage of our fear of physical and emotional starvation and turns it into a weapon to create panic, but also lust, greed, and envy. Propagandas meant to recruit and swell the ranks have a highly vulnerable psychographic to exploit – those who lack experience in the ways of the world, brains that are not fully developed as it struggles with the onset of hormone levels, and a strong desire to love and also to lust. It is an insidious form of manipulation, and it is often difficult for those in abusive relationships to see the reality of the abuse they endure, misclassifying it as love and refusing to get out. Abusers exploit it. Cults exploit it.

Wars exploit it as well, and when we begin to hear sex-based narratives during times of conflict and violence, we must begin to look at information through a critical lens by looking for evidence to support the often sexist perspective of the stories:

1. **Are in-groups being portrayed as being morally superior toward women than the out-groups?:** In some cultures, to be morally superior is to take an alleged "feminist" perspective, while in others, superiority comes from adhering to alleged "traditional" perspectives. In either case, we are being deliberately divided as we fail to question our own sexism for the sake of decreeing another group will harm our women through their political, religious, or ideological sickness.

2. **Are women being portrayed as prizes or trophies the out-group wishes to possess?:** This is a dangerous notion whether it comes from the in-group that wishes to control the freedoms of their female population in the name of "protecting" them, or from the out-group that wishes to frighten one half of the population to keep them frozen in place. Women are not helpless children, but adults who can devise plans, defend themselves and their country, and be equally productive as men. Whenever the narrative begins to infantilize women, it is a red flag that a war propagandist wishes to bring manipulate the populace based on sexist stereotypes.

3. **Are women being portrayed as damsels in distress who need in-group men to save them?:** Whenever women are portrayed as weak and helpless, we must take a closer look as to the motives for such deceptive practices. Are men being incited to enlist in order to protect their "fragile" women? When we are being encouraged to see women as lesser beings incapable of contributing to their societies, we must begin to examine the motives behind it.

4. **Are in-group women being idealized morally, while being infantilized simultaneously?:** In-group women will be seen as having beauty and morals, but when it comes to intellect, they will be portrayed as helpless and unable to help themselves. While women are vulnerable in times of unrest and war, we should also remember that there are women in the military and law enforcement who face the same dangers as men. When we see an entire segment of an adult in-group

being placed in the same category as children, it is a sign that the intent is to make the out-group rivals seem horrific and bent on our destruction by going after the "weakest" segment first.

War exploits sex as a gateway into becoming a pawn on a chessboard, but it isn't the only way the ways of Eros are manipulated to keep potential pawns in check.

Chapter Ten
When men were men
and women were women

Modern Western gender roles have gone through numerous transformations over the decades, even if much of the progress is only skin deep and in a perpetual state of flux. For example, the #MeToo movement had two distinct subtexts: when it first took root after Ronan Farrow's 2017 *New Yorker* exposé on Hollywood mogul Harvey Weinstein, women who spoke out against sexual harassment were portrayed as active agents of change who were using social media to bring their tormentors to justice.

But by the time the contentious confirmation hearings for US Supreme Court Justice candidate Brett Kavanaugh began in 2018, something dramatically changed with the subtext of #MeToo: women were portrayed as helpless victims of male abuse, not powerful agents of change with one editorial cartoon portraying Lady Justice as a shapely blonde as Republican arms in a suit cover her mouth with one hand and one arm with the other.

It was a form of sexist propaganda that drew from *war* propaganda posters of the Second World War when US, German, Italian, and French posters depicted enemy soldiers as rapists who ploughed through young, comely, and shapely in-group women. If Justice herself was reduced to being a helpless victim, then what chance did the American Everywoman have?

Suddenly, women were no longer active warriors, but helpless victims in need of rescue, yet no one asked the hard questions. They did applaud the dubious cartoon, as one September 30, 2018 piece from *CBC News* did as it extolled the fact that it was a *Canadian* cartoonist who got the attention of the US press:

Lady Justice is on her back, blindfolded. And above her, a man with the Republican Party's logo on his shirt cuffs, is pinning her down with one hand and covering her mouth with the other.

Bruce MacKinnon drew the cartoon for Nova Scotia's Chronicle Herald newspaper, inspired by Christine Blasey Ford's Senate judiciary committee testimony last week against Supreme Court nominee Brett Kavanaugh.

"I understand it's hard for people to look at, especially people who might be survivors of sexual assault," MacKinnon told CBC News.

The same tone deafness to the manipulative image could be found in September 30, 2018 article from the *Huffington Post*:

But some social media users were critical of the image, commenting that it is re-traumatizing for victims. One person tweeted that the cartoon made her feel like she couldn't breathe.

Few questioned why there was a sudden and breath-taking *shift* in the narrative: when #MeToo was a grassroots and organic movement, women were seen as heroes and fighters pushing back against the barriers of the past as they stood up to people more powerful than they were, but when it came to a political battle between the Democrats and the Republicans, it turned into choreographed political propaganda where women depended on politicians to save them from another political party. The movement was no longer grassroots or organic, with various political operatives and PR firms taking advantage of a primed demographic as they altered the message and drowned out the original intent. It was a stark contrast, but one the press never questioned.

The polarizing cartoon did not have Justice fighting back in a rage, or have other women come to assist her. Justice may be blind, but so is the *Marvel* character Daredevil and *Mortal Kombat* character Kenshi, yet both young and attractive white males are powerful fighters who can take down hordes of sighted adversaries without fuss. Justice is supposed to be a *stronger* force against the corrupt, yet a single image denied women even that one iconic woman of power. Once #MeToo was seen as an effective movement that resulted in, according to the *New York Times* in one year of #MeToo, 201 men in power lost their positions with almost half of their replacements being women (while *Bloomberg News* the tally of accused in men power at 429 one year after the original Farrow piece), and in some cases, face criminal charges, it was co-opted by an institution as a strategy to wield power by turning a legitimate message into exploitation.

If one gender's deepest fears are exploited for political gain using their own progress and strength during times of peace, then what can we expect during times of *war?* We are placed in precarious emotional quagmires with threats of death, starvation, and rape, and then asked whether we wish salvation or to be left as helpless as Justice in an editorial cartoon. While starvation, homelessness, and death are common universal triggers, a war propagandist will often use primitive gender-specific threats to aim a message at a particular target, even when a society has improved its environment for women.

It is the hunter-gatherer motif that runs deeply in war propaganda: men are portrayed as the hunters, while women the gatherers. In propaganda posters during the Second World War, women were to summoned to farm in the fields and build weapons in the factories. One 1943 Australian war poster featured a comely woman look at the viewer and said while holding neatly pressed shirts, "Our job to clothe the men who work and fight." Women have distinct roles to play in war propaganda: if the message is targeted at women, it is about gathering – food, clothing, weapons, and other staples for survival. Maslow's lower-level needs are their domain. If the women are targeted at men, however, they are to either fawn all over him in uniform, or be victims who must be saved from the enemy. At no time is a woman to be seen as attempting to defend herself from harm.

She is always beautiful and young. She is nubile and meant to arouse the young men who are potential soldiers, but should she be a damsel-in-distress, he must also be incited to want to cause harm to those who rape and torture her. It is Eros and Thanatos in a single image. He must be lured by his baser desires as he simultaneously is repulsed by the image. Jane Gay, a cartoon character created by Norman Pett to serve as a morale boost to British troops in the Second World War, had a penchant of always shedding her clothes – but she was comely and a hyper-sexualized ideal that reminded the men that their delicate women at home couldn't keep their clothes on when left to their own devices.

Often, the young women are *mothers* who have died by hideous means trying to protect her children. In one Fred Spear propaganda poster of the Second World War, a drowning woman is sinking to the bottom of the ocean holding her child with a single word: *Enlist.*

She cannot fight; ergo, it is up to the men to protect their women. The image of horror and sexual arousal are not done by accident: the goal is to establish a *misattribution of arousal.* In 1974, Dutton and Aron discovered that fear triggers also resulted in sexual arousal, and gives credence to the old teenaged ruse of taking first dates to horror movies to spark *romantic* ideations. The adrenaline rush and physiological changes of fear and hate can be misattributed to love and lust.

In 1962, Schachter and colleagues demonstrated the dilemma of arousal misattribution when experimenters injected subjects with adrenaline and had them witness confederates in a waiting room behaving in a variety of ways. However, the confederated behaved (elated, angry), the subjects believed they were feeling the same way as they had felt the rush of adrenaline. All it takes is a single shot of artificial and covert arousal to be paired with a specific image, and the process of misattribution begins.

It is not difficult to see how simple a matter war propaganda becomes. We can watch a movie which we know is a work of fiction. We can watch or read the news, and we will emotionally respond to the stimuli, meant to arouse our biochemical responses. Advertisers also know it and spend billions of dollars in refining more effective marketing campaigns, as do politicians. To rouse a crowd and whip them into an adrenaline rush can translate into increased sales or votes. Charismatic politicians and celebrity endorsers bring out our aroused emotions as they are paired with a party or product, respectively. We associate the rush with their affiliation and wish for the good feelings to continue.

War propaganda also relies on pairing adrenaline rushes with specific images to rig outcomes. Love and hate are fused together to spark strong emotions that require certain actions to satisfy. Young childless men are sexually aroused, enraged, and then asked to commit violence in order to fulfill the cycle in the hopes of surviving victorious, and returning home where his baser desires will be the reward for his risks.

The backbone of any war propaganda campaign is always based in fear. Regardless of gender or identity, fear stimulates the mind in specific ways. It makes learning more accurate, even if it clouds our understanding of our own emotions. Too much stimulation of fear brings sensory overload, but when the siege is optimal, it allows for reactions and makes the audience forget about creative alternatives to assumptions.

The imagery of terror when it comes to the abuse of women is graphic in times of war, such as was the case in the May 24, 2018 edition of the *Washington Post:*

> Nigerian soldiers and self-defense forces have raped women rescued from the Boko Haram extremist group, Amnesty International alleged in a report Thursday that Nigeria's military dismissed as "false."

> The report alleges that thousands of women and girls were separated from their families in camps in northeastern Nigeria and abused. Some were raped in exchange for food, the report says, and others were beaten and called "Boko Haram wives."

When there is no escape from the terror, coherent thought can be easily lost, and yet the article was not based on primary sources or first-hand interviews, but an appeal to an authority. The lack of detail or verification gives us no inside workings of what happened, how, or why. We have no faces, nor names. We have two foreign groups: the Nigerian soldiers and Boko Haram, making the fear of the unknown that much greater, and is no different than when a victim in a horror film hears ominous noises and can only shout a trembling "Who's there?" before the inevitable gratuitous slaughter. In this case, we are given terror to the point we are forbidden in asking who is there.

There are psychological and biological differences between the sexes, independent of gender identity. Jiménez, Aguilar, and Alvero-Cruz demonstrated in 2012 that while men and women have increased hormone levels when victorious, but increased cortisol levels when defeated, men's levels for both are greater in either case. When there are biological differences to the same stimuli, we can expect different responses as a result, and as war propaganda targets men more than women, its strategy banks on those differences to achieves its goals.

How men respond to fear, lust, love, victory, losses, gains, threats, child-rearing, and aggression, as opposed to women responding to the same stimuli, especially when cultural norms are overridden by other factors is intriguing. While Archer in his 2004 meta-analysis demonstrated while boys and girls possessed the same levels of anger, boys were far more likely to demonstrate physical *aggression*. Men are consistently the instigators of conflict and its greatest victims. As Van Vugt noted in 2009:

> Across all cultures, almost any act of intergroup aggression and violence, for instance, warfare, genocide, rebellion, terrorism, street-gang and hooligan violence, is perpetrated by coalitions of men. Evidence of male-to-male intergroup violence goes back as far as 200,000 years (e.g., mass graves containing mostly male skeletons with evidence of force).

We often assume that cultural differences play an important role in our beliefs and behaviour, yet war propaganda disproves our self-assessments time and again. There are different biological triggers and icons which elicit different responses from the sexes. Men, for instance, exhibit greater psychological and physiological distress when their partners are unfaithful to them, and as Buunk, Angleitner, Oubaid, and Buss discovered in their 1996 study, this reaction was consistent across nations and cultures. The idea that in-group females may fall by choice or by force to a rival alters not just thoughts, but biochemistry as well. War and sex are *linked* if the enemy wins, he gets to control the environment, including who will mate with whom – or if they will mate at all. When primates go to war, the victorious leader will take the mate of the defeated leader as a prize. Humans do not usually partake in those practices, but the *fear* of it being meted as a form of punishment can serve as a powerful propagandistic tool to ensure that the in-group complies – or that the out-group trembles at the prospect.

Boko Haram succeeded in instilling such fear when they kidnapped young Nigerian schoolgirls, and of those freed, many found themselves scorned by their former in-groups lest they were infected by the ideology of their captors.

Men and women can be psychologically manipulated in different ways as they have biological and biochemical differences. For example, men respond to fear differently than do women with their cortisol levels increasing. Zorawski, Blanding, Kuhn, and LaBar's 2006 study showed that while men shown an increase in cortisol after fear conditioning, but women did not as estrogen seems to play a role in suppression in women. What it means if that psychosocial stress improves memories in men, but suppresses memories in women. Cortisol's effect on the prefrontal lobe, the part which regulates focus and planning, as well as personality, impulse control, modifying complex behavior, emotional reactions, a prioritizing incoming information as it ignores extraneous information. It is a critical part of the brain which plays a significant role in information intake and processing, meaning any disruptors can seriously impair our ability to judge and make decisions. For women, it hampers their memory. Cortisol impacts both associate learning and declarative memory, meaning to increase stress is to covertly add intellectual static preventing an audience from using their intellect to assess information they are given.

While there are similarities in how men and women respond to war propaganda, there are stark differences between the sexes. When it is a threat to reproduction, men are triggered into aggression, while women are driven to fear. Both humans and animals respond with violence when their children are under threat: animals take aggressive stance and attack potential predators. Animals with developing broods are territorial. Males are primed to keep predators away from the territory, while females defend the nesting area. There is no time for negotiation or thinking: every second matters when it is a question of saving the next generation or losing them to a predator.

War propaganda brings false rushes with its cold terror: young men are told they will never be able to reproduce as their pool of potential mates will be raped and slaughtered. Women are reminded of the knives at their throats and must do as they are told to ensure their survival. Whether it be a terrorist attack or a war, the threats are presented in vivid detail befitting of a horror movie. Images of abused and confined women have been an effective staple of propaganda posters and unconfirmed rumours in every war, and the message is clear: the more brutal our response, the faster we will do away with the enemy.

If men and women are to break free of the forced and often *rigged* terror, calm will bring down the levels of cortisol, for instance. Liberation gives space and the right physiological mindset to reflect, analyze, think, and demand *specifics*. In public speaking, for instance, a large crowd intimidates, but should the speaker make the effort to speak beforehand with members of the audience, to get their names, motives of listening, and personalize and *individualize* the mass of listeners, it breaks down the horde and makes public speaking less stressful. The war propagandist thrives in presenting daunting crowds to terrorize either the in-group or out-group: personalize the mass and stop the frenzy and the truth and reality of the situation begins to emerge without the imposed filters of the propagandist, regardless of the sex of the audience. Men and women can bypass the filters, albeit in slightly different ways. Men are at risk of allowing their aggression to fail them. Women begin to *forget* salient information under stress. Yet both can find the solution in creating enough space and static to reflecting and devise counterstrategies against the influence of professional emotional manipulators, so long as they understand the calm must come within, and not to expect institutions, which very often have vested interests in stirring their adrenaline levels, to do it for them.

The further manipulation of sex roles is an important factor to explore when dealing with potential war propaganda. We need to establish provenance of the origins of where initial information has come from: it is from victims or eyewitnesses who are primary sources? Is it through visual or audio evidence? Or it is filtered through firms and groups that have a vested interest in altering the perceptions of events in order to control a large group of people into complying with destructive and violent solutions that are both sexist and bigoted?

In order to prevent us from falling from such ruses, we have important questions to ask when confronted with information:

1. **Are our in-group women being presented as moral and physical ideals?**: If women are suddenly lithe and scantily-clad beauties without flaw, we know this deviates from the more textured reality of what women are. When we see women as saints rather than human beings with flaws, pasts, and even folds and wrinkles, we are being primed to see

ourselves with halos who are genetically-superior to out-groups. As no one can live up to so impossibly-high standards, there are emotional consequences that a war propagandist can easily exploit.

2. **Are narratives targeting female-centric fears?:** If tales of horror target women, we need to take extra care to ensure this is not a gambit to terrorize a demographic to agree to being confined to ensure their survival. If unnatural habits are formed, we need to ensure not to fall for them in the first place.

3. **Are hormonal and adrenaline levels beings manipulated through narratives?:** If we are having our own cortisol levels being provoked, there will be psychological consequences that may impair our reasoning abilities. We must take any emotionally-provoking information and find reason and facts to put it in perspective in order to verify the claims objectively.

4. **Are sexist stereotypes being used to describe our in-group?:** During times of peace and prosperity, women are seen as independent and capable of achieving great things. The more volatile the circumstances, the more regressed the narrative becomes, and women are portrayed as increasingly incapable of any defensive actions.

Yet it is not just manipulation of the sexes that a war propagandist relies on to rig consensus – there is also a question of threatening the welfare and fate of children as we will see in the next chapter.

Chapter Eleven
The lost generation

The biological point of procreation is to restock the in-group with the next generation; however, as children require much parental investment, it is hoped the new generation will respect and honor the ways of the in-group. Ideally, we seek children of morals, intelligence, progress, and peace who are constructive and innovative, improving the lot and standing of the in-group.

But we also hope the children of the out-group are not indoctrinated to focus hatred on us and then harm us or our future.

The idea is a most shocking threat to the animal within: how does the in-group deal with violent out-group *children* incited to cause harm to their peaceful in-group offspring? What chance do the child who have never held a gun or know the ways of survival supposed to survive? When there are "helicopter parents" who cannot cope with being barred going to their children's school to supervise their lunchtimes, what chance do their progeny have if there are peers who are trained to destroy them?

And as an article in the September 21, 2006 article in the *Sydney Daily Telegraph* warned readers, the out-group children were being dutifully trained and indoctrinated for such horrific purposes:

> A video game for "terrorist children" where the player fights US soldiers before attempting to kill President George Bush is spreading on Islamic extremist websites.
>
> Pictures of UK Prime Minister Tony Blair adorn the walls of a US military camp in Night of Bush Capturing, apparently produced by a group said to be a mouthpiece for several jihadist groups, including al-Qaeda.
>
> The player's character is a militant travelling through the camp and then mountain terrain picking up weapons, according to the SITE Institute, a research group which monitors terrorist internet video releases.

At the end of the game, the player faces a battle against Mr Bush.

The levels have titles such as "Jihad beginning", "American's Hell" and "Bush hunted like a rat".

The theme would come up again in a May 2018 edition of *Reason* magazine:

> Ever wonder what it would be like to participate in an Islamic holy war? Hezbollah has you covered. A Lebanese media company affiliated with the militant group has released *Sacred Defense*, a first-person shooter video game in which players defend Shiite Muslim shrines and take down ISIS warriors. It's "a tool to confront the savage culture that invades our markets through games that are stripped of feeling and belonging" and "a tribute to the souls of the martyrs," according to a *Newsweek* translation of the official description.

While the article makes a brief mention of a similar US recruitment game, it fails to mention that most military-based video games have always found an enemy to take down without questioning the motives. When it is out-groups who do it, then we express shock and repulsion.

Yet the message is clear. We are not safe. Our children are not safe. The war propagandist liberally uses images of children to remind parents of the young that their parental investment will go down the drain unless they take a more hardened and calculating approach to the problem.

The exploitation of children is a common theme to frighten out-groups as well as in-groups. Singer in 2003 discussed the practice:

> Among Iraqi dictator Saddam Hussein's human rights violations was his policy of recruiting children into Iraq's armed forces, in clear violation of international law and moral norms. Already, U.S. and allied forces have faced child soldiers in the fighting around Karbala and Nasariyah.
>
> Since the mid-1990s, thousands of Iraqi boys have attended military style summer boot camps. During the 3-week-long sessions, boys as young as 10 years old went through drills, learned the use of small arms, and received heavy doses of Ba'ath political indoctrination. The camps were named after resonating current events to help galvanize recruitment and add to the political effect. For example, the 2001 summer camp series was titled the Al Aqsa Intifada, to link it with the

symbology of the Palestinian uprising that started earlier that year.

The war propagandist may wish to frighten the in-group to prime them to fear out-group threats, in order to parents to *agree* to having their children take up arms to save the nation. There is a dual purpose to the games, and the sight of small children with weapons represents the loss of innocence for both the in-group and the out-group. As Kincaid noted in 2017:

> The most extreme issue facing boys under Islam is the recruitment of child soldiers by the Islamic State. A series of photographs and videos released in 2015 and 2016 featuring children as young as four or five years old, depicted either watching or conducting gruesome acts of war, has propelled this epidemic into the spotlight. The Islamic State has dubbed these child-warriors "the Cubs of the Caliphate".
>
> A study by the Combating Terrorism Center (CTC) in February 2016 has analysed photographs and videos released by IS between January 2015 and January 2016 eulogising eighty-nine "martyred" child recruits...
>
> "What this database points to is the fact that use of children is far more normalized," [one researcher] revealed when interviewed about the study. "They are not just being used to shock people in execution videos. They are being used for their operational value as well. This is something that sadly we have to expect to increase and accelerate as the situation becomes more precarious for ISIS in the years to come."

Both sides of the conflict will equally exploit the image for different purposes: the out-group will use it as an example of the dangerousness and barbarity of the enemy, while the in-group will justify it as necessary for survival as their enemies drive them to protect themselves in such extreme measures. Each side manipulates the narrative for their own ends.

There are countless ways to manipulate adults by threats to their children, such as making them orphans. Without protectors, children are vulnerable to death, abuse, and exploitation. The terror of the plight of one orphan in Mosul was detailed in a October 24, 2017 broadcast of *All Things Considered*:

> In this camp for displaced Iraqis near Erbil, boys and girls play games led by a child-care worker. Across the road in a trailer

used by social workers, a little girl named Kawkab sits down. She's wearing fuzzy, pink pants and a matching top with hearts on it. She's 10 now. She doesn't remember if it was two or three years ago that her mother was killed. But she can't forget the images because she was there.

It was the mother's altruism and doing the right thing that helped facilitate the tragedy:

> Kawkab's talking about ISIS. We're not using her last name because of security concerns. She and her mother were in Mosul when a cousin in the police came to their house and begged her mother to help him escape. ISIS was killing policemen. She agreed to take them, and they were caught in an ISIS checkpoint and her mother killed as punishment, while Kawkab watched.

In a December 23, 2001, the *Sunday Times* recounted how some war orphans were forced into prostitution:

> A look of outrage settled over the features of Abdul Habib Salim, head of the Allauddin orphanage, as he recalled how children had become spoils of war for Taliban officials who took over his institution in late 1996, writes Matthew Campbell.
>
> On his first day in the job, the Taliban commander appointed to run the orphanage in place of Salim showed an interest in three teenage orphans. "They were very pretty girls," said Salim. "Fereshta was 18, a talented seamstress, Maleha was 17 and Mariam just 15." The next day they were gone.
>
> The commander had taken the women as concubines for his brother and two other relatives. "The Taliban didn't care about orphans," said Salim. "They were just loot. They were forcibly married. There was nothing anybody could do."

Using names and vague details do not make the narrative any less harrowing. We do not look for facts: we look for narratives, and yet still, not all war orphans are what they are purported to be. In 2014, one chilling image of an alleged young Syrian orphan lying in-between the graves of his dead parents made the rounds of social media, until the original Saudi photographer corrected the account as it was taken in his home country, and the young boy was his nephew posing for an art project. More photographs showed the boy was also smiling for the cameras, and he was not an orphan.

As the photographer recounted:

Look, it's not true at all that my picture has anything to do with Syria," Al-Otaibi says, "I am really shocked how people have twisted my picture...

I love photography...Every artist has ideas in his head. So I had the idea to make a project whereby I show in pictures how the love of a child for his parents is irreplaceable. This love cannot be substituted by anything or anybody else, even if the parents are dead.

Yet what the photographer wished to capture as homage is what a war propagandist seeks to exploit as a means to an end. The complex and multi-faceted dynamic of parents and children is filled with vulnerabilities that a manipulator can co-opted and distort to rig outcomes in favour of violence.

Orphans and child soldiers are only a small part revolving around propaganda exploitation of the icon. The very notions of child-rearing and reproduction are key to manipulating an audience to believe the solutions proffered by those sending distorted messages to them.

Child-rearing in the animal world has much in common with their human counterparts. Parenting in the animal kingdom revolves around creating a fortress for the offspring, ensuring a safe birth, feeding the offspring and guarding them from threats, and then teaching the offspring to feed and protect themselves. It is a cycle of life. There are countless threats to this cycle, particularly if parental confidence is diminished: male animals often kill offspring that they detect is not their own.

It is similar among humans: parent raise their children, feeding, clothing, and providing them shelter as they instill their own values and beliefs into their offspring through political, ideological, and religious beliefs as they educate them themselves, or through academic institutions. When there is a threat toward children by an out-group, the ability to protect the offspring and instill our own belief system becomes weakened, and worse, our own previous in-group values are in peril of becoming a source of shame to future generations who will now be primed to repudiate them.

But an ideological hijacking is not the only source of fear. The notion of in-group women becoming enslaved and raped by the enemy hints that there is a very good chance there will be offspring with the enemy as the father. It increases their stock at the expense of our own. The

Second World War repeatedly used this icon to incite young childless men into enlisting.

And there is a good reason why the icon is effective. When paternity confidence is diminished, men are biologically primed to reactive negatively, but when there is higher paternity confidence, the area of the brain to regulate emotions alters. Plateket al in 2004 demonstrated that men had different physical and *biological* reaction to images of infants that resembled them:

> [M]ales respond favorably to children as a function of facial resemblance when making hypothetical investment decisions… [W]e extended these results and found a sex difference in neural substrates activated by seeing children's faces that resembled the viewer. Unlike females, males showed significant neural activation in the left frontal cortex, which has been hypothesized to be involved in the inhibition of negative responses. In another recent investigation of the neural correlates of facial resemblance and face recognition in child and adult faces, using fast event-related fMRI, also found a sex difference in activation associated with facial resemblance— specifically when responding to child faces that were morphed to resemble the participant. It would appear, therefore, that facial resemblance in children may activate neural substrates associated with the inhibition of negative responses in males.

The need for both resemblance and mate fidelity in men is strong. In 2004, Apicella and Marlowe went to explore the relationship between "men's perception of the degree of resemblance between themselves and their offspring and their perception of their mates' fidelity" and found that the less their offspring resembled them, the less investment they made, and if they suspected their mates were not faithful, they invested even less in their children. If the men were no longer involved with their mates, the degree of their children's resemblance to them became an important factor on how much they chose to invest in their children.

War propaganda exploits these notions in men, and stories of the rape of their in-group women is a strong and common theme that spans cultures, countries, and eras. The Second World War produced numerous rape-themed posters and stories, with illustrations of enemy soldiers with exaggerated features, making stark contrasts between the facial features of the in-group and out-group. Fascist propaganda posters used images of

African-American soldiers in such posters, yet when it came to their posters of soldiers murdering their children on the battleground, the out-group US soldier was overwhelmingly white.

But there is another reason why the rape icon is powerful as it manipulates both men and women: there are reproduction differences between r-selectionist species (i.e., the parents are promiscuous, their offspring is of high quantity, low quality, and there is low parental investment), and K-selectionist animals, such as humans (i.e., they are relatively monogamous, and their offspring are of low quantity, high quality, and the parents are atricial). When an enemy is portrayed as a r-selectionist beast, we see them spread at a faster pace, threatening to overpower us in sheer numbers. It is not just that enemies are portrayed as rapists, but *vermin* rapists. They are drawn as rats and snakes who will quickly overtake us by sheer volume alone as they not just impregnate their women, but our own.

We often see xenophobia complaints about immigrants during times of peace: *they* have "too many" children that *they* expect *us* to support. *They* are criminals who will rape *our* women. When xenophobia turns into civil unrest, the icons become more overt. Such images of immigrants have been used in modern times in Canada, the US, UK, Denmark, Norway, Spain, South Africa, and France, for example.

But if we have emotional bonds to children we identify as being part of our own in-group, the fear of the dangers that can harm them can bring terror, as was the case of a US couple worried about the fate of their own two children – and the 10 Sudanese orphans they took under their wing on December 31, 2013:

> The eyes of the American parents living at a United Nations camp alongside thousands of South Sudanese refugees fill with tears as they describe their options: Remain and risk another rebel assault or fly to safety, leaving behind the 10 orphans who call the couple mom and dad.

> For nearly two years, Brad and Kim Campbell have been feeding, clothing, educating and parenting 10 South Sudanese children whose parents were killed by conflict or sickness. Their missionary lifestyle was upended after violence broke out in South Sudan's capital, Juba, Dec. 15. Now the Campbells, their two American daughters and the 10 orphaned children live

in an ad-hoc U.N. refugee camp that is low on food, water and sanitation.

The former Omaha, Nebraska residents are grappling with ensuring that daughters Katie and Kassidy Talbott are safe, and also protecting their South Sudanese children, who range in age from 5 to 16. Mother Kim Campbell, 54, said it is a tough balance to strike.

"I have two of my own children here," she said in an interview at the refugee camp on Monday. "We know the situation is bad. There is no food or water in Malakal."

We are at the mercy of not just the enemy, but our in-group authorities. When there are dangers to vulnerable children from multiple angles, how does the propagandist propose that parents respond when there are physical threats to offspring? Their answer will be to follow their decrees to the letter, make personal sacrifices, and gear up for battle. Children can be abducted, starved, and abused during times of civil unrest, and as a propagandist's tool, children are valuable pawns.

The terror strikes hardest when children are felled en masse doing the most mundane of routines, such as what happened in Yemen on August 9, 2018 as recounted by the *New York Times:*

An airstrike from the Saudi-led coalition struck a school bus in northern Yemen on Thursday and killed dozens of people, many of them children, local medical officials and international aid groups said.

The attack sent a flood of victims to overwhelmed hospitals struggling to cope in what the United Nations considers one of the world's worst humanitarian crises.

The coalition said it had hit missile launchers and called the attack a "legitimate military operation," but the attack and the justification for it were condemned and drew new attention to the tremendous human toll of the war in Yemen, especially on children.

"No excuses anymore!" Geert Cappelaere, Unicef's regional director in the Middle East and North Africa, said on Twitter. "Does the world really need more innocent children's lives to stop the cruel war on children in Yemen?"

An attack on children is not just an attack on our in-group's future viability and progress: it is a loss of innocence. Child survivors are damaged and often physically broken. The trauma lasts for years, and is found across cultures, nations, and eras.

Yet what a war propagandist suggests will create more childhood victims of war, causing more bloodshed and loss. Preventing carnage through proactive means while not taking the bait of violence stems trauma, and yet is rarely an option seen at the table.

Whenever we are dealing with information regarding the safety and well-being of children, we must take extra care to ensure the information we are receiving will not impede our ability to find constructive solutions by asking the following questions:

1. **How are children being portrayed in the narrative?:** Children are vulnerable, by definition of their undeveloped minds and bodies and lack of experience; however, if we are given too much detail about the alleged acts, but have vague details of the victims – and also the *villains,* it is a sign that there is something dishonest about the story itself. Verification is crucial here.

2. **Is the child or teen is too well-rehearsed?:** Is their performance too pithy? Are they overly-articulate? When their stories are well-rehearsed and choreographed, we must determine if they received media-training, and if they have, it suggests the story may be a fraudulent one. Children are vulnerable to exploitation, and in this case, they are being exploited toward a propagandist's cause.

3. **Can the information be verified?:** While grim stories about atrocities toward children can be real, other times, the over-the-top stories are too bad to be true. We need to establish when it happened, where, and who was involved. Are there satellite images to back up the claims? What forensic evidence has been provided?

4. **Are infants part of the narrative?:** The most vulnerable of children are infants, but they are also unable to speak or provide details. On the one hand, this makes them easiest target for abuse during conflicts, but their built-in anonymity makes them simple conjured figments to a war propagandist's canard. We do not believe or dismiss without verification, but we need to break down the story, separate fact from filler, and then look to confirm or refute the information given, the same way police do when investigating a peace-time crime.

Threats to children are a parent's worst nightmare, and nothing threatens a child's physical, emotional, and psychological well-being than war. The propagandist exploits the massive threat to keep both in-groups and out-groups in check, but the threat is made all the more serious and vivid when plague narratives are brought into the mix as the following chapter explores.

Chapter Twelve
Plagues

What we cannot see can kill us. Bacteria and disease strike silently as they are too small for the eye to see, but once sickness strikes us, if we have no defense against it, we are finished, and it can spread to masses in short order. We can be walking out in the street one day, and dying in the hospital under quarantine the next. The notion of such a death is one thing, but if we are denied the tools, medicine, and personnel who can save us, we have no hope of survival.

Such was a case presented of killing vaccination workers as was recounted on Australia's news program *Lateline* on November 27, 2014:

> Taliban gunmen in Pakistan have killed three female polio vaccination workers and their driver in the country's south-west.

> Another three of their colleagues were wounded when two men on motorbikes intercepted the health workers' van before they could meet up with their security detail.

> The Taliban often targets health workers carrying out immunisation programs, claiming the campaign is a cover for Western spies or an attempt to sterilise the population.

The notion of killing healers is a far worse than merely dying of a potential plague: the enemy has the power to not only spread disease, but undermine our solution permanently. Our advances are meaningless and the out-group will throw us back in a more primitive time, bringing out the animal within us to cower at its own helplessness.

It is not just the spread of disease that is concerning: it is the spread of an out-group's ideology that can destroy us and our way of life. War propaganda draws attention to the horror overtly, as it did in a January 8, 2011 article in the *Toronto Star*:

> In Pakistan, that moment has already arrived. The Taliban disease is metastasizing into the interior, encroaching even on

the capital, Islamabad. And the governor of Pakistani Punjab, a moderate figure, was gunned down in Lahore this week by a religious assassin.

For Canada and other Western nations, the growing instability in Afghanistan and Pakistan will be a major concern in 2011, threatening all of South Asia at the very time that our partnership with India is blossoming.

It is a cancer that has *metastasized,* all but announcing that it is *too late.* The danger is beyond critical levels. We have no choice but to fight with our strongest medicine, in this case, violence as chemotherapy.

Yet the notion of the out-group threatening us with the pain and suffering of illness is nothing new, but in the early Aughts, it was standard fare, with the term *bioviolence* used to describe it. The phrase had a chilling effect as it warned the Western in-group May 1, 2008 article in the *Futurist*:

> A looming danger confronts the world—the threat of bioviolence. It is a danger that will only grow in the future, yet we are increasingly failing to confront it. With every passing day, committing a biocatastrophe becomes a bit easier, and this condition will perpetuate for as long as science progresses.
>
> Biological warfare is as old as conflict, of course, but in terms of the objectives of traditional warfare— gaining territory or resources, compelling the surrender of an opposing army— biological weapons weren't very effective. If the objective is to inflict mass death and panic on a mixed population, however, emerging bioweapons offer remarkable potential. We would be irresponsible to presume that radical jihadists like al- Qaeda have ignored said potential.

Although the article acknowledges some unknown experts to dismiss the notion, the warning is that the reassurance is a lie, adding to the terror:

> Some experts argue that terrorists and fanatics are not interested in bio- violence and that the danger might therefore be overblown. Since there have been no catastrophic bioviolence attacks, these experts argue, terrorists lack the intention to make bioweapons. Hopefully, they are correct. But an enormous amount of evidence suggests they are wrong. From the dawn of biology's ability to isolate pathogens, people have pursued hostile applications of biological agents. It is perilous to ignore

this extensive history by presuming that today's villains are not fervent about weaponizing disease.

By the sounds of the warnings, one would believe scores of people would have already fallen to the silent and invisible plagues surrounding us in that era. Even *People* magazine took time off from gossiping on manufactured celebrity shenanigans and publicity stunts to deliver a dark message on November 25, 2002:

> The post-9/11 world raises no end of worries to keep us awake at night, and one of the most disquieting is: Could some enemy attack the United States with a massive dose of smallpox? This question took on new urgency Nov. 5, when government officials acknowledged that, along with the U.S., Iraq, North Korea, Russia and France have probably cultured the lethal virus. More disturbing, some of a stockpile amassed by the Soviets during the Cold War is missing, inciting fears that the potential biological weapon may have fallen into the hands of terrorist groups such as Al-Qaeda.

We are to be denied sleep thinking about potential violence and disease, but even here, the word is *probably*. We have no hard evidence or facts. Just an idea that it *could* happen, and it is bad enough. War propaganda thrives on terrorizing people even when the threats are slight or even nonexistent. One bad act of violence occurs, and then the worst-case scenarios begin to surround us more than the actual out-group threat.

Why are threats of the non-violent kind as terrorizing to us as the idea of bombings and shootings? These threats are evolutionary and primitive in nature, and it is something the animal within understands. We respond to catastrophes, droughts, famines, plagues, floods, and other natural disasters with fear as there is very little we can do to prevent a colossal disaster from swallowing up the entire in-group. Tsunamis and floods have killed scores of people. Tornados and hurricane tear down our fortresses with ease. When we begin to equate an enemy with being a natural disaster, we are turning them into more than just a villain: but a god and a force of nature as well.

The massive nature of a destructive out-group can suppress our willingness to see them as individuals. Mob riots in times of civil unrest conjures up a dystopian world where there is no humanity or reason. We cannot negotiate with a group that is infected with violence and hatred.

They are feral and reduced to searching for the bottom needs of Maslow's hierarchy.

Such as was a daylight riot to be found in Iraq as recounted in the July 10, 2006 story in the *New York Times:*

> A mob of gunmen went on a brazen daytime rampage through a predominantly Sunni Arab district of western Baghdad on Sunday, pulling people from their cars and homes and killing them in what officials and residents called a spasm of revenge by Shiite militias for the bombing of a Shiite mosque on Saturday. Hours later, two car bombs exploded beside a Shiite mosque in another Baghdad neighborhood in a deadly act of what appeared to be retaliation.

Mob mentalities are not the only things to fear. Riots and mass panics bring out the worst in people. They are no longer themselves. They are desperate enough to do anything to survive. They are merely responding to hardships that affect hundreds, thousands, or even millions of other people. If food supplies are cut off, how will they feed their children who will become weak and malnourished? The Second World War often saw food supply lines become a weapon in and of itself: cutting food off from out-groups often brought their defeat far more effectively than did bombs, guns, or tanks. In North Africa, Germany has been defeated by the Allies as they focussed on cutting off critical supplies until they felled the enemy.

Human behaviour radically shifts when disaster strikes, and panic and fear takes over. As Weinbaum noted in 1980:

> [A]s long as city people have food in their stomachs, political leaders need not fear popular uprisings; but it has become apparent that, in the absence of food security, no regime...can have a firm grip on power.

If we are weak, our immune systems are stressed, and we become exponentially weaker. When there are rations, we are made aware how close to the precipice we are, and how simple a matter an enemy can take us down with the absence of staples, even more so than the presence of soldiers. In 2001, Hinton, Chau, Nguyen, Nguyen, Pham, Quinn, and Tran showed that there were panic attacks from Vietnamese refugees attending a psychiatric clinic as memories of starvation during the days of Pol Pot regime stayed with them and significantly altered their behavior.

But the notions of disease and starvation are commo threats from the war propagandist. Any icon that can be equated with such devastation is used and frequently. As Connors noted in 1998, Saddam Hussein was compared repeatedly vermin in various US editorial cartoons, being portrayed as spider, rat or other creatures. He was a carrier of disease that could spread around the world and destroy it.

So persistent was the motif, that the *Sydney Daily Telegraph* kept the analogy going until the end on December 17, 2003:

> In his eight months as a fugitive, the ousted Iraqi dictator – who once boasted 68 palaces – was reduced to living in a filthy hideaway, eating only rice and chocolate.
>
> While every one of his former bathrooms boasted ostentatious gold fittings, he had to use an open trench as a toilet.
>
> And every time danger approached he disappeared down his pathetic rat-hole, hardly bigger than a grave.
>
> The ultimate humiliation for Saddam was not the fact that he looked like a beggar when caught by US soldiers on Saturday, but the hovel in which he was hidden.

Pairing the enemy with such insidious icons impacts not just our emotions, but our memories and perceptions of future events, ensuring we do not forgive or forget. Dutta, Kanungo, and Freibergs's 1972 experiment showed that subjects had selective memories: they were more likely to remember unfavorable traits of out-groups, but more favorable traits of in-groups. We see those who caused us terror as evil, long after the threat has either been resolve or even disproven. We see out-groups with suspicion, but in-groups as our salvation. We must stick together, or else we will fall apart. We are helpless if we dare stray away from the boundaries set for us by the war propagandist: we can easily starve or die from disease if the out-group sniper doesn't get to us first.

Morewedge, Gilbert, and Wilson's 2005 experiment demonstrated that atypical events are more vividly recalled than mundane ones, and they also used their past emotions as filters to future events, leading the experimenters to conclude that "the impact bias (the tendency to overestimate the affective impact of future events) may be due in part to people's reliance on highly available but unrepresentative memories of the past." In other words, we remember traumatic events clearly, and then expect for them to happen again and be more likely to occur than what it logically or physically possible.

It was that kind of mental manipulation that went into the symbolism of 9/11 by Osama bin Laden's operatives. It was more than a terrorist attack: it was propagandistic theatre. The mundane routine of air travel was turned into a weapon that could fell thousands with shocking visuals. Damaging the Pentagon and the Twin Towers in New York was a form of cold terror that was to prime the audience and impact their thoughts, emotions, and most importantly, *future* expectations. An encore would be near impossible to pull off as measures would be immediately put in place, and yet after, the idea of terrorism, gripped citizens who expected the act to become a regular part of life, even if the expectations never lived up to reality. The plague hit US soil without warning to the middle-class, and then altered the narrative for them.

And the act itself suddenly became a creature that could strike us with its venom as one September 26, 2001 piece on NPR's *All Things Considered* showed:

> The United States briefed NATO allies today on the direction of its military and economic strategies to capture those responsible for the September 11th attacks. At a meeting of allied defense ministers, Deputy Defense Secretary Paul Wolfowitz said the US is planning a multifaceted, long-term battle against terrorism in which military tools are only one aspect.

The analogy was quick in coming from authority sources:

> Deputy Defense Secretary Paul Wolfowitz summed up US thinking, saying, "We are going to try to find every snake in the swamp," but the essence of his strategy is to drain the swamp. Wolfowitz did not come to NATO for the purpose of laying out evidence of who the United States believes the so-called snakes are.

When danger strikes unexpectedly, it will be likened to a snake. When it can reach a large part of the populace, it will be likened to a disease or a rat. We can never rest or feel confident as we cannot predict when the danger will strike again. The war propagandist exploits our fears and keeps the in-group dependent on their directives while keeping the out-group cowering in the corner with its own threats.

Finding the truth during times of unrest and conflict is a slow and laborious process, yet the war propagandist insists on rushing our thoughts and feelings. In cases such as these, we must take extra caution in determining if a piece of information is true and realistic, or a fabrication and distorted exaggeration. In this case, we need to be careful what to ask in order to make the proper determinations:

1. **Does the threat level align with reality?:** How many people have been harmed? Is there a solution? Often, a handful of people have been in contact with a threat, but then suddenly, the narrative insists that it has been thousands and that it is already "too late." Looking for an accurate picture gives us a better idea of whether there is a threat – or a threat of a threat.

2. **What evidence has been presented and how specific are the details?:** The vaguer the accusations, the less information we have to make a judgement, which will make the probability of finding the correct solutions lower than if we had a clear and accurate picture of events.

3. **Is the out-group being likened to a disease or vermin?:** This is classic war propaganda, and whenever it is employed by the press or authority, it is a troubling sign that a third party may have been employed to make a group of people seem like primal threats.

4. **Are out-group leaders being portrayed as evil despots unmoved by moral arguments?:** While there have been many leaders who were brutal and even psychopathic, when the coverage seems cartoonish or has fairy tale qualities, it is a sign that we are being re-aligned to think in terms of war.

When it comes to the darkest of threats, the war propagandist ensures that our minds are primed to panic, and we will look for saviors and salvation, but even then, the manipulators of war have prepared the script of what and who to look for in a hero, and we will examine next.

Chapter Thirteen
Heroes and angels

War propaganda must paint a picture of despair, but not so desperate that the in-group all surrender to the enemy. If there is no hope, then the in-group will turn on one another, on their leaders, or just give up. While an enemy propagandist may desire this outcome, those with the in-group are not wasting talent and resources for defeat. The end goal is always victory.

But to achieve victory, there must be models who an audience can mimic their actions and memorize their scripts. Originality and creativity must be suppressed. Ingenuity requires free and critical thinking. Sanctioned behaviours are needed in order to control the in-group to engage in predictable behaviour and strive for the same rewards and ideals. To rig behaviour requires a behaviourist approach: provide a hero who has the qualities to be rewarded, and positively reinforce those who follow the protocol. Those who don't are to be shunned and be portrayed as lazy, ignorant, treacherous, and immoral.

The brave are heroes, and guardian angels. They are easily identified by uniform. They are young, virile, brave, handsome, and desirable. They are tough and capable, yet most importantly of all, altruistic. Without them, we are doomed to fall to the enemy who will destroy us and our way of life.

Both men and women are given their directives on how they should model their behaviour. The Second World War produced no shortage of propaganda posters from various countries on all sides of the conflict: male soldiers looked robust, alert, with determined looks and erect posture as they slew the enemy. Women were glamourous cheerleaders to the men who did not gossip lest enemy agents got wind of important information, worked the factories, donated their modest pay to fund the war effort, and did not put up a fuss looking after children as they made no effort to talk their mates out of joining the army. As one Canadian propaganda a poster declared with a smiling glamour girl holding a weapon of war, *I am making bombs and buying bonds!* Another US one presented a somber-looking woman holding an infant and a toddler, *I gave a man, will you give at least 10% of your pay in war bonds?*

The "10% rule" was displayed on other such posters, with one comely young woman in a factory uniform putting money in an envelope with the slogan, *This is my fight too! Put at least 10% every pay day in WAR BONDS.* The 10% can be seen in various places on the poster. It is obvious the young woman does not come from wealth, but she is doing to heroic thing making ammunition as she gives as much as she can to the cause, at least $25 in an era where such an amount would be a dear sum. While her arms and neck are dirty from the work, her finger have a perfect manicure and she still has lipstick and looks fresh.

War soldiers could be smiling or serious. They could be wounded, but still freshly-pressed, cheerful, and powerful. They hold weapons, and in many cases, *swords.* These men fight with every breath and are in the middle of a chaotic battlefield taking on any and all threats.

These images are the *ideal.* They are the gold standard of what is considered heroic and angelic. Their faces are clear and expressive. They are muscular and proud. They alone take on armies of faceless and brutal enemies. They give their lives, their labour, and even their last cent to rid the in-group of the threat. They are everything an altruistic is expected to be, but the question is whether or not the images are *realistic.*

In Chapter 9, we explored the criteria for an ideal sexual partner through the filters of the war propagandist. The gold standards were also ones who were not just exceptionally attractive and sexualized, but were also unobtainable standards to achieve. The images are rigged so that the audience must work hard toward it, but never quite hit the mark, leading to self-doubt and feelings of fear and *inadequacy.* Yet when we are seen as emulating the ideal by the in-group, there are perks of praise, rewards, and should we fail and perish in our efforts, there will be processions, and perhaps even statues and our efforts memorialized in history books. There will be journalism articles of our heroic deeds and our sacrifice for the greater good. Should we survive, we will still be praised and written about through a positive lens, at least until the danger is past. As we have seen through the ages, heroes with statues of their likeness and buildings erected in their honors have often had those same statues and buildings taken down and renamed when a new authority overseeing the in-group has a different agenda and wishes to disparage the ideals of a previous era.

Movies depict heroic images in times of peace, but during times of war, they are more confined and clearer in their roles. In the US during the Second World War, the US Office of War Information (OWI) was the government agency vetted scripts for films, and was in operation from 1942 until 1945, and came four years after the US Justice Department's anti-foreign propaganda law Foreign Agents Registration Act (FARA) was established to ensure that enemy nations did not employ US companies or agents to disseminate their anti-US narratives to the public.

The OWI had its tentacles in every facet of communications, from print to broadcasting to film. The message was power as it was consistent with the goal of not just defeating the plans of their enemies, but ensuring the US was in a powerful position post-war. Entertainment and news was highly politicized. Films during the era relied on handsome actors fighting against caricatures of racist stereotype enemies who were mindless, homely, and indistinguishable from one another. Major movie studios had interchangeable films such as *Mr. Winkle Goes to War, Pilot No. 5,* and *The Purple Heart* all had the same underlying current: the hero is distinct and valiant. The enemy are wicked vermin out to destroy all that is good and would succeed without our in-group heroes.

Soviet Cold War propaganda had slight variations, but while their females were depicted as sturdier and more robust, and were more forceful than their daintier Western counterparts. Yet the men were shown as strong and valiant as were those in other nations, from the US, UK to China. The ideal man is more defined by his brute force and confident gaze, but also willingness to engage in front-line combat with the enemy.

The universal qualities do people look for in their heroes are universal throughout cultures and eras. At an early age, we see those close within our personal in-group as heroes. White, in 1999, surveyed youth from kindergarten to Grade 12 to ask about their perceptions of what is a hero. Most came with close personal members, such as relatives, as defining their notions of the concept. We seek those who are both extraordinary, yet *average*. An Everyman or Everywoman who we can relate to, but who goes beyond the confines of the mundane to protect us.

Yet it should not be surprising that athletes are often equated with heroism. They are strong, fast, and fit. They compete and aim for victory. From ancient Grecian Olympians to the present figures, we seek those with physical might, even if there is little use for them. They are still combatants, regardless if the athletes lean Left or Right. Colin Kaepernick may be a politically polarizing and controversial figure, yet he is revered for the same kinds of propagandistic notions of bravery that Allied soldiers were during the Second World War. Those who identify within a certain in-group see him as a hero, even if other groups do not – and see him with the same propagandistic hatred reserved for enemy out-groups. Polarizing figures often serve as both hero and villain and their image is co-opted for political narratives, regardless if the truth is less extraordinary than it is presented.

Yet athletes are not soldiers. They are not in charge of protecting us during times of war. Soldiers are the guardians, and often a propagandist will exaggerate the valiant ways of them. Any who break or disavow the cause are seen as under the spell of the enemy.

But the heroics will go over and above what is logically and even physically possible. In 2003, a British marine by the name of Eric Walderman was praised in the UK press for his ability to cheat death with his smiling picture of his helmet that protected him from no less than four bullets, as the March 27, 2003 edition of the *Times of London* reported:

> Royal Marine Commando Eric Walderman yesterday showed how he cheated death after taking four shots in his bullet-proof helmet.
>
> Marine Walderman's life was saved by his Kevlar helmet after he was caught in Iraqi gun sights during a gun battle at Umm Qasr.
>
> His relieved partner, Lindsey Robinson, 25, said: "I can't believe it. He is the luckiest man out there. I'm just so glad he's still alive."
>
> The 25-year-old soldier had the incredible escape as the Marines drove out the last Iraqi fighters from the key port town.

The four bullets ripped through the outer camouflage of the standard- issue helmet, but were stopped by the ultra-tough protective Kevlar shell.

Three weeks later, the story was revealed to be a hoax, but it was not the only one that found its way in the mainstream Western press.

Private Jessica Lynch was a 19-year-old US supply stationed in Iraq who had the misfortune to be ambushed by enemy soldiers after the vehicle she was riding in took a wrong turn. But the press painted her a hero worthy of the silver screen as was recounted in the April 3, 2003 edition of the *Washington Post:*

> Pfc. Jessica Lynch, rescued Tuesday from an Iraqi hospital, fought fiercely and shot several enemy soldiers after Iraqi forces ambushed the Army's 507th Ordnance Maintenance Company, firing her weapon until she ran out of ammunition, U.S. officials said yesterday.
>
> Lynch, a 19-year-old supply clerk, continued firing at the Iraqis even after she sustained multiple gunshot wounds and watched several other soldiers in her unit die around her in fighting March 23, one official said. The ambush took place after a 507th convoy, supporting the advancing 3rd Infantry Division, took a wrong turn near the southern city of Nasiriyah.
>
> "She was fighting to the death," the official said. "She did not want to be taken alive."

Like many other journalistic propaganda pieces, it relies strictly on unnamed experts, authority, and in this case *officials.* It was later revealed that the story was a complete fabrication, and that Lynch, who had no part in the false heroic narrative, was too wounded to be firing weapons or even moving, and was cared for by Iraqi doctors who did not harm her. The narrative was too good to pass up, but the truth came out later on.

Yet the narrative followed the rules of heroic narratives perfectly. Good and evil are defined across cultures and eras in specific ways, but all show an all-or-none dynamic of being completely devoted and loyal to the in-group. They are up against *inferior* enemies who are evil, dangerous, deviant, and lazy, and must protect the in-group from starvation, rape, torture, and murder. Soviet propaganda often showed female farmers producing mounds of wheat and staples to feed the collective: this was a woman who mothered the in-group while the men took care of the brutes who would harm them.

Regardless of culture or era, the hero protects an in-group at the highest possible risk. A Good Samaritan warns the in-group or helps those vulnerable members of the in-group, such as children get away from danger. Physical and moral heroes are defined as those agents who have altruistic properties and will sacrifice themselves for the protection of the in-group. While physical heroes are expected to also be moral agents, moral agents are not always expected to use physical strength to protect the group.

Yet both must not seem me-centred. We look for certain qualities and narratives in our heroes and saviours. Martyrs will die for us. Guardians will kill for us. They can do so with confidence as we are the morally superior group in the conflict, and there is no doubt of our superiority. Their memoirs (should they survive to have a ghostwriter pen one) or biographies (should they not) will recount a certain *folksy* charm: they saw the obvious dangers and were compelled to act for the in-group's survival, and then *glory*. To win is not just an act of ensuring that our basic needs are met: it propels the entire in-group to the top level of Maslow's pyramid of needs: the collective becomes *self-actualized*. We have won the future. The OWI has already set the narrative for a Post-War narrative for the US even before the war was over, for instance.

While politicians must write a concession speech in case of defeat, though they also hope their victory speech is the one they use, the war propagandist does not ponder concession speeches: their point is to manipulate the in-group to win, not lose. They move pawns on to a board through imagery and narrative. Heroes are carefully crafted to be a balance of extraordinary, but also mundane. We can relate to them, and hope to become them, yet the price of honor is most likely our lives, and while we may dream future generations will see that we tried to reach and impossible ideal, often those who tried to emulate the propagandist's script are reviled and disavowed by future generations who are under the judgmental spell of a new war propagandist with a new agenda who must erase the past to provide no reference as to not to taint their carefully-crafted directives.

One of the most difficult feints to detect and overcome, when the in-group is presented in glowing terms as being heroic, we often wish to believe our side has not anything heinous, and even when we are forced to confront it, we may create out-groups within our own group to blame *them* for the acts, as we distance ourselves from those atrocities; however, when we are presented with heroic tales of in-group acts, we must still verify information by bypassing the self-adoration, and thinking critically:

1. **Are in-group members being portrayed as super-human in terms of strength, cunning, and morals?:** While real acts of heroism exist, we must take care not to assume that our side hasn't done anything questionable to the other side. Timing of these stories also give us clues: if there has been bad or demoralizing news about our losses, often times, a "feel-good" counter-narrative is used to keep in-group support in a healthy range.

2. **Are these feats physically or logically possible?:** Often, these stories are exaggerated or even fabricated to give an impression that our in-group is super-human, and haven't suffered losses or committed atrocities. It is important to look for confirming and refuting information to ensure we are not having our attention deflected from the reality of the situation.

3. **Are in-group atrocities being hidden through heroic tales?:** Often, questionable acts are framed as heroic ones, while other times, they are manufactured to hide what the in-group is doing. It is important to verify or scrutinize information with a skeptical eye to prevent our interpretation of reality from being skewed.

The heroes of the in-group are the protagonists in the narrative, and there are clear and defined differences from the enemy. There may be show trials to display captured enemy leaders, but these courts do not follow the standards that peacetime criminal courts do, and even in-group attorneys who are asked to represent enemy out-group defendants often find due process is not the point of these flawed trials: it is theatre to assure the public that the in-group's propagandistic narrative was correct: the in-group were just and hence, victorious, while the out-group are guilty without a shadow of a doubt. If the hero is the ideal of good, the enemy is the antagonist and obvious defective villain who must be destroyed at all costs, as the following chapter explores.

Chapter Fourteen
Us versus them

What is often forgotten about war propaganda is that usually there are at least *two* disgruntled parties, and *both* will engage in the practice of mass manipulation. Bombers will find righteous justification for their carnage, for instance. The US has often been accused of using mass communications to put forth a narrative for the case for war by scholars who commit a confirmation bias of ignoring the other side's propaganda. War propaganda is war propaganda. There has been no shortage of anti-US propaganda from the USSR to North Korea to Al-Qaeda and ISIS. The Nazis whipped their citizens to fear Jews before going on to instruct them to fear US soldiers, particularly African-American ones.

Strangely enough, we do not always have empirically studied direct side-by-side comparisons, though books such as Sam Keen's *Face of the Enemy* has taken a more holistic approach to looking at war propaganda through universal eyes, and regardless of the ethnicity, gender, race, religion, or background of the propagandist, the methods are the same: patriarchal, antagonistic, and distorted. It is a dichotomy using shaming, fear-mongering, and virtue-signalling to tell a simplistic tale of how the righteous and flawless in-group must resist against the forces of the out-group. There is no group, nation, region, or people who do not use propaganda to gain mass compliance and have used war propaganda in one form or another. When we are led to believe that there is only one group who employs it, our perceptions become distorted and we become vulnerable into thinking we have found a simplistic rule that will forever make us immune from it.

But it is that very belief that is the foundation of war propaganda: *we* do not have propaganda, but *they* do. *I* do not believe propaganda, but *they* do. We may define our own in-group based on Right and Left politics within a nation, but outsiders do not see our divisions: they see the whole nation as *they*. We do not have to look any further than the US's left ideations of Russian agents meddling in the 2016 presidential campaign: there was not a single differentiation on *which* Russians were to be distrusted: it was just *The Russians*.

It is this track where the seeds of war propaganda become planted: *we* are diverse, while *they* are homogenous; ergo *we* are immune from bigotry, while *they* are bigoted toward *us*. Once we begin to divide groups, we begin to *compare* them, and comparisons bring adjectives with connotations and judgements based on a pecking order. *Our* superiority makes *us* a target, and the inferior *them* will seek to destroy *us* because *they* cannot compete with *us*.

We were on the edge of perfection when *they* destroyed *our* dreams.

The narrative has been employed time and again, and when it sparks or incites war, the violence seems to justify that narrative, even when we are no less culpable than the out-group. When we begin to examine mass communications during times of conflicts and clashes, one of the most important first steps is to determine how the narrative is rigged to contrast two opposing sides: how does each one see itself as *superior* and the other side as *inferior*. Is it based on language or religion? Is it based on race or nationality? Is based on economic or educational factors? Is it determined by political ideology or moral differentiation? Once we begin to chart how each group weighs their identifying traits and contrasts it to another group, we can begin to see how propaganda will be devised to reinforce the notions of in-group superiority and out-group inferiority.

Propaganda's content has not changed over time: *They* will always be brutal, evil, and behave as *one*. *We* will be the benevolent contrast who are fighting for freedom against their oppression and brutality. *They* are the threat. *They* are animals, and many propaganda posters over various wars have portrayed enemies as rats, snakes, any other form of vermin. They are the snakes who devour worlds as if they were morsels to be consumed whole. They are the brutes who will rape our women and slaughter – even cannibalize our children.

We, on the other hand, are civilized, and benevolent. We are valiant and embrace freedom. They are aggressors. We are peace-keepers.

They, in turn, see themselves as peace-keepers and us as the aggressors. It is this mirror image narrative that creates an impasse as no side wishes to lose, be in the wrong, or at fault.

How we begin to divide the Us into the camps of Us versus Them is simple: we have conflicts when our own rigs stand in someone else's way the way their rigs stand in our way. Logically, the optimal and logical course of action is to negotiate to find mutually beneficial common ground.

But when there are finite resources, pride, jealously, and greed, it becomes too easy to want to take the whole rather than just a part. Competition sets it, whether it is for land or for natural resources, such as oil. When a small in-group lacks the brute force to take more or at least keep more, they need to create a cause in such a way that they can *recruit* more members into identifying themselves as part of the in-group. They may be on a lower rung to be exploited and then discarded, but recruiting more into an in-group requires skill. Some will see themselves as satellites or allies, whiles others will wish to be included into the in-groups. What a war propagandist does is no different than a religion, cult, or even political party: preach to a potential flock to bring in more members, but the difference is that the war propagandist offers larger promises, but asks that the in-group or *flock* make a far bigger sacrifice.

How to cultivate and expand an in-group is a challenge, but with mass communications, it is possible to reach a larger audience with a targeted message. There can be fear-mongering if the danger is probable. There is inciting hate if violence is the goal. There are hints or even outright promises of utopia should the goal succeed, and when there is likely death, the build-up to utopia must be convincing, and it is the reason the in-group must be deified: they must see their actions and beliefs as *worthy* of reward.

Speeches often are tool of the propagandist. A live audience can be caught up in the idea of belonging to an action group and feel the cause is larger than themselves. They see the potential leadership up close: if it is one who is charismatic and can memorize the names of potential recruits, the sense of belonging and *mattering* to an authority often is enough to convince individuals to join, particularly youth. In the early days of Soviet Russia, the strength of a speaker's persona was emphasized as it proved to be an effective tool to convincing youth to identify with and join the ranks.

In the US, by contrast, one 2001 study, Deluga had subjects rate 39 presidents on "American presidential Machiavellianism" and charismatic leadership, and found that raters gave those with high presidential Machiavellianism high ratings for charismatic leadership and saw those leaders more favourably. Speeches are an important tool to orient groups and create an instant on-site in-group. If the speech is memorable enough or received attention, it is seen as a watershed historic moment for those who attend.

Posters and articles were once the other form of recruitment, but with social media, it is simpler to recruit on a global scale. Al-Qaeda and ISIS have employed such measures as have various factions of white supremacists.

Social media has become a powerful tool for war propagandists as Columbia University Political Science Brigitte Narcos noted in a 2000 paper:

> [T]he violence for political ends had triggered what one might call the calculus of terrorism: extensive media coverage of an incident that in turn results in public attention, and, most important, reactions by decisionmakers...

In-groups can be manufactured. So, too, can out-groups. The sense of belonging and group affiliation is a drive for many. War propaganda draws the lines in the sand, and elevates the in-group at the expense of the out-group, and does this in a variety of public forums to reinforce the message and give a sense of dire urgency: *if We do not act now, They will win.* We are pressured to trust the leaders of the in-group or risk expulsion and danger if we see common ground with the out-group. It is not just belonging, but also psychological ambush. You are either with the in-group or against the in-group. Common ground and middle ground do not exist.

The gambit is a common one during political campaigns with frenzied fear and misplaced hope as no matter who is victorious, the rich remain rich, while the poor remain poor. For those who are older, they have enough experience to see how past leadership has fared, but to the war propagandist's target audience, the naïveté of youth allows them to promise that *this* group will be the turning point who is superior to their parents and grandparents: it is even within in-groups that divides take place. Respect for our forefathers and foremothers is discouraged for a *new* and by default, *superior,* if untested way of doing things.

War propaganda exploits more than just the unknown future: it isolates factions of the in-group and primes them to view the source of the problem as being outside the chosen faction of the in-group. It actively encourages xenophobia. It is ageist toward those of the in-group, but bigoted toward those outside the in-group. Nazi Germany created the Aryan ideal to differentiate the in-group with others, such as Slavs. Western propaganda posters in the Second World portrayed the Japanese with overtly racists features that made them look inhuman and gnarly next to the robust Caucasian soldier. The teeth was exaggeratedly large and fang-like, with one poster overtly turning the head of the Asian enemy into a ball to be punched by a strong white fist with the word "American labor" written on the arm with the phrase *Don't save his face! Every blow counts!*

The out-group must be dehumanized before they are to be obliterated. North Korean anti-American propaganda posters have portrayed US soldiers as ghost-white monsters torturing the in-group with wicked glee. The out-group are not just homely people: they cannot be trusted to do anything else but harm us in inhumane ways.

It does not take much to create in-group perceptions and biases against any out-group. The mere grouping and labeling of two random clusters of people is enough as we have seen earlier. People view members of their own group (whether the group is national, ethnic, religious, or some other designation) as superior to others, and even within in-groups, there are castes within them and skirmishes. We label generations, such as Baby Boomers, Gen X, Millennials, and Gen Z, with each group seeing themselves as superior to the others. We do not see evolution or progress from one generation to the next: we see previous generations as being inferior in their beliefs than the current group, until they are disavowed by their children as being ignorant and discriminatory. The divide among in-group generations isolate targeted groups, preventing them learning from the past errors and wisdom of those who were fooled by the same messages in previous conflicts. The inexperience of youth makes them a premium group to court, but not for their superiority, but natural credulity that comes from a lack of experience and empirical observation.

Human nature views strangers and those who are different than us with suspicion. We see out-groups as potential threats, and as some scholars have noted (Volkan, 1985), humans have a need not for just allies, but enemies. We need to have a tangible group to blame when we are in conflict or feel impeded. As we have no emotional investment in strangers, they become easy to turn into designated enemies. If we are incited by a third party, such as the press, we are more likely to cause harm. In one 2014 study, Yanagizawa-Drott, examined one Rwandan village's behavior during the country's 1994 genocide and found a correlation between propagandistic messages and bloodshed: after state-sponsored broadcasts were aired, there was an immediate marked increase in violence against the out-group.

How and why do people dehumanize their enemies and rivals? The answers are inter-connected: in-groups look to an official source and authority to guide them, and show there be impediments, the leader can transfer blame onto an out-group that can be identified. The authority will justify vilifying the real and perceived foes by equating danger and hardship to the destructive ways of the out-group. Conflicts begin to arise, and while one group begins to demonize and dehumanize the group, the targeted group will begin to do the same in retaliation. Tension builds as anecdotes of terrible deeds bring real skirmishes and the idea of resolution becomes increasingly difficult. That is the point: the gambit cannot work if two sides see their common traits and begin to humanize one another.

We see shades of this deteriorating dynamic whenever there is anti-immigrant sentiment: the newcomers do not know the area's Shibboleths. They see their own ways as *normal*, but are seen as an affront to the in-groups own ideas of *normal*. The immigrants or refugees are not personalized: they are referred to as a large *collective*. Nations may begin with noble intent, but should there suddenly be an economic downturn when jobs are scarce and resources become finite, and that same group is seen as a threat to life and way of life. The isolated newcomers are suddenly seen as the enemy with news stories making note of any government programs these groups received at the expense of the in-group. Propaganda encourages the dehumanization of out-groups in order to justify violence, even genocide as being a moral and courageous solution. Out-groups are seen as leeches and vermin who must be exterminated to prevent our crops from being taken by them.

However, when times are prosperous, people are less likely to turn on a geographically close out-group; it is when the animal within feels its needs *threatened* does it begin to make its calculations. Economic struggles and hardship provide the environment for the propagandist to operate; however, when an out-group attacks our land, once again, our needs are threatened and we are more likely to become a receptive audience, even if the wrong out-group is identified. In modern times, some mass killings were initially linked to terrorist groups before it was later discovered that it was a member of the in-group that had their own reasons to express their hatred. We are more likely to believe an out-group member will cause us harm than one of our own. As Fluckiger (2006) noted, immigrants have been portrayed as criminals in reports in North America, Britain, Western Europe, Russia, Costa Rica, and South Africa, while are seldom seen as actors in other types of news reports.

We seek assurances and look for those who most like us. We are primed to judge qualities in people to determine both inclusion and exclusion. We seek those who speak like us, look like us, believe like us, dress like us, but also understand the subtle rituals of the in-group. Fraternities and sororities at universities separate students as they partake in different rituals and pledges, and it should be no surprise that this age group – when they are away from home for the first time – are prone to in-group creation and affiliation. Students who do not join such groups are often excluded from group activities and bonding rituals as a result. We seek affiliation, and then compare our in-group to others.

But group affiliation is not enough. We need authority to sanction the in-group and guide it. The in-group turns to an expert or official for advice and guidance when deciding whether to trust strangers from their authorities, and appeals to the authority. News reports use experts and officials as their staple to assert what they report is the truth, yet many reports do not name a single expert or official by name when doing so. The

Jessica Lynch hoax was predicated on the word of unnamed officials yet time and again, the assurances of veracity turn out to be deceptions, yet many continued to believe the original claims.

Should someone in the in-group become alarmed and challenge the narrative, their loyalty will be in question, and accusations of treason and treachery will plague them. In 1972, actress Jane Fonda's trip to North Vietnam during her own country's war with the area resulted in a backlash and turned her from an insider become an outsider, and the actress was dubbed *Hanoi Jane* for her perceived disloyalty as the August 14, 1972 edition of the *New York Times* made clear:

> If the Justice Department de cides not to prosecute Jane Fonda for her radio broadcasts from Hanoi, it should recom mend legislation to provide criminal penalties for similar cases in the future, the House Internal Security Committee said today.
>
> Representative Richard H. Ichord, Democrat of Missouri, in a letter to Attorney General Richard G. Kleindienst, said, "In the event the Justice Department determines that the broadcasts of Jane Fonda from Hanoi during July, 1972, do not constitute treason or sedition, or that her conduct cannot be reached by existing statute for any other reason, then the department is requested to furnish a report to the committee with recommendations for legislation which would be effective to impose criminal sanctions under similar circumstances in the future."

John Walker Lindh, otherwise known as *The American Taliban* was captured in 2002 in Afghanistan fighting for the enemy side, but it was not just Lindh who would be questioned for loyalty. Jesselyn Radack, a "duty" lawyer in the Justice Department's ethics office discovered that Lindh's father hired him an attorney, and she advised that Lindh could not be interrogated without his lawyer present. When her emails were leaked by *Newsweek,* she found herself unable to find employment despite her credentials and background. She merely advised the government about its legal obligations, yet found herself being accused of sedition and disloyalty. She did not defended Lindh, yet the notion of possibly aiding an out-group during times of war is enough for severe repercussions.

In times of peace, we take our in-group affiliations for granted, but should there be war and we are not mindful of the fragility our bonds when the animal within feels threatened, we can find our lives turned inside out as we are labeled treasonous for aiding and abetting those who wish to destroy us. Even those who proclaim to support us will not risk harm by risking their well-being to show tangible evidence of their solidarity.

When we see an Us Versus Them narrative, we need to establish whether the linear divide is real or manufactured. Furthermore, we need to see whether there are inter-group relationships, such as inter-marriage and offspring with multiple affiliations. "Purity" of ethnicity is a dangerous motive for violence, but it also often serves as a red flag that there are propagandistic narratives in play. We need to look very a skeptical eye whenever such divides have been constructed as we asked the following questions:

1. **On what variables has the Us versus Them divide been constructed?:** Is it based on racist or bigoted elements? Is it a form of religious, political, socioeconomic, or ideological bigotry? The bigotry can be *two-sided,* meaning both sides are appealing to chauvinism. We do not take one side as the "correct" one by default.

2. **Is there a history of tensions?:** Knowing how long the narrative has been in play gives us valuable clues of the built-in triggers and justifications used to sustain conflict.

3. **What are the motives for creating the divide?:** We cannot dismiss monetary or geographical gain, and, in fact, would be wise to begin our working hypothesis by confirming or refuting that this battle is merely a distraction in order for one entity to gain financially or politically from weakening the other. While nationalism may be a ruse or justification, the truth is that there are those who profit from the distraction of violence and exploit frenzied and uninformed citizens by overwhelming them and encouraging them to plunder and murder for gain. Should the factions be wise to the ruse, they would be less likely to engage in the scheme in the first place.

4. **What political operatives, lobby groups, and PR firms are behind the stories? Who is paying for the coverage, and how much are they paying for it?:** To begin our journey to the truth, it is best to follow the money trail. While the US has FARA, other countries do not have similar laws, and in a world where stories can be disseminated through any nation's

media outlet or social media network, it is important to establish provenance of every fact and anecdote. In fact, an inventory of information and its origins can help us devise maps of webs of information as well as disinformation.

5. **Do the stories or speaking structures sound too rehearsed or too much alike?:** If everyone in a story provides succinct and profound pithy quotes, we know the polish must come from an outside professional source. If stories have the same patriarchal structure and have the same change in plot twists at the same junctures, we can be certain they have originated from the same propagandist. Timing of stories are also crucial – when did these stories begin and where did they originate? When we see coordinated efforts with too much refinement, we can be certain the stories, if they are not out-and-out frauds, are gross exaggerations meant to distort and manipulate.

There is still a peculiar irony to in-group and out-group dynamics: while we may see ourselves as superior to the out-group, we also dehumanize them as we erase their individuality and their very faces, as the next chapter shows.

SECTION THREE
Mindtrapping

Chapter Fifteen
Erasing faces

In the words of Aldous Huxley, "The propagandist's purpose is to make one set of people forget that certain other sets of people are human." The war propagandist must erase the faces of the out-group to prevent us from see common ground, or worse, sympathizing with the enemy. We cannot bond with an enemy, nor are they allowed to bond with us. We may begin to question the violence and the carnage. We may begin to fall in love with one another as we begin to question the narrative that this is an unreasonable people who wish to harm us. Take away the common ground and unreasonable requests seem logical.

The civil war in the former Yugoslavia was a peculiar example of erasing individuality and presenting an entire nation of people as a single entity. As noted elsewhere, the Serbs married other ethnicities, but they also had clashing political beliefs with one another. Today, there are at least eight viable political parties with wildly different platforms, there is ideological diversity in the region and has been for years. During the Second World War, when Serbs fought alongside the Allies, they were various factions, from the Partisans, Monarchists, and Chetniks among others. It is a collective with a long history of internal debate and headstrong conflicts.

Yet the Western press did not seen this group in those terms. They were repeatedly referred to as *The* Serbs, and the narrative assumed the group was single-minded and marched lockstep together. Yet if we were to look within our own mundane collectives, we would clearly see we have different opinions and beliefs, as well as our own principles and ideologies. We have different politicians who preach different solutions and could not be mistaken for their rivals. We have our own heroes, from celebrities to athletes. We have different collectives within our own who have various affiliations, based on careers, race, ethnicity, religion, sexual orientation, and socioeconomic status. We would be amused if an outsider were to tell us that our wealthiest citizen thought the same way as the local poverty activist, yet when it comes to war, that is precisely what we do to out-groups without thinking.

Yet the above is a minor example of it, nor is it the only example of one group being turned into a single entity without faces that express emotions other than hatred, wickedness, and anger. With each of the Gulf Wars, the press wasn't concerned about putting a face on the various regions and factions of Iraqis, but merely presenting *The* Iraqis.

Often, the war propaganda will take advantage of a group to show they are a people without faces. When there is military conflict with Muslim nations, for instance, much will be made of niqābs covering the face of women, never mind that those without covering their face are also made to seem *faceless*.

As one UK journalist mused to Canadian journalism students in 2004:

> ...British journalist and author Roy Greenslade, who maintains the world may have been a different place if war correspondents had written the truth about the horrors of World War I instead of playing the patriotism card, accepting government propaganda and suppressing facts.
>
> "It is surely fair to speculate that if newspapers had done their job then people would have pressured their governments to negotiate a compromise settlement," Greenslade told Ryerson journalism students at this year's Atkinson Lecture as he talked about the powers and perils of patriotism and war coverage.
>
> "Millions would have lived; Germany may not have been saddled with crushing reparation; Hitler's Nazis may never have risen to power."
>
> By adopting an attitude of "country, right or wrong," Greenslade said journalists "may well have done a gross disservice to their countrymen and women, not to mention the rest of humanity."

But for the in-group to be absolutely certain of their own rightness, they must be presented with a single narrative about the enemy that seems absolutely wrong. The less human the enemy seems, the less we believe they could be right. They become unverifiable entities who seem robotic, and devoid of a soul and we begin to fear what this horde of heartless enemies have in store for us.

Biologically, humans require faces to process information, and we begin to recognize faces early on. Infants as young four months and show preferences to seeing faces. Journalists talk about the importance of putting a "face" on their stories: nebulous concepts are less likely to serve as a "hook" than when there is a person who represents the "face" of the event or issue in order for the story to be relatable and comprehensible.

The war propagandist knows this as well as the psychologist and journalist, and focusses on the important task of dehumanizing an enemy group: that is, the targeted out-group must be made to look like a dangerous outsider. By isolating the target and making him (or her or they) seem inhuman, and therefore, they must be different than us: we have hope, dreams, goal, family, love, opinions, and connection, but the enemy out-group does not. They are all the same. It is the reason, for instance, why the niqāb was prominently used as a symbol of Islamic untrustworthiness: the enemy is watching us and it could be *anyone* hiding underneath. In 2019, Kabir examined Australian newspapers and found an increase use of the "Muslim Other" narrative to isolate the designated out-group. The black clothing and head coverings made it simple to frighten many Western citizens by equating the out-group clothing with facelessness.

Sometimes an enemy knows that facelessness strikes fear in his targets and will deliberately hide his face for such purposes. During the height of ISIS's campaign in 2014 and 2015, they had one of their operatives, known simply in the Western press as Jihadi John, a British man of Arab extraction who beheaded various foreign hostages all while obscuring his face. His victims, on the other hand, had their faces in clear view of the camera, wearing orange jumpsuits, which was a symbolic piece of propaganda in its own right.

The March 2, 2015 edition of the *Independent* drew attention to his lack of face:

> "It's about creating a mythology and the name is a big part of that," says Raffaello Pantucci, a counter-terrorism researcher at the Royal United Services Institute. "[He] was never masked to shield his identity – he must have expected to be identified at

some point – but to create the myth of the faceless butcher, the avenging hand of Isis. The nickname plays into this to create a cartoonish figure."

It was macabre live theater war propaganda, baiting those targeted groups to go after the terrorist group, but most forms of propaganda switch the roles to incite the *in-group* to ready for battle, not the other way around, and when he was later confirmed killed in a drone attack, the Western press had their narrative pre-set by the out-group with whom they were at war, as the *National Review* did in a November 13, 2015 piece:

> Few individuals deserved to eat a Hellfire missile as much as Mohammed Emwazi —a.k.a. Jihadi John, aka the Masked Coward. Responsible for torturing and slaughtering Western hostages and innocent Muslims with grotesque zeal, Emwazi has been a human metaphor for the Islamic State. But even aside from this righteous fulfillment of justice, his demise — reported and highly likely, though not yet officially confirmed — would be a significant strategic success.

> For a start, U.S. and British Intelligence Services have been working hard to locate and kill Emwazi. Hiding in the Islamic State's Syrian fortress capital, Raqqa, and cognizant of U.S.-U.K. intelligence monitoring, Emwazi, like other ISIS leaders, would have made great efforts to avoid … Indeed, as the BBC's Frank Gardner reports, Emwazi "took particular care not to leave a digital trail to his whereabouts." And took "enormous efforts to intercept and decipher any encrypted messages that might reveal his location or those of his associates."

When faces are erased, we can impose whatever narrative we wish, and when the in-group hunts down and kills the enemy, it is seen as a success: *our enemy cannot triumph over us because we will hunt them, kill them, and expose them on our path to victory.* In-groups seek the removal of faces to build up their drive and desire to prove their superiority to the haunting phantoms.

Erasing faces is a real form of othering: it allows the in-group to pass judgement on the out-group's motives and assumes the out-group has less than pristine motives for their nebulousness. On April 18, 2011 one Fox News Channel opinion piece made an interesting case for banning religious headwear for women:

> The face-veil (niqab or burqa) presents both a security and health risk to others. Imagine a doctor or nurse who is veiled in

terms of spreading deadly superbugs; imagine the awkwardness of a face-veiled courtroom witness, judge, teacher, or bank manager.

Most important, from my perspective, the burqa is a "prison," a "coffin," a "moving sensory deprivation isolation chamber." I have argued that it is a human rights violation and constitutes both a health hazard (to the wearer) and is a form of torture. Burqa wearers have no peripheral vision and only limited forward vision. Hearing and speech are muffled. Facial expressions remain hidden. Movement is severely constrained. No eye contact can be made.

Those who wear the gear are potential disease spreaders – never mind that the practice has been in existence without incident for this long. They hide their faces from us. They avoid eye contact with us. It is a security risk. They are deprived of sensory stimuli; ergo, their perceptions and experiences are inferior to our own. That is the argument used to create a pecking order, and justifies imposing our way because the in-group knows better and needs to end the ways of the out-group before it is too late.

The op-ed piece argues that the out-group does not move or see the way the in-group does. The faceless cannot be seen as having any feelings, families, doubts, hopes, fears, or dreams. In this case, the out-group women are so deprived of stimulation they do not know how tepid and weak their perceptions are and must be instructed how to dress by the in-group. We must assimilate the faceless before they do it to us. The out-group in this case has been isolated, and in the words of the author, are hiding in living in a prison of their own making. These out-group members are isolated from the correct ways of the in-group and are less trustworthy because of it.

There is one more detail to the article: it does not quote or interview a single out-group woman. There is no *face* to the argument, not even a quote to react to with a rebuttal. We do not put words to the faceless because there may be a chance the in-group sees the other side's point.

Once an enemy has been made faceless, the real work to dehumanize then demonize begins. Creating a faceless enemy requires overt or covert censorship: we leave the out-group's personal diversity and texture away from our narrative. They must all be made to be the same, and the rig must ensure they have no humanity inside them. After isolating the enemy, the out-group must be made to seem cold, barbaric, brutal, and most importantly of all, faceless. The enemy is equated with sheer brutality, and a heart of stone; the more depraved the image, the easier it is to get public opinion on side to be willing to impose violence on those they fear.

It is a common motif in journalists' war stories as was the case in this March 31, 2006 front page article in the *Kitchener-Waterloo Record* about Canadian soldiers in Afghanistan:

> War is waiting and drinking tea, then running and waiting some more.
>
> War is driving into roadside bombs and having the limited satisfaction of shooting at distant figures slipping over a mountain ridge.
>
> The enemy in this war looks like almost every other Afghan until he strikes.

It also was a central theme in a December 14, 2005 Canadian Press piece:

> For the division, which fought the Taliban in Afghanistan and helped U.S. forces drive north into Baghdad during the March 2003 invasion of Iraq, there is the frustrating reality that otherwise friendly village leaders could be behind the bombs.
>
> Anyone could be an insurgent, and ahead of this week's parliamentary elections, the attacks showed no signs of waning: Four American soldiers were killed Tuesday in a bombing northwest of Baghdad.

The article also equated facileness with enemy cowardice and cunning:

> "I can accept the fact that the guy got the draw on me. But not being able to see the enemy, it ain't fair," said 1st Sgt. Andre Johnson, 38, of Baton Rouge, La. "Just show me your face. Let me know who you are."

Yet turning an out-group into a faceless horde speaks more of the war propagandist's cowardice: when we feel guilt or shame, we avoid eye contact with those we wish to harm, and when we try to manipulate our own mental images by denying those faces exist, we know what we are proposing is wrong. When we deny the existence of texture and variance within out-groups, we are dehumanizing an entire group of people. There can be no face-to-face negotiation without first acknowledging those who do not agree with us have faces, feelings, ideas, and goals. To overcome the drive to create a faceless enemy, we must first see them as they are – as another group of Us.

When one side is taking pains to erase faces and personalities of other groups to homogenize the perception of them to others, we must ensure we do not follow the same bigoted path. It is a brazen act of chauvinism, and to see the picture of reality clearly and accurately, we must ask hard questions in order to restore those faces before we proffer solutions to conflicts:

1. **Is there an attempt to make one side look interchangeable with one another?:** If the answer is yes, then we know that there is propaganda at play. The out-group has people who have families just as the in-group. If they are aggressors, we should still see them as human beings. It will be how we relate to them, find common ground, and devise solutions that are realistic and will not haunt us later on.

2. **Are out-groups identified by a collective label?:** The labelling of collectives conditions us to accept vague information instead of hard and falsifiable facts. Group X is a nebulous term. Fifty members of a group who come from a specific region with the following leadership gives us an opportunity to verify information and know the extent and spread of hostilities.

3. **Are there too many frivolous details about the in-group presented and too few of the out-group?:** This is a form of misdirection to ensure we are focussed on the real and perceived injustices we are suffering and not notice we do not have evidence to confirm or refute the claim, nor will we believe we are the aggressors or have caused harm to the out-group.

4. **Are we left to use our own imaginations to paint a picture of the out-group?:** The fewer details we are given about the out-group, the more likely we will imagine the worst about them, and if our brain chemistry is being manipulated through stressful messages, we will be hard-pressed to be able to pull back and see the situation rationally. Sometimes it is members of the in-group who wish to create monsters to gain mass

compliances, other times, it is the out-group trying to seem more powerful than they actually are.

5. **Are stereotypes used to describe the out-group?:** The less realistic the portrayal, the more likely a propagandist has exploited our own inner fears and prejudices to paint the narrative ourselves.

6. **Is the term "villain," or "aggressor," or "enemy" expressly used to describe the out-group?:** While they may be any or all of the above if their intent is to cause harm to us, over-use of the terminology hints that there may be deliberate distortions used to describe an out-group and the situation is more nuanced and complicated than what it presented.

7. **Do in-group members covering a conflict understand the ways of the out-group?:** How well-versed are they in terms of language, history, culture, and Shibboleths? Often in-group chroniclers impose their own filters on groups they had very little contact with or knowledge about, and rely on stereotypes and generalities rather than helpful information.

To remove the face is also the first part to paint over those faces with one of our own making in order to elevate our standing at the expense of the other as the following chapter explains.

Chapter Sixteen
White knights, dark shadows

Justification for evil actions is at the heart of war propaganda. The propagandist gives us licence to kill, and the arguments are persuasive when they are not tested or scrutinized. Voltaire who said best when he mused, "anyone who has the power to make you believe absurdities has the power to make you commit injustices." One of the surest ways of getting an in-group to believe absurdities to have them commit injustices is by assuring them that they are morally superior to another group of people and they have the right and duty to cause harm to the out-group.

While the structure of war propaganda is Us Versus Them, it must take the narrative to an extreme. Our perceptions of reality must be hijacked and filters must be placed to superimpose over reality. We are transported to a fairy tale where we are the white knights who must battle the dark, faceless shadows in order to survive and stop the evil from winning.

We suddenly forget our in-group has prisons filled with murderers, rapists, child molesters, and torturers, but see the out-group as having nothing but brutes among them.

The differences between the in-group protagonists and out-group antagonists are stark, as they were presented in a June 10, 2010 piece entitled "We heard the blast that killed our boys --- AUSTRALIANS AT WAR" about an attack on the Australian forces by the Taliban:

> Major Jason Groat the Officer Commanding Alpha Company 6RAR told me two soldiers had been seriously injured. Within the base atmospherics was soon heard a ricochet of frightening words: 'One member, no vital signs'. . . 'EDD deceased'.

> Complexions paled. This tight-knit company, as close as only soldiers become, had trained together since last September and fought together since February.

From the ramparts we saw a helicopter land 2 1/2 kilometres to the west as another hovered above. We saw the evacuation chopper wing back towards the main base at Tarin Kowt.

The time span between incident and arrival was 38 minutes. And then we heard worse. Two soldiers had died, the second in transit.

They were well known to the company. They were part of the company. They were the company. You could not miss them. Sapper Jacob Moerland, better known as Snowy, a lean Queenslander with white hair and moustache stood out for more than his looks. A "character" is how his mates put it. In contrast Sapper Darren Smith, "Smithy", the dog handler, new to the company was shy, but no less keen to make Herbie a star.

The Taliban caused harm to *our boys*. Our soldiers are *boys*. The word brings positive connotation and humanity. The soldiers in the piece are all humanized. They have nicknames and are a cherished part of the in-group. We know nothing about the individuals who killed the in-group soldiers. They are the collective known as the Taliban. They are nameless and faceless. The fallen soldiers of the in-group have names, faces, personalities, and families.

The assaults on our in-group will reinforce the idea that *our boys* are in the right and must vanquish the out-group threat, even if they are harmed. In one March 24, 2003 article, presented such a narrative:

After a sober weekend that saw both British soldiers and journalists killed in Iraq, polls indicate a striking turnaround in public sentiment here.

A YouGov poll released Sunday shows 56% of 2,116 respondents feel Britain and the United States were right to take military action to force Iraq to disarm, while 36% disagree – the exact inverse of a similar poll taken before the war.

"Since the fighting started, there has been a rallying around," polling analyst Peter Kellner says. People "want to back the troops."

That back-our-boys mood could explain the comparatively modest turnout of 100,000 protesters at Hyde Park Saturday. Many of the marchers were schoolchildren, and some touted other causes ("Don't go ballistic, go solar," read one sign).

We are saints. We are angels. Even when we feign skepticism, we side with the in-group and disparage the out-group. March 10, 2003 article from *Newsweek*:

> I spent a few days in December on an aircraft carrier in the Gulf. My bunkmates were Palestinian journalists from the Mideast Broadcasting Co. (MBC), all of whom acknowledged that they refer to suicide bombers in their reports from the occupied territories as "freedom fighters." Hmmm... It turns out these guys (or their colleagues) are going to be hanging with U.S. forces again when the shooting in Iraq starts. But that's a smart thing for the military to allow. Under its new policy, the Pentagon will "embed" 500 correspondents for up to two months with American combat units, 20 percent of whom come from the foreign press. Will some media "embeds" end up "in bed" with their military protectors? Will others be so hostile they are forced to leave? Not clear, but one thing we know: for now, anyway, the anger that military officers felt toward the news media during the Vietnam War has subsided. They need every reporter in the region – no matter how skeptical – to help fight Saddam Hussein in what may be the mother of all propaganda wars.

The press is not there to be objective – neither side as both have their own terms to describe their in-group and out-group. They are there to tell a *narrative.* The journalist admits as much above. He then goes on to justify the spin:

> That could happen again. Truth will forever be the first casualty of war. But maybe this time the military can stay focused on its larger aim – making sure that Saddam doesn't get away with lies about the effects of U.S. bombing. "What better way to combat those lies than having impartial observers right there?" Lt. Col. Mike Halbig told me. Even the Arab crews from places like MBC and Al-Jazeera will at least broadcast the good pictures they get with the Americans. They'll toss in their spin, but TV pictures – as the U.S. military has finally learned – speak louder than the words of some official behind a podium.

The "pictures" will prove our in-group is right. There is no question, just a mere justification why journalists are agreeing to be babysat by an authority.

"Embedding" was doublespeak for guided censorship and spin. It allowed for those chosen journalists to brag as they mentioned their adventures *first.*   As one journalist wrote in 2005 about the process of "embedding":

> Welcome to our generation's battle for hearts and minds, born in the shock and awe of America's invasion of Iraq. It's driven by politics, ratings, the sheer number of news outlets and Web sites available these days and, most importantly, the unquenchable thirst for power in Washington. This is the propaganda war within Gulf War II. Its roots are in Ground Zero, and I have been a willing participant. So, too, were many other reporters. A month after the terrorist strikes on the East Coast, I sat in the cargo hold of a C-17, its bay door open and our crew wearing oxygen masks as the Air Force dropped crates of humanitarian rations in the dead of night from 25,000 feet over Afghanistan. A few weeks later I was in Kuwait with a 1st Cavalry Division brigade.
>
> These military events were legitimate stories, but also our coverage of them contained an obvious rah-rah component. We were, after all, reporting on events certain to reinforce the patriotism of Americans already supportive of President Bush and the war. It harkened back to the simpler era of Ernie Pyle journalism, and I relished it as any patriotic American at war would—especially with an enemy as easy to hate as al-Qaeda. But I also knew it couldn't last as I stepped on the bus that took NBC's David Bloom, *The Washington Post*'s Mike Kelly, and a dozen other journalists to our assembly areas in Kuwait's northern desert.

Even during an admission of what was clearly happening, name-dropping and reminding readers how "easy" it was to hate the enemy. *Yes, there is propaganda, but we are the heroes in this one* was the message (what is not mentioned in the report was that the US government was been warned about al-Qaeda's methods when they injected themselves in the Yugoslav war in the late early aughts, but ignored the signs).

What is interesting to note is it was no secret that the US government was overt in their attempts to control the message of war, which should have made the press skeptical of the notion of embedding. As the Associated Press recounted in one December 17, 2002 article:

> Less than a year after they shut down a propaganda office, Pentagon officials are debating whether the U.S. military should engage in covert opinion-moulding in allied nations.

...Operations could include paying European journalists to write favourable stories about American policies or secretly financing books or schools to counter radical Islamic thought being taught at some Pakistani religious schools, defence officials said on condition of anonymity.

A previous Pentagon program created after the Sept. 11 terror attacks to centralize information operations - such as spreading messages on a battlefield by leaflets - and to win over anti-American foreigners died quickly in February when the new Office of Strategic Influence was shut down.

Its closure followed an uproar prompted by reports that the office had proposed giving false information to foreign journalists to further the U.S. war against terrorism.

The problems would not end there, particularly after the Weapons of Mass Destruction – the impetus for the war – never materialized. The *New York Times* assured readers that there was WMD, and yet, when they were proven to be wrong, the apology they proffered on May 26, 2004 editorial merely entitled "The Times and Iraq":

Over the last year this newspaper has shone the bright light of hindsight on decisions that led the United States into Iraq. We have examined the failings of American and allied intelligence, especially on the issue of Iraq's weapons and possible Iraqi connections to international terrorists. We have studied the allegations of official gullibility and hype. It is past time we turned the same light on ourselves.

In doing so – reviewing hundreds of articles written during the prelude to war and into the early stages of the occupation – we found an enormous amount of journalism that we are proud of. In most cases, what we reported was an accurate reflection of the state of our knowledge at the time, much of it painstakingly extracted from intelligence agencies that were themselves dependent on sketchy information. And where those articles included incomplete information or pointed in a wrong direction, they were later overtaken by more and stronger information. That is how news coverage normally unfolds.

But we have found a number of instances of coverage that was not as rigorous as it should have been. In some cases, information that was controversial then, and seems questionable now, was insufficiently qualified or allowed to stand unchallenged. Looking back, we wish we had been more aggressive in re-examining the claims as new evidence emerged – or failed to emerge.

No matter that the crux of the issue is that the *Times* spread war propaganda and was wrong in the coverage, the narrative halo is still in place. The meant well. They did many things right (an *enormous* amount, whatever the term means), and they deserve the pat on the back that they gave themselves. They are still the heroes. They are unrepentant. They were just a bit lax, but that is *normal* according to the piece.

Nowhere do we have any mention of the *consequences* of that false narrative. How many innocent people perished in the war? How many were harmed? Why did the *Times'* coverage perfectly align with a propaganda narrative?

How do we have no means of challenging a narrative or have ways of admitting that the in-group can behave in villainous ways? How do we maintain balance when we are being forced to take a single side, regardless of what the facts happen to be? For instance, we have at our disposal forensic psychiatry which examines the likelihood of a person's truthfulness based on what they say and how they say it, yet during times of war, we have no vetting process to scrutinize what various parties are claiming. We have an in-group that is deified, and an out-group that is demonized, regardless of the circumstances.

War propaganda must convince its target audience that the enemy group all act as one entity and are all unteachable and interchangeable. Because the enemy is portrayed as a threat *en masse,* the level of danger the enemy possesses must seem swift, certain, and severe. Our boys Snowy and Smithy died a valiant death, but the out-group the Taliban was responsible. We do not know the nicknames of the individual enemy soldiers who did the deed, or whether they liked animals or were shy. It is not as if the out-group cannot do heinous things: after all, they are just as likely to absurdities that will compel them to commit injustices just like everyone else.

But it is Hero versus Villain, not People versus People. This angle does not serve a propagandist's purpose, however. The "other side" must be equated to the dark side. It is not a question of right and left or looking across at an equal: it is staring down at someone who is beneath you, and yet challenges your supremacy with evil intent. We cannot just say we disagree with an out-group: they must be seen as *monsters.* Even as recent as 2013, one *New York Times* editorial on the Syrian conflict ran with the headline, *"When to talk to monsters."*

The war propagandist exploits both our egocentrism and our xenophobia, and our own toxic stew makes us vulnerable as it prevents us from seeing people as people, as we can do more easily during times of peace. We see the out-group as a villain who is in conflict with our heroic side. We see their flaws and we see illusions of their brute force and their WMD, even when none exist.

On the other hand, the in-group's flaws and sins must be ignored in order to serve as a contrast to the target enemy. The egos of the in-group are stroked and heroes are manufactured to boost morale. We are *brave* and courageous, never monsters. We are knights in shining armor. War atrocities from our side or allied side are ignored by us, or justified. When we have a press that cannot admit becoming a vector that spread misinformation, we cannot expect them to challenge a narrative that appeals to our worth as heroes.

Because there are biological changes when an audience's emotions are being manipulated (when the ego is stroked, or when hatred is induced), propaganda can be an effective tool to manipulate perceptions of interpretations of reality. For example, in 2005 Schultheiss, Wirth, Torges, Pang, Villacorta, and Welsh showed that hormonal levels were impacted in both men and women depending if they were victorious in a task or failed. It was more than just emotions: it was *biochemical* changes as well. When we are told of our glory and victories, we are being primed on a biological level, not just an emotional one.

It is this last point that we must be aware of any time we are being groomed through praise and heroic narratives. We may have responsibilities and duties as citizens of our in-group, but we are also citizens of the world as well.

When the in-group automatically places itself higher than anyone else in some pecking order, we need to acknowledge our own subjective biases and begin to look at a battleground as flat where we are dealing with other human beings and not a pyramid that is rigged for us to be placed on top, whether or not we earned it. It is here where we need to ask the most self-critical of questions, or else, we will either over-estimate our power only to be felled, or we will cause harm to others where the rest of the world will wish to make us accountable for our own hubris and brutality:

1. **Are reports looking at our in-group objectively or are they justifying our behavior?:** Scandals have hit various governments and armed forces precisely because propaganda at the beginning hid darker deeds. In Canada, for instance, their armed forces were subjected to a 1996 federal inquiry after disturbing pictures of Canadian soldiers were released showing horrific abuse and torture of innocents. The 2016 Chilcot Report in the UK outlined that multiple governments were aware that there was no imminent threat to the West by Iraq, yet journalists from the Western world did not question anything they were told. US soldiers abuse of Iraqi detainees in Abu Ghraib prison also revealed that the in-group were instigators of horrific crimes against a captive audience.

2. **Are our in-group fighters and politicians being deified?:** It is one thing to acknowledge acts of bravery and kindness of individuals and groups. It is quite another to use those acts to hide the sins of the in-group. It is not a competition: both sides will have both good and bad individuals, and in order to find a workable solution, it is important to keep that balance and reality in mind.

3. **How accurate are reports of our in-group?:** How well is the information sourced? Are refuting facts presented as well as the confirming ones?

4. **Is the source an unnamed official in authority?:** If officials sources are anonymous, it is very likely the story is inaccurate and deceptive. Nebulous sources are most likely manufactured ones.

We must take care not to allow ourselves to be flattered as we are being encouraged to passively fear an out-group. If we are not careful at this delicate stage, we may find our own inner animal and machine being taken over and rewired as the next chapter shows.

Chapter Seventeen
Animal and machine

Prosecutors have to find it to secures convictions. Advertisers have to exploit it to fatten their clients' bottom lines. Actors are constantly pestering their directors about it to give a more convincing performance.

But it is also the one crucial atom of human behaviour that propagandists must understand to gain mass compliance. At the core of everything that we do, lies the spark that compels us to think, believe, and ultimately act in certain ways, and we call that "it" motive.

Knowing how to effectively change and manipulate the motivations of others has the power to drive people to create or destroy the lives of millions. Motivation can spark wars, or sweep in peace, but how a propagandist can effectively exploit the drives of groups of people with differing educational and socioeconomic backgrounds is a difficult question to answer. After all, how does a person quickly nudge one group of many to radically alter their differing (and often competing) motives, interests, and beliefs? What's in it for any of us to change our thoughts, beliefs, values, and behaviours? Why do we change the way we think and behave, especially behaviour that would normally go against our established beliefs – or could even cause us irreparable harm? Why go the more dangerous, primitive, and violent route when our pacifistic and routine ways have worked so well for us in the past, especially if there is no direct threat to our well-being in the first place.

For example, the aught's have shown us any teens and young adults, who grew up during peacetime in North America, suddenly and inexplicitly became radicalized to the point of changing their beliefs, religions, and made the decision to commit violent acts in their home country, or go abroad to fight as soldiers for DAESH. Their motives for joining and targeting strangers for death are not typical: they faced no danger at home. They were mundane youth with unremarkable upbringing, and yet, through social media, had slowly transformed into someone else.

They did not face imminent danger. They were not protecting loved ones, or were under threat. Martin Rouleau was a Canadian who had no overt natural motive to run down people with a vehicle, yet he is one of many who have followed the same path.

Yet it is not just "lone wolf" operatives whose mindsets became altered. When Iraq invaded Kuwait in 1990, there was little reason for most nations to fear for their lives or well-being. Citizens from countries such as the US or France were nowhere near the explosive region. While developments of the invasion made international headlines, there was little public support for liberating the small, wealthy nation with the reputation for hedonism and human right violations. Though the human rights watch group Amnesty International publicized its report on the chaos in Kuwait, polls continued to show a tepid support for international military action. So what would nudge various nations into committing troops to the small region?

It would take no less than the shocking tale of the slaughter of newborns to finally snap apathetic citizens into supporting military intervention against Iraq. One December 18, 1990 wire service article began in this blunt and dramatic way:

> It was a slaughter of the innocents.
>
> In the days that followed their August 2 invasion of Kuwait, Iraqi forces killed more than 300 premature babies by removing them from hospital incubators, Amnesty International reported Tuesday.
>
> The living-giving machines were then looted and shipped to Iraq.

How did the reporter know this story to be true? The article went on to describe the source of the cowardly and peculiar atrocity:

> On October 10, one fifteen-year-old Kuwaiti girl testified before a US congressional committee in Washington that she had seen Iraqi soldiers come into Kuwaiti's al-Addan Hospital and go into a room where 15 babies were in incubators.
>
> "They took the babies out of the incubators, took the incubators and left the babies on the cold floor to die," she said.

However, by this time, this story was hardly new: US News and World Report cited the same atrocity in its October 1, 1990 edition:

> On the sixth day of their invasion, Iraqi soldiers reportedly entered the Adan Hospital in Fahaheel looking for hospital equipment to steal. They unplugged the oxygen to the incubators supporting 22 premature babies and made off with the incubators. All 22 children died.

The sordid tales of the senseless killing of infants circulated as early as September, but was finally "confirmed" by a young eyewitness in mid-October. Though the eyewitnesses in question had either been exiled Kuwaiti ministers or vaguely identified civilians, their credibility was not scrutinized by either the press, nor the public. The stories were taken at face value and liberally embellished in various news reports. As one Associated Press article on November 28, 1990, recounted for readers:

> An infant's head crushed under a soldier's boot, a retarded girl gang-raped by soldiers, babies torn from incubators and from their mothers' arms and mass graves for babies were stark images in the testimony delivered by four men and two women.

The raw atrocities were allegedly witnessed by one teenaged girl who testified in front of a US Congress Human Rights Caucus, but her story was seemingly supported by Amnesty. It seemed as if her account was verified by credible institutions, but that was a clever feint.

The problem was that concrete and verified concrete evidence was sorely lacking, nor did the press or public know anything of this young girl's background.

No matter, public opinion began to shift from ennui to outrage. For example, one *San Antonio Express* editorial on December 23, 1990 played up the dead baby card without skepticism or corroborating evidence:

> The Iraqis apparently moved quickly after the invasion to suppress widespread opposition in Kuwait. No one – not even children and babies – was spared the wrath of Hussein's henchmen.
>
> The Amnesty reports says more than 300 premature babies died after the Iraqis stole their incubators from Kuwait City hospitals.

In a country whose population was then 2.1 million, 300 infant deaths were a significant blow. As was seen in chapter eleven, the girl's harrowing tale was a hoax. Yet the story was powerful enough to quickly spark international support for military intervention against Iraq. The tale of the slaughtered newborns was repeatedly used by both journalists and politicians alike in their daily missives to their public, though concrete information could never be found, and Amnesty's claim of 300 murdered infants was proven to be false.

Whether the incited are the lone wolf terrorists, or a general public, propaganda has proven to be an effective means of altering both perceptions and beliefs repeatedly.

Yet concrete and verifiable information is almost always lacking from the war propagandist's yarn: it is the emotional details that matter the most, though on first inspection, the propagandist seems to have provided some proof of his claims. Sometimes the proof is in the form of a seemingly credible eyewitness or detailed description filled with colour and powerful imagery. But on closer inspection, the propagandist's "facts" are frequently sketchy, or even nonexistent: forensic proof is replaced with more flowery descriptions more readily found in emotional fiction novels rather than police reports. In the above example, none of the numerous press reports about the alleged infanticide named names: which soldiers were responsible for the deaths? Why did they pick on newborns, and not the more threatening adults? Where are the bodies buried? What forensic tests were conducted to confirm the claims? What about satellite images (that were in existence in 1990)? Where are the stolen incubators and why did the soldiers need them over other medical equipment?

Of course, asking those basic and rigorous questions would ultimately lead to the truth, which is precisely what a propagandist does not want to happen: the purpose of the story is to spark outrage and reaction, not skepticism. In a way, the propagandist is like the magician who wants the designated mark to pick a certain card from a deck: the magician will use sleight of hand to force the pigeon to pick a predetermined card of the magician's choosing, even though the mark may believe that it is fate or free will, and that the mark has full control over what card is ultimately chosen.

Magicians refer to this sleight of hand as a *force*. The magician forces the selection, but gives the illusion of choice. The act is rigged to work in the magician's favour. The pigeon is mere window dressing.

The war propagandist also tried to "force" his marks to opt for a certain course of action that is strictly of the propagandist's – and not the audience's – choosing. But the manipulator cannot make the trickery obvious. There is a desired outcome that is needed quickly before anyone has a chance to question the story. The manipulator must make it appear as if the forced option is a natural and moral one that the marks chose based on facts and their own free will. In other words, the propagandist must nudge the targets to think in the precisely same way he wants them to think, without their knowing that they are secretly being manipulated.

It all goes back to motivation: why change an audience's motivation? Because their manipulator needs his audience to think and feel in a certain way that will lead them to wittingly follow his set script – one that has the potential to cost them their lives. If the targets all think and behave differently from one another, then they are more likely to disagree with him and balk at the extraordinary demands; therefore, mass compliance hinges on ensuring the majority of a targeted audience feel the same way about a course of action. There is strength – and comfort – in numbers: if the majority favour a certain solution, people are more likely to go along with (and feel secure about) the final *forced* decision.

But the psychological manipulator also has to ensure that the chosen solution (a) seems logical, doable, active, and moral to the majority, (b) seems to be one chosen of free will and consensus, and not trickery, (c) virtually guarantees victory over the enemy, and (d) is one of the pigeon's choosing. There is no point manipulating people if they all decide to go with another option that does not benefit the propagandist – the optimal "solution" has to be one that appears to be the most auspicious alternative by the majority of the target audience.

Meeting the requirements needed to change public opinion is no small feat: finding the right stories and images to spark outrage and fear, getting the desired consensus of diverse people, and maintaining momentum can easily backfire in the wrong hands. Motivating a sizable number of people to agree to opt for violent and potentially fatal measures takes careful planning, strategy, and a clear grasp of deep-seated fears and needs of people. The most important step is the *first* one: if the story or image doesn't provoke strong primal emotions and fears immediately, all else fails. If the audience has a chance to reflect on the information they are presented in an objective and calm way, then they are given too much leeway to analyze the misinformation they are given, and may rebel; ergo, propaganda must appeal to the primal, not the intellectual motivations of the manipulator's marks.

Those problems are the key obstacles for the propagandist to overcome if the goal is to quickly and effectively change the opinions and convictions of thousands, millions – or even *billions* of individuals, or at least stigmatize and isolate the potential resistance he or his superiors are likely to face. Different people have different agendas, experiences, backgrounds, knowledge, vulnerabilities, morals, philosophies, interests, cultures, and worldviews. Healthy and normal minds are unpredictable, individualistic, and question the unknown. More sophisticated thinkers or rebels will be skeptical of almost any declarations made by authority figures, whether the authority instructs them to deify or demonize a target. Mass persuasion is no easy feat: to procure broad consensus and action takes much more than mere persuasive parlour tricks or charming manipulation. For the war propagandist, the message isn't merely a way of communicating with his marks; it is the way of *controlling* his targets and stifling his potential detractors. A manipulator needs his targets to willingly give up their autonomy and their rationality so that they will blindly follow his orders.

Psychologists Stanley Milgram, Solomon Asch, and Philip Zimbardo proved how simple such compliance could be created. Milgram merely wore a laboratory coat when he insisted subjects give "electric shocks" to a confederate whenever the man gave "wrong" answers (the shocks were fake; however, the subjects were unaware of it). Subjects would be distressed, but continue to administer them, even when the confederate suddenly went silent, with the implication that he was dead or unconscious. Thought subjects were free to defy the experimenter who told them that they must continue, they increased the voltage as they believed they were bringing harm to a stranger.

Asch's experiment was not as distressing, but showed that subjects would overwhelmingly agree with the experimenter's confederates who would deliberately give obvious wrong answers to simple tasks. The subjects were fully aware that the answer was incorrect, but preferred to appeal to a group than rebel against their lunacy.

Zimbardo's prison experiment was as disturbing as the Milgram experiment as his subjects were assigned to groups of "prisoners" and "prison guards." Behaviour radically changed, and those who were designated leaders began to manipulate and abuse their prisoners, with weaker guards following their lead, and demonizing the groups of prisoners. The experiment was terminated early, but the results were devastating.

There is one more experiment worth mentioning: Elizabeth Loftus demonstrated the same dilemma in a subtler way: by merely using loaded language in a questionnaire, subject's memories of a televised event greatly altered. After viewing a car accident, the subjects who were asked how fast were the car going when they *crashed* gave faster estimates than the ones who were asked how fast the cars were speeding when they *collided.* Other experimenters replicated the findings in other ways: asking subjects whether they saw "a gun" during a videotaped robbery would not generate as many positive replies as those who were asked whether they saw "the gun" – regardless if a gun was present during the event. If subtle nuances in language generate vastly different replies, then we are a species who follows leads more than defy them.

What these experiments suggest is chilling: humans can be tamed and alter their perceptions of self and others by mere authoritative decree.

A war propagandist goes beyond decree: a manipulator targets biological motivators in such a way that other propagandists do not. Advertisers are targeting different human wants, needs, and insecurities, but their messages exploit an entirely different set of personal neuroses and competiveness: toothpaste with whitener promises a more attractive smile which can translate to more dates and admiration for beauty and health, while a more expensive car means flashing your elevated status among your jealous peers, again signalling your superiority within peacetime. It is meant to solve problems by the passive act of spending resources on a specific product. A powerful vacuum or antibacterial soap means cleaner surroundings that are resistant to potential germs and malodorous emissions, preventing weakness and social scorn.

In these cases, the target audience is promised a better way to enhance their potential assets, but on the whole, the audiences' safety and well-being won't come to an end without those products and services. A life without whiter teeth or a flashy car won't impede anyone's chances of survival. Even a vacuum cleaner or antibacterial soap isn't truly necessary for human existence to thrive, though they are helpful accessories that most of us (barring teenaged boys) have come to appreciate and take for granted. Most items that are subject to advertising save for (certain food, medication, and basic clothing, heat, and shelter) are not essentials for those of childbearing years. Formal education is also not an essential for a society to survive to reproduce. In fact, the majority of people in this demographic can survive and function without most medications.

Most advertisers merely promise a *better* way to life a life, whether better means safer, prettier, cleaner, sexier, richer, or happier. While fresh breath and trendy clothes may help a twenty-something improve his love life, those luxuries will prove useless if the person is being bombed by enemy troops. Disposable diapers are heaven-sent to any parent, but diapers will not save an infant from barbaric, drunken soldiers determined on annihilating their target. The propagandist does not deal with trivial insecurities or vanities such as looks or peer status. He deals with psychological and physical bare necessities – not only promising survival for the individual, but for the very survival of future generations of the in-group, and ultimately the in-group itself. It is life and death he peddles, not a clearer complexion or longer eyelashes. Propaganda thrives in chaos and repressed instincts; in peacetime, most citizens do not have to worry about the ravages of cancerous anarchy – they have police forces, courts, and active governments worrying about the feral minority from them. Instead, people can worry about better educating themselves, raising their children and social status, indulging themselves, improving their appearance or health, and earning more money to stay solvent.

But if the threats of war, economic devastation, and lawlessness interfere with the mundane reality of the established social order, mass psychological priorities change to the propagandist's advantage: everything that was once established and taken for granted is either being threatened, or is now *destroyed*. Here, a propagandist can deftly fill a void: he or she provides them with the critical information the in-group needs to know about an enemy – and it is the manipulator who can decisively show and clear the route that leads the in-group away from the enemy's lethal clutches. People fear for their lives and safety: an assured, informed, and powerful voice (or more likely, a chorus of voices preaching in unison) will get their attention.

The voices may also get attention and credibility for another reason: as many experts in communications and crisis management have noted, the message that is disseminated first is the one which sets the terms of debate in the public mind: retractions can have almost no effect on public opinion (particularly if the voices are weaker, less credible, or more disorganized than that of the opposition), and the message may be dismissed or simply ignored. First impressions are crucial in crisis communications: if the seasoned exploiter plans carefully, or at least quickly takes advantage of a chaotic situation, he can immediately disseminate his message to his targets first, thereby spinning reality the way he needs. With his audience fraught with trepidation, they are in the right mindset to listen and obey.

We have seen such a stunning example during the war in the former Yugoslavia, where international public opinion went squarely to the sides that invested greatly in public relations. Ruder Finn Global Public Affairs represented warring sides. There was a void of knowledge of the region, and the firm took full advantage, and set the narrative from then on. The less an in-group knows about a region, nation, or peoples, the easier it is for the war propagandist to fill in the blanks with whatever narrative will demonize the other group as prior ignorance will serve as a barrier to seeing the lies and slander.

As also in the case of Iraq's 1990 invasion of Kuwait, foreign interests of regular citizens were hardly threatened; in fact, the bigger danger lay in invading rather than staying out of the line of fire. Kuwait was a small, obscure Middle East nation that was nowhere near North America or Europe (the civil war in the former Yugoslavia hit closer to

Europe, and its interests were more immediate). How can a war be sold to disinterested, sheltered third parties? Why did the babies and incubator hoax work as well as it did?

There may be many reasons why unaffected citizens believed a dubious yarn and agreed to risk the lives of their troops to liberate a distant nation, but two important features stand out: so long as a propagandist can (a) argue that stopping a potential threat will prevent an enemy from growing more powerful, and more importantly, (b) appeal to the latent raw, primitive instincts of his audience, he still has an excellent chance of persuading his marks. In the Gulf War hoax, the emotional descriptions of the senseless "murder" of newborns sparked outrage, yet, the logical problems of the story hardly sparked the intellectual skepticism that the take should have immediately provoked. Why did the hoax seem credible enough, and be powerful enough to serve as a rallying cry for war? What was so special about that hoax?

The war propagandist has a different arsenal of psychological tools to manipulate and shape his audience than does the advertiser: someone may feel apprehensive about his thinning hairline, but that level of shallow anxiety cannot be compared to the fear of torture, starvation, rape, or murder. It's as if the war propagandist and advertisers are with extreme alternate worlds. For propaganda and other persuasive messages to be successful, the target message needs to appeal to people's basest needs and fears, but to do that, the manipulator has to understand human behaviour at its most basic level.

People may have different levels of education and income, they also may have a different set of ideological beliefs, but everyone needs food and fluids to survive. Extreme cold will kill the professor as readily as the janitor. Both the Republican and the Democrat will die in the same agonizing way if they are shot in the head, and both know a foreign agent does not seem them as separate entities. The wealthiest socialite and the poorest homeless young girl will not be able to have children of their respective lovers for the next nine months if they are impregnated beforehand by force by enemy soldiers. Economic, ideological, and class divisions are virtually illusionary: while money can provide better access to superior medical care, education, and standard of living, wealth is not a fail-safe shield for everything. Facing the business end of a rifle reduces everyone to the same level of helplessness: the Olympian and the quadriplegic suddenly have everything in common.

It's not simply the threat of assured death that keeps the more primitive portions of our brain preoccupied: on some level, the mind worries about fulfilling the purpose of our existence; that, is, making certain we reproduce and ensure that the next generation lives to reproduce as well. So far, societies can expand in only a single way: by ensuring women and men of childbearing years and capacity actually have children. Even with immigration, the younger immigrants still need to make babies to make their inclusion into the in-group worthwhile. In other words, instincts drive most of us to avoid enough dangers to survive to the reproductive years – and then ensure that our offspring survive long enough to continue the cycle. The urge to merge is there for a reason.

In a functioning and peaceful society, this cycle usually runs relatively smoothly, whether the cycle involves a prearranged marriage of a young man and woman, or a same-sex couple employing a fertility clinic or surrogate mother to achieve the same ends. But within the two ends of the spectrum, the typical cycle involves a man and a woman uniting – and at least one of the parents raising the children themselves. While cultural norms and sex ratios play a crucial role on how this cycle will run for the majority of the in-group, the end result needs to be the same: enough safety for the in-group to produce the next generation, regardless of a couple's sexual orientation. The bottom line is reproduction. A threat to this cycle can mean the destruction of the in-group – not just for human in-groups, but even for the simplest of animals.

If the instinctual goal is to secure the next generation, then the question becomes *what does an in-group need to make certain that the reproduction cycle functions smoothly?* At the most basic level, the in-group must have space, provisions, safety, and trust, meaning an in-group requires the following criteria in order to survive:

•Enough physical land to support an expanding society;
•Adequate shelter to protect the in-group from outside threats and extreme climate;
•Enough food and clean fluids to survive;

Adequate weapons and defenses to keep enemy out-groups at bay;
•Enough healthy, fertile young women of childbearing years to ensure the next generation;
•Enough fertile in-group men to impregnate them;
•Enough protection to keep newborns and children alive, safe, and healthy;
•Enough parental confidence to prevent infanticide;
•Adequate communications systems to not only ensure cultural indoctrination and loyalty to make certain the in-group stay as a cohesive unit, but also ensure that the in-group are warned of any potential dangers.

Without any and all of the above provisions, an in-group will eventually die out, whether the in-group is a tribe, nation, or continent, and it is up to the in-group to keep themselves unharmed as best as they can at all costs, both for the safety of the individual, as well as the collective. But there is one more provision that an in-group needs to keep themselves functioning as a single unit, though the quality itself can be completely arbitrary, nor is it essential in any way for *personal* survival: an in-group needs a distinct set of customs, beliefs, and other differentiating characteristics to separate themselves from outsiders. It is a form of sanctioned insanity: certain dress or rituals may have no other function other than serve as a Shibboleth so the in-group know who is one of their number, and who may be a potential threat. While humans can survive in both permissive and restrictive systems, the idea of group preservation and survival is essential for the collective as will be discussed in more detail later.

Yet the drive for collective adherence, loyalty, and trust remains strong, even if it is not always an objective and rational process. In one 1984 experiment, researchers told two groups of college students who were randomly assigned to two separate groups that they were, in fact, a separate "group" before they were asked to rate each group on intelligence and attractiveness in comparison to the "other" random group. Logically, the groups should have rated themselves higher on some levels, but the other group as equal or higher in others since the groups were randomly chosen.

However, when it came time to rate each other, each group rated itself and other members of their own temporary "group" as being superior to the other "groups" in *every* way – quite an interesting assessment considering that subjects were arbitrarily thrown together. There was no design or pattern in mind. Merely being told by an authority (in this case, the experimenter) that someone was part of their "group" was not only easily accepted by subjects, but suddenly, the members of the group seemed prettier, wittier, and more urbane than those peasants in Group B. Group formation is a natural process: people divide themselves according to religious beliefs, race, age, gender, profession, political affiliation, past trauma, wealth, musical tastes, hobbies, residence, geography, language, favourite sports team, and even telephone area code. Add the fact that we are primed to hold a more favourable view of our in-group, and the potential for inter-group conflicts becomes greater. Ours is always better than theirs, but then they have the gall to always think that they are better than us.

So then, at the most basic of human concerns are two things: one, that we can live long enough to procreate, and two, that we belong to a group. But how do those two urges have anything to do with propaganda? What's the connection, and why is it important?

War propaganda is no ordinary negative communications system: its purpose isn't merely to insult a target enemy, or smear him for wearing off-season shoes: what would be the point of calling an enemy group meek or merely rude? What outrage can the insult "slacker" or "garish" bring? There is none, and that is why a war propagandist doesn't employ superficial put-downs. The propagandist doesn't waste his time that way: he accuses his targets of being rapists and murderers who are out to destroy the in-group because he knows that is the quickest and most assured way of getting attention.

By treating the enemy as both a feral animal, and a heartless killing machine, the psychological manipulator can dehumanize his target, and in the process, exaggerate the differences between the in-group and the target out-group. Enemies are portrayed as rapists and murderers who threaten to destroy the home team's women and children (thereby threatening the reproductive success and existence), while expanding at the in-group's expense. As we have seen in previous chapters, starvation is a popular theme for propagandists. During the Second World War, British and American posters made it clear that food shortages were the doing of enemy forces; thereby justifying the reason why food rations were needed to be imposed (the posters served two purposes: to ensure compliance, while placing blame on another party so that the in-group would not blame its own government for the action). Fast forward to the Balkan War of the 1990s where Bosnian Muslims in the region were reported to be so hungry that they were forced into cannibalism to survive, though the story was later to be proven a hoax.

If basic biological drives are important for enforcing certain messages, we should expect to see many propagandistic messages appeal to these forces. We should also expect to see a strong reaction to propaganda, which appeals to our evolutionary drives, such as accusing enemy soldiers of raping and impregnating the in-group's women (meaning the males have lost the chance to expand the in-group), starving us, driving us from our land, expanding on our territory, and ultimately, killing us.

An enemy who can take out ten of us is dangerous. An enemy who can take out a hundred of us is a force to take seriously. But an enemy who can quickly and efficiently murder tens of thousands or millions of us is one who has the power to not only kill us, but can also destroy the existence of the in-group. It is the big numbers that the war propagandist is interested in since it will get him the most attention, and likely the biggest support to implement his chosen solution any way he wishes. The specter of big threats looming over an in-group is most likely going to a near *carte blanche* for the ruling regime.

It was a big threat that brought quick and deceive support for the 2003 US invasion of Iraq. Then Iraqi leader Saddam Hussein needed to be stopped, not just because of his government's record on human rights abuses – but because he would soon be capable of slaughtering citizens in faraway countries with his Weapons of Mass Destruction.

Reporter Judith Miller seemed to know the frightening truth as she stated in a March 19, 2003 *New York Times article*:

The administration has assigned top priority to the hunt for weapons of mass destruction, officials said. After months of relatively fruitless international inspections, the discovery of such arms, officials said, would vindicate the administration's decision to go to war to disarm Iraq. Conversely, failure to find them would leave the administration vulnerable to charges that it had started a war needlessly.

The same narrative was seen again in her numerous articles, including one on November 22, 2003:

Such intelligence information is particularly vital at the strategic level. "War has become so much more destructive through concealment and long-range strikes that the warning time before an attack has diminished considerably," Mr. Pollack said. ["]Terrorists armed with weapons of mass destruction, states and other nonstate actors could inflict terrific damage in a much shorter time frame than ever before."

Hussein was once again seen as a serious threat to countless other in-groups, though United Nations inspectors did not find the evidence to support the accusations. Dr. Hans Blix, who headed the UN inspections stated as much: that there was no "smoking gun" found in Iraq, according to Dr. Blix. However, supporters for the invasion insisted that the threat was real and it was big.

But just how big was the threat? As big as a mushroom cloud, according to US President George W. Bush. That message was aired on most American news programs, as it was on the October 8, 2002 broadcast of *The CBS Evening News with Dan Rather*:

GEORGE W. BUSH: Facing clear evidence of peril, we cannot wait for the final proof, the smoking gun, that could come in the form of a mushroom cloud. Understanding the threats of our time, knowing the designs and deceptions of the Iraqi regime, we have every reason to assume the worst, and we have an urgent duty to prevent the worst from occurring.

However, the "clear evidence of peril" wasn't clearly outlined, yet the "smoking gun-mushroom cloud" metaphors would be used again and again, as it was in the September 9, 2002 edition of *USA Today* when then national security advisor Condoleezza Rice was quoted as saying, "But we don't want the smoking gun to be a mushroom cloud."

The macabre idea was repeated in another speech on November 12, 2002:

GENERAL TOMMY FRANKS: What I believe that means is that a great many nations on this planet will line up with the United States of America – I didn't say to go to war – I said will line up with the United States of America, in our view, as part of the international community when we say, "The road ahead will not continue to look like the road just behind us," because the stakes are too high, and the sight of the first mushroom cloud on one of the major population centres on this planet is something the most nations on this planet are willing to go a long ways out of their way to prevent. And that is the position of strength which I believe we occupy right now.

The "mushroom cloud" just wouldn't go away – it was hovering over the November 26, 2002 edition of the Fox News Channel's *The O'Reilly Factor*:

US ARMY COLONEL DAVID HUNT: This pre-emption has – we have to have this in order to protect ourselves. This – the United – the Middle East is a very volatile place, and we've got one of the most volatile men in the world sitting there with – trying to develop weapons of mass destruction. I don't need to wait for a mushroom cloud in Houston to know that we've got to hit this guy before he gets going.

There's no doubt in my mind we're going to have to do this.

That latest buzzword also reared its ominous mist on the October 7, 2002 edition of CNN's Lou Dobbs' Moneyline:

MAX BOOT, COUNCIL ON FOREIGN RELATIONS: The question in my mind is, are we going to have to see a mushroom cloud over Manhattan before we realize that we are not containing Saddam Hussein?

That's a risk that I'm not willing to take, And I think we need to act pre-emptively, before he requires nuclear weapons to go along with his chemical and biological stockpile.

Boot repeated the same phrase on CNN on October 30, 2002, "I wouldn't give it too much time, because if we give it too much time, Saddam Hussein will develop nuclear weapons, and then he will be free to do whatever he wants. And the only way we'll find out that containment isn't working might be perhaps if we see a mushroom cloud going up over Manhattan."

The ubiquitous mushroom cloud proved so popular, that one Canadian columnist repeated it on September 24, 2002, "America and its allies could wait and see what Saddam Hussein does next. But inaction has its costs. As national security advisor Condoleezza Rice crisply states, 'We don't want the smoking gun to be a mushroom cloud.'"

By 2003, a solid number of Americans clearly favoured invading Iraq – even though the Iraqi government did not even declare war on the US, but no matter, it was the mere *possibility* that persuaded enough people to support a war, though as of this writing, those tools to make the mushroom cloud was never found.

But the threat of mushroom clouds is hardly new: propaganda posters from the mid-1940s on have also used images of the mushroom cloud as a dire warning to its target audience that an enemy has the potential and the desire to wipe out the in-group on a mass scale. Ironically, many scaremongers from other nations (from the Soviet Union, then Czechoslovakia, East Germany, Vietnam, and China) have used the same ominous symbol to describe what the US has the potential to do to them and others.

Yet it doesn't have to be a WMD that is used as a reliable in-group bogeyman: the threat of biological weapons, such as the spread of HIV, or the use of nerve gas or anthrax can also be invoked to strike fear in the target audience; just so long as the threat seems swift, certain, and severe. However, there is another advantage to employing scare tactics: when fear is deftly used as a persuasive tool, critical thinking skills on the part of the audience can be suppressed, and they may fail to notice that the propagandistic tale is, in fact, riddled with logical errors. Fear is used as a misdirection: it draws the audience's attention away from the poor sourcing and shoddy reasoning, and toward the more sensational and emotional parts of the story. For those who are skeptical, they can be isolated, silenced, demonized, and accused of treason, or at least heartlessness and sympathizing with the designated devil.

Ironically, those who believe a propagandist's likely story too often refuse to consider whether it is they who are sympathizing with the wrong group or person. If that's the case, then how can so many war propaganda stories be so readily believed over and over again, when many of those tales fall apart on closer inspection?

Millions around the world readily believed that Iraqi soldiers stormed a hospital, left the more threatening adults alive, left important hospital machinery that could have used behind, but stole incubators, took the trouble to gently take the newborns out of these devices, placed them (as opposed to tossing them) on a floor, left with the equipment, and the hospital staff just stood passively without bothering to pick up those helpless infants to save their fragile lives.

The story is so faulty that it is laughable, but it didn't stop many intelligent, shrewd, or even cunning people from believing the tale without question. After all, the story was told by a pretty, fresh-faced teenaged girl, and for many, those traits alone made her seem credible. It wasn't.

Propaganda of this sort doesn't appeal to logic or intellect: it must appeal to raw and intense human emotion for it to work effectively. Blinding emotion prevents the mark from seeing the obvious, but even so, the tales need to appear logical on the surface. There is logic, and there is illogic: some call it sophistry, while others refer to it as "smoke and mirrors," but what makes war propaganda so worrisome is that it heavily relies on faulty and folksy logic that *seems* right. Questioning the bias or the lies seems wrong, immoral, insensitive, and downright paranoid – the logic errors work to the propagandist's advantage. As we've seen in previous chapters, even the most convoluted tale has incited its target to hate and harm various out-groups.

That propaganda can suppress critical thinking to even those who are trained to spot faulty logic and have expertise is unsettling. For example, the incubator hoax was given credence by Amnesty International, activists, politicians, and journalists. Ironically, the propagandist must make his chicanery seem plausible by using logic himself: he must know how and by how much to exaggerate, downplay, ignore, and shade his stories in order to make them sound more believable than the truth. Strangely enough, very rarely will the unvarnished truth be enough for him to make his case: if there is a real threat plaguing his people, he will still likely take some creative license to intensify the tale, inadvertently making real atrocities seem tame, and even less believable in comparison. His horror stories must be more intense, more grotesque, and more savage than the truth, even though real documented cases of atrocities should be enough to spark outrage, or at least, concern.

Parsing words and spinning phrases become important tools to make the yarn seem both brutal and realistic enough to his marks. It must conform to stereotypes of the out-group – exaggerated caricatures will be believed over realistic portrayals. Language will be manipulated to serve the exploiter's own ends: the in-group's soldiers will be labelled "freedom fighters" while his enemies will be classified as "terrorists" or even "*the* terrorists" as if there was only one variety available. His containment institutions will be knowns as "detentions centres". But the opposing side will run "death camps." The measured labels will make much sharper contrasts between the in-and-out-groups, while suppressing inclinations to questions whether the labels or accurate, objective, or even productive.

Adjectives and other descriptive words become crucial "keywords" to describe the enemy: brutal, butcher, barbaric, evil, murderous, vile, horrendous, savage, and vicious are commonly used words in the propagandist's lexicon to describe the target, while words such as innocent, brave, valiant, humane, peaceful, and resolute are designated to describe the in-group. Language is exploited to differentiate the "us" from the "them" to stifle skepticism and restrict debate. Whether "saintly" would be used to describe our in-group imprisoned serial killers, or "barbaric" to describe the out-group's altruists doesn't matter: in times of crisis, even our bad guys are good (or at least ignored for the sake of narrative for the time being).

But propaganda is riddled with other logic errors that normally should be immediately recognized as such:

1. **An unmovable force can trump an unstoppable object.**
   The question might make a philosopher give a complex answer to this old paradox, but for the propagandist, it is a question that is easily answered: his illogic dictates that the immovable force will ultimately be the victor in a battle with the unstoppable object.
   How so?
   For the psychological prevaricator, he will build up his bogeymen to be extraordinarily evil and powerful: these enemies are the ones who will kill, steal, and expand at the

expense of the in-group. The enemies have only one goal, and that is to destroy and/or enslave their target. In other words, they are the unstoppable force that must be feared or hated. There is no negotiating with them. They are no minor threat, and with their numbers, power, and determination, they have the ability to exterminate their marks. They are worthy opponents who the in-group must resist against to survive. An enemy who is a lesser threat is less likely to cause instant outrage; ergo, the threat must be big.

If the enemy is truly an unstoppable force, it poses a problem: if anyone is that powerful, resistance is futile, and morale plummets, which. Makes disseminating propaganda another futile exercise, and the dire warnings of doom become meaningless. If the enemy can win with absolute certainty, then what is the point of stirring the in-group when the only option left is to surrender, flee, or ready for death and submission?

If, on the other hand, there is a way for the in-group to rally and defeat the threat, then there is a reason to incite the group and manipulate their emotions to serve a purpose: to transform them into the weapon that defeats the out-group. It is this "ray of hope" that compels young men (and to a lesser extent women) to enlist and fight, and compels the others to support their in-group's leaders as well as their strategies for defeating their enemy. The group must be resolved and stick together to defeat the common threat: the in-group becomes the unmovable force that must stop an unstoppable object.

According to the propagandist's illogic, an enemy nation who has the ability to make and launch a nuclear weapon may be dangerous, but there is always *hope* of stopping him if the in-group follows his directives to the letter and act as one *before* the enemy can complete their plans. It doesn't matter if there is a political or ideological schism plaguing the in-group or discontent over the chosen leader: once a propaganda campaign begins, they will put aside their differences as they realize they all are facing a larger and bigger threat. Propaganda does not merely instill fear; it instills fear with a *motive*, namely, to change the way people think and behave. Survival of the superior group is the incentive for mass compliance, and any inter-group clashes need to be suppressed.

2. **Simplistic lines must be drawn for mere survival.** The Manichean world of war propaganda means there can only be two groups: Us and Them. We are naturally the good guys and the protagonists, so by default, the bad guys must be Them. The key here is "we" and who "we" represent: "we" are the ones in the right who seek right for the right reasons. If "we" are fighting for freedom, then who are we fighting against? It cannot be another group who are also fighting for freedom, or then we begin to question our own binary stance. Therefore, all opponents are the opposite of who "we" are.

   The arbitrary lines seem to be believable, even if the two opposing groups coexisted together during peacetime (as in the case of civil wars). Facts about the intermarriage rate will be conveniently ignored and suppressed in order to pit one group against the other. During the civil war in the former Yugoslavia, even though all warring sides of the conflict with sizable populations who married each other and had children for decades prior to the war, as do other multicultural nations (especially in the larger city centres. In this case there were over one million mixed marriage in the nation prior to the war), suddenly the war became a battle among *the* Croats, *the* Bosnians, and *the* Serbs, as if those were three separate and distinct entities – or even rival football teams – who never intermixed. During the Holocaust, German citizens with a single Jewish great-grandparent found themselves perilously cast as the "other." Those who are members of more than one group may find themselves either pressured to divorce themselves from the opposing groups, or are labeled as being one of the enemy.

3. **We can either sink or swim.** This black-and-white worldview gives rise to another logical fallacy: there is only one way to beat the enemy, and that is with brute violence. Propaganda makes the forced-choice sound rational, and the only alternative available. By downplaying alternative strategies, there is also a *confirmation bias:* ignoring all evidence that would refute the propagandist's hypothesis. We either fight the enemy or lose; negotiation is fruitless, as is other methods of conflict resolution. Related to the "sink or swim" is the "you are either with us or against us" reasoning: alternative solutions and views of the situation are nonexistent; therefore, suggesting otherwise means that

dissenting voices side with the enemy, not the home team, as Jane Fonda infamously discovered when she went to Vietnam an A-list celebrity, and came back as "Hanoi Jane" for decades. During times of crisis, the marketplace of ideas is closed and acceptable beliefs are rationed to but one.

4. **To survive the enemy, "we" must appeal and defer to our authority figures.** If the point of propaganda is to gain mass compliance, then there needs to be a leader who will lead the group to victory. Leaders cannot be questioned since it means it increases the chances of alternative solutions gaining momentum and credence. Leaders will be portrayed as strong, resolute, intelligent, brave, knowing, and dynamic, even if they were previously seen as the opposite. Reputational transmutations happen frequently in times of war. That photographs of leaders in military fatigues near tanks and air force planes become commonplace during times of crisis is no accident, nor is it coincidence that leaders will also be photographed with folders, papers, and other "intelligence" paraphernalia: we need to have confidence that the drastic solution our master has devised is the right one. He must be seen as brave and informed enough for us to gain our trust and goodwill. Jacques Louis David's *Napoleon Crossing the Alps* may had Bonaparte's cape in a logically impossible placement, but he certainly captured the spirit of a confident, valiant master. George W. Bush's "Mission Accomplished" photo op also portrays the same image. Without a hint of irony, Nazi propaganda posters during the Second World War showed Adolf Hitler gallantly leading his troops to battle wearing nothing but a crisply pressed dress shirt and tie. The tradition continues: other modern-day leaders, such as Vladimir Putin and Kim Jong-Un have also been preened and posed to look masculine and heroic. If people are asked to relinquish their intellectual autonomy, they have to be reassured that they leave their fate in capable hands.

5. **We must surrender our freedom and employ violence to preserve our freedom and peace.** There is an assumption that it is better to be restricted by our own in-group than be restricted by outsiders – and that the only road to peace must be paved with blood and bone. The propagandistic paradox assumes that the only language the enemy understands is violence, and in this case, "violence" isn't merely a method of

self-defence, but an effective communication tool to let the out-group know their targets won't be pushed around – and that they prefer peace over war. It also means that the in-group will also have to sacrifice their freedom, privacy, and relatives (as one American Second World War poster blared with a young woman holding her infant and toddler, "I gave a man!") to ensure the group's ultimate survival and triumph. There may be other benefits of curtailing personal freedoms, which will be discussed later on.

6. **We must rely on the confirmation bias.** A *confirmation bias* simply means that we looks for evidence that *supports* our theory, while ignoring evidence that may refute it. For example, we may want to believe that someone who claims to have psychic powers really is psychic: we may actively look for evidence that "proves" their "abilities" (i.e., they correctly guess your zodiac sign), while ignoring evidence that would refute our hypothesis (i.e., they incorrectly guessed the zodiac sign of eighty people before us). As an evaluation method, only looking at confirming evidence can lead to potentially dangerous mistakes.

    Yet that sort of thinking is actively encouraged by propaganda: in-groups are to look only for evidence that corroborates the theory that the outside in question is evil, faceless, and in the wrong (or, in the case of WMD, the in-group were encouraged not to bother to look for it at all, lest the mushroom cloud get them); it does not attempt to look for evidence that may show the outsider has redeeming qualities, is human, or may have a legitimate grievance against the in-group. During wartime, propagandists ask their target audiences to commit the same error: while evidence that supports negative images of the enemy are touted, while proof of the opposite are disregarded,

    For example, in 1914 during the First World War, German soldiers were accused of murdering young Belgian girls at Liege; worse, the soldiers had apparently eaten an infant in front of the horrified crowd. However, the glaring fact that there was no credible firsthand witnesses or survivors – nor corpses, or other forensic evidence was completely ignored until the yarn was no longer needed to incite citizens, and was determined to be false. Similarly, in 2005, US soldiers were accused of flushing the Quran down the toilet at Guantanamo

Bay. While the story sparked immediate outrage, few who became angered bothered to find or ask for evidence to confirm the story, which was later to be proven false and retracted (note that the yarn was trivial in comparison to how prisoners were confirmed to be *treated* in the facility, but like many other cases of propaganda, the false tale is elevated at the expense of real cases of brutality).

7. **Emotional appeals outweigh intellectual ones.** Propagandistic stories are rarely ones that appeal to facts or logic: they appeal to very strong emotions, such as fear, paranoia, and anger. Facts are not allowed to get in the way of an emotionally manipulative story no matter how ridiculous the tale is on closer inspection. Soldiers are credited with more strength than is humanly possible, and casualties are higher than the actual population of the group. To question these stories violates all the rules of propagandistic logic: to question the credibility of anyone in the in-group, and especially the in-group's leader can be seen as being akin to treason. But there are two other less-than-noble reasons for the emotional appeals: first, strong emotions are needed to emotionally manipulate an audience. While appealing to an audience's logic is a more effective long-term persuasion method during times of peace, the propagandist doesn't generally need a long-term change: just an immediate one. By the time cooler heads prevail, the audience will have long ago already done what their exploiter has asked them to do.

A deft propagandist gets away with spinning bogus, biased, and exaggerated tales to further his own agenda, whether the agenda is legitimate or not. Other times, the threat is real, and his already frightened group sees (and are victims of) the dangers firsthand. But in either case, he doesn't waste his efforts for nothing: he has set up his various stories for a pay-off. He hopes that by pressing the right buttons, he will get the desired response from the decisive majority. If he has done his job well, he will get his people on his side.

The psychological manipulator has spent a considerable time bringing out intense and irrational emotion (or, in the case of a real attack, enhancing it), suppressed skepticism, and dissent in his own people, and has made alternative solutions to the problems seem immoral, unrealistic, and wrong. In one real way, the group is encouraged to turn on their primal emotions, while simultaneously being encouraged to turn off their minds. The strange contradictory requests ask that the audience behave as if they were both feral animals, but then behave like machines (i.e., do what they are asked without questioning why or how they are being utilized and exploited). The "hard" decisions are seemingly made only by the leaders, and not the public (though the decision to agree to go to war on someone else's terms is, in fact, a hard one in itself). While the enemy becomes faceless, we are encouraged to become mindless.

Though propaganda can manipulate people regardless of their age, gender, nationality, educational level, or socioeconomic status, it seems as if one specific demographic is targeted more than the others: young healthy, fertile men who don't have children or have very young children. Since it is still mostly men who fight wars on the front lines, then we should expect to see propaganda messages appeal to their biological drives more than women. There is no need for those selling a war to waste their energies on scaring the elderly; on the other hand, frightening energetic and strong young men enough to enlist and defend their nation's self-interests has its benefits.

But how do we know that propaganda primarily appeals to men in their prime? On the surface, it seems as though everyone would be frightened and outraged by the threat of an outsider, and generally, people across borders do feel that way. However, there are signs that much of propaganda speaks to strapping young men. For example, in various propaganda posters from different eras and cultures, many show comely, young, and well-endowed female nurses tending to the bedridden, but still healthy-looking, but slightly wounded male soldiers are the patients. One of the more iconic propaganda images of the Second World War was a female icon posed seductively, looking at the viewer, and declaring *I want you – to join the army*. Interestingly, when females are used in propagandistic images (usually beautiful, exaggeratedly curved, and well-endowed, such as posters and cartoons, she is typically looking at the viewer and is posed in a sexually suggestive manner. The British cartoon character "Jane" was used to boost British morale in the Second World

War: she was the naked sex object who usually surrounded herself with military paraphernalia.

Others have used pornographic enticements to first attract the man's sexual attention (showing a pretty young girl with a heaving bosom and disheveled bed hair), then then show images of those same young women being tied up, beaten, and raped (or report allegations of mass rapes, or rape camps); thus asking the man to deplore the behaviour enough to enlist; after all, if the outsiders are defiling "our" women, their victims will most likely be murdered or impregnated, meaning the pool of potential female mates is dwindling quickly.

Defensive and inter-male aggression are also central themes of propaganda: it uses extreme images of terror, usually of men against other men. Propaganda is used to rouse enough hatred and aggression in men to want to fight. The opponents depicted or described are other strong, young men; far less common are images of women fighting men, or women fighting other women. Whether the images are illustrations or photographs, the soldiers on both sides seem preternaturally strong and confident. "Our boys" will be particularly robust. In March 2003, during the Iraq War, smiling British Eric Walderman made international headlines when it was reported that his government-issued helmet saved him "after being blasted in the head four time." While the story later proved to be a hoax, Walderman's appealing rugged face and winsome smile were genuine: he looked the way an invincible soldier should look. In November 2004, the photo of twenty-year-old James Blake Miller, a cool-looking US soldier with a cigarette dangling from his lips who was stationed in Fallouja, also became iconic and was dubbed "The Malboro Man" by the press who repeatedly noted that the "gritty" Miller was a "country boy from Kentucky." Propaganda almost always proclaims in various ways that the in-group's soldiers always look collected, eager, and ready for their bloody battles.

Just like punk music or action films, propaganda heavily relies on both sex and violence to move its audience. But propaganda does it in a different way: images of the "good guy's" women being seduced by the enemy tries to encourage the audience to want to kill the enemy, since the outsider is taking away potential mates from the audience. Sex and aggression are almost always used together to both sexually arouse the man, and to encourage his violent streak. In some species, many appeasement postures are the same ones used as sexual postures. The sexual images used in propaganda are stereotypical with women being shown in very specific poses, almost always in an appeasement posture. Even Nayirah al Sabah, the young teenagers who falsely claimed to have witnesses the brutal murder of Kuwaiti newborns looked submissive and meek, though she herself was well-dressed in white, fresh-faced, and comely.

Instinctual manipulation is meant to spark reaction, and there are several types of male-centred propaganda that aim directly at basic male drives: infanticide, rape stories, threats to life, and specific deprivation icons. The purpose of each one is to convince the pool of potential soldiers that they must not only join the battle, but that it is in the best interest to fight to the best of their ability as they ignore their more hedonistic drives. Effective propaganda does not need logic to be believed since many such stories are completely illogical, yet they are still believed without question.

Baby-murdering is a powerful icon that can almost instantly galvanize any public, but why is it used for war, and more importantly, why would it appeal to men more than women? On the surface, infanticide should appeal to women more than men: after all, women, being seen as the peace-loving nurturers, give birth and bond with their children; so, we would naturally expect the propagandist to frighten mothers. Mothers are generally the primary caregivers of children of any era or culture; it stands to reason that this form of horror story should be aimed at them rather than young men, many of whom have yet to marry, let alone think about raising a small child.

However, since it is men who have not reproduced (hence have not passed on their genes to the next generation), or men with young children who go into battle, they still have not reached one of the most crucial biological goals. That is, if the entire purpose of surviving up to the reproductive stage is to reproduce, then this type of propaganda is exploiting the fear that one's efforts to pass on his genes will be thwarted by the enemy. It is a patriarchal narrative that is binary: there can only be one hero, and one villain, and the natural assumption is that "we" are the heroes. Reproduction is a very strong drive, and any threat to a male's reproductive success will likely bring on aggression, particularly, when the environment is unstable and under threat.

In nature, animals fight off predators who threaten their offspring with vigour; it should be no surprise that people react strongly to this kind of propaganda. If the enemy is seen as an entity that is out to destroy us by preventing us from reproducing, then we will want to aggress against the enemy, just like the mother or father animal will automatically ward off predators who want to eat their young. Thwarting natural human functions usually results in increased aggression, as we have seen in previous chapters. It is not necessarily cruelty to helpless little children that motivates men, but the real possibility that an enemy will reproduce at our expense, while we are denied to do what nature intended up to do does motivate. The drive to reproduce is powerful, and any disruption from the natural flow during times of chaos and uncertainty causes anger, aggression, and real biological changes in brain activity, muscle movements, and hormonal balances.

Images and tales of civilian women being raped and murdered by the enemy is also a powerful image which is heavily used in propaganda, but why would this appeal to the male biological drive when the icon shows women in danger?

First, reduced parental confidence occurs if the male partner believes the child born was the result of a rape (i.e., the child is not yours, but of your enemy). Since animals wo are not confident of their paternity kill the young, and human stepfathers are more likely to kill offspring that is not theirs compared to biological fathers even in peacetime, this vein of propaganda incites hatred because men subconsciously do not want to risk the possibility that the parental investment they make is for the child of an enemy. If our r-selectionist enemy (the one who quickly produces litters of inferior offspring) is contaminating our k-selectionist gene pool (the one who slowly raises and invests in fewer, but higher quality offspring), then it seems that it is only a matter of time before we are consumed by the feral outsider.

Once the in-group mate is impregnated, she cannot mate again until her gestation period is over, and she give birth. Ergo, if enemy soldiers are raping and impregnating "our" women, we may become angry because (a) some foreign entity is invading our land and space (thus forcing us to retreat or flee), and impregnating our mate; the chance of passing on our genes to many more offspring is reduced, and (b) our enemy is passing on his inferior genes at our expense, meaning the enemy state is expanding while our own is being actively reduced.

Propaganda is not used to instill fear in the female population as much as it is used to instill hatred in the male population, since it is the men who usually go to the front lines, and not as many women, and in many countries, not at all. Even in cultures that do see women in combat, most images and tales still directly speak to men rather than women: from the valiant images of male soldiers shrugging off combat, to nubile young damsels in distress, to the threats of losing the chance to become a father. By treating men as both feral animals and efficient machines, the war propagandist suppresses thought and manipulates emotions to ensure his potential soldiers are primed to fight to the best of their abilities against an enemy. No matter how progressive a culture or era may be (such as progressive era of the *fin de siècle* Art Nouveau era that saw a more masculine shift during the First World War as well as the return of progressiveness after – until the outbreak of the *Second* World War), during times of crisis, the methods that seem to work best are those that exploit our most primitive thoughts, fears, and urges.

The propagandist finds the animal within us to convert us into a reliable machine that serves as a weapon: we are primed to defeat through *destruction,* without independent thought or freewill. While the animal is natural to us, the machine is not, and the ramifications of inducing unnatural thought have cost millions their lives over time.

Chapter Eighteen
Apocalypse reigning

War propaganda thrives in big threats. It sanctions fear and paranoia as it actively encourages its audience to indulge in every irrational logical fallacy to keep facts and reason away from their thinking. It thrives in becoming over-the-top, and it is not just threat of war, but complete annihilation. The enemy will conspire to subjugate us, enslave us, torture us, and then rule the world as they destroy the entire planet and doom the whole of humanity, themselves included.

Of course, these threats make genuine atrocities look *trivial* in comparison. No true victim of torture can compete with the phantom ones who were abused far worse than a losing opponent in a *Mortal Kombat* game. The excuse for exaggeration is often to "get attention" for a plight as if the ends justified the means; however, if atrocities are being committed on both sides, then one side is willfully casting themselves as victims in a misdirection to shade the other side as heartless and mindless killers. The propagandist deliberately obfuscates the truth to shade the culpability ratio. It is a bid to give other collectives a legitimate excuse to form an alliance with you, or, as the third stratagem of the thirty-six decrees, *kill with a borrowed knife.*

When the world becomes outraged, they will move to isolate the demonized out-group. It is the way of forming coalitions and alliances. The end is nigh, and everyone surrounds and isolates the threat, the threat will surround and isolate us. We must not allow the Apocalypse to reign is the message: to ponder or debate wastes seconds as the threat annihilates without opposition. It is an old ruse, but has been effective time and again.

For it to work, there must be a tight control over the flow of information, and using certain experts on one side of the debate, while shutting out others. If we see the "threat" and have the chance to assess it ourselves, we may decide there are worse, or we see the threat is not one who will destroy everyone in their wake.

The Cold War is such an example of two groups painting the other as a *global threat* who would destroy the world with nuclear bombs. The US and the USSR were both ruthless and relentless with their campaigns aimed at their own citizens and allies. They could *never* trust the other, as people were repeatedly warned, until the 1980s, and then suddenly, it was declared over.

Yet the propagandistic indoctrination of that era still persists. When Donald Trump won the 2016 Presidential election, besting the Democratic contender Hillary Clinton, suddenly, there were accusations of Russian *collusion* with the Trump team, and millions of dollars and three years later, an investigation showed the premise to have been unfounded. Nations meddle and snoop in one another's affairs as we will see in Chapter 22, but those other sordid episodes were never considered to look at a bigger picture to compare and contrast how genuine soft influencing occurs over the narrative constructions that present a more cinematic version meant to frighten.

Yet the bigoted narrative was a mere replay of Cold War propaganda, with many in the press spreading misinformation. There were countless flaws with Trump, from his political inexperience to his simplistic views to his uneven business acumen to even his chaotic and disruptive methods of strategy, any of which could have been used, but it is interesting to note one of *war propaganda* was employed, one with riffs of a "nuclear-threat" level of a previous demon.

BuzzFeed News, an online publication most noted for its nonsensical, gif-filled quizzes and kitsch aesthetic and over-indulgence of pop culture references, suddenly presented itself as a legitimate news outlet, and published various "scoops" linking the president to Russian agents, only to be debunked repeatedly. The *New York Times* also indulged in the practice, particularly in one December 12, 2017 article with the headline, *Fingerprints of Russian Disinformation: From AIDS to Fake News,* an article with a strong confirmation bias that ignored that their *own* media had spread disinformation on the same topics, such as AIDS, homosexuality, and employed a journalist named Jayson Blair who wrote fake news stories in the *Times* until he was exposed.

As journalism has yet to develop and employ empirical methods for their industry at the academic or professional level, it is a discipline vulnerable to deceptions and propaganda as we have repeatedly seen in this book. It is a discipline poorly equipped to detect it or challenge it, especially as its narratives follow the same ones as war propaganda, even though those in the business of optics and deception, such as PR firms, have highly sophisticated methods of using neuroscience tools to tailor-make their campaigns for their clients. It is a highly uneven match, and when citizens, who have very little expertise in media literacy, are dependent on news reports, and even less reliable social media reports, the results can be violent and destructive.

But the Cold War frightened the masses in numerous ways: Hollywood films depicted the Soviets as a single entity (not differentiating Russians with its numerous satellites, including Latvia, Lithuania and Estonia, who all broke away from the Soviet Bloc in the early 1990s as they were decidedly *not* like the whole) who were devious and determined to harm the world. Popular television programs such as *Mission: Impossible* Had the theme of a small group of American agents who could outwit these brutish menaces with ease: even being able to go so far as to fool the natives by speaking English to them in a poor and inconsistent accent. As the enemies were gullible and credulous, they always followed authority, wore uniforms, and could be fooled by simple means.

It was hardly the only method of manipulating the public in fear of a doomsday. In 1951, *Duck and Cover*, a short "social guidance" film played in classrooms across North America, warned children that a nuclear attack could happen at any moment, and the best course of action was to hide under their desks and cover their head with their hands. Distributed by the US government's Civil Defense branch, it offered no useful information or explanation to children, nor did its dire scenarios come to fruition.

While Wikipedia, itself an inaccurate online resource, insists the film is not propaganda, it has all of the elements of being precisely that. It warns of an impending apocalypse, and worse, it is aimed at children. The notion of hiding under a school desk in the event of a nuclear attack defies logic and common sense, but it is meant to instill fear. Showing the film in classrooms where children are primed to learn, it was a crass method of sending a message of imminent destruction. While shows such as *Mission: Impossible* At least showed active creativity to face a designated enemy head-on, *Duck and Cover* instilled a message of passivity, and showing that the correct response is fear and retreat.

After all, the threat is too large and too sudden, and even a collective can do nothing to stop it. When the Apocalypse reigns, it is the end. It is a form of *learned helplessness.* It is a psychic shock, but its damage is greater than the physical variety.

Martin Seligman's classic 1967 experiments consisted of three groups of dogs who received shocks: some of the dogs could stop the shock by means of pressing a lever, while another group received them whenever the other group did, and could not do anything to stop the shocks. They had no control over their surroundings, and not surprisingly, groups with control of their environments could move away from unpleasantness, while those who could not stood in place and cried, never realizing the condition suddenly changed and they were now free to move to avoid the shocks.

War propaganda seeks to teach helplessness. If the threat is too big, then we are helpless. We are frozen in place, and sensory overload takes over. We cannot move or act, let alone think and reason. Why *Duck and Cover* is a case of war propaganda is simple: it presents a patriarchal narrative of helplessness. The children were not taught to question, or seek answers, let alone demands. They were not encouraged to ask their governments about their decisions, and they were not encouraged to write to the Soviets to ask them the same questions. It goes beyond sink or swim: it is merely, when it comes, drown.

But it is also the way to frighten those within the in-group. The method of poisoning our active and critical thinking is key. There is no escape they *They* arrive, and the natural response to loss of life is agreeing to a loss of freedoms and liberties, as we are not encouraged to ponder whether a life of self-imposed imprisonment and self-perpetuating terror is a life worth living. We are to fear and react to threats, not be brave and reflect on proactive plans to investigate and assess before coming face-to-face with what frightens us and be find solutions in a confident and open frame of mind.

The enemy must be portrayed as a group that is capable and willing of destroying and killing on a mass scale, whether the method of weapons of mass destruction, an invincible army, or biological weapons. The Cold War fueled this cold terror, and allowed millions of people to agree to oppression by not the "enemy" side, but their own. Popular culture was an effective method of guiding daydreams of the people. The patriarchal structure of there being a single Chosen One who is heroic, while the opposing side was villainous by default, prevented anyone from questioning the narrative. The villain was not just out to harm us, by to destroy the world.

Yet it is not always destruction by nuke or army that is meant to terrorize. Destruction by an enemy who keeps populating the planet with their own is also a war propagandist's method of instilling terror. It is not just their men who are untrustworthy and whose motives are destructive, it is also their women who keep giving birth to more and more of their kind.

The Second World War propagandists had a fondness of portraying enemy soldiers as snakes, rats, lice, and creatures that not only were common fodder for phobias, but were the kinds of vermin that reproduced in large numbers in a short amount of time. There are r-selectionist animals that have promiscuous parents who produce high-quantity, low-quality offspring and give low parental investment. On the other hand, K-selectionist animals have relatively monogamous relationships, and produce low-quantity, but high-quality offspring with high parental investment and are altricial. In nature, we see the differences. We are in awe with the majestic lion, and shudder at the rabies-infested rats.

The propagandist draws the line in the sand for us and makes the comparisons: the enemy is portrayed as a r-selectionist creature, while the in-group is portrayed as noble K-selectionists. By portraying the enemy as a r-selectionist creature, the target group is seen as promiscuous, undesirable, ugly, evil, and as quickly expanding, while we are portrayed as monogamous, loyal, noble, civilized, benevolent, and kind Mary Sues, and our low fertility rates (whether true or not) threaten our existence next to the enemy's alleged high rate of fertility. We feel that our enemy is taking over the world at our expense, and they will literally swallow us up like a snake swallows their prey.

For example, the Second World War had its share of posters portraying enemies as snakes *devouring* the entire planet. They would overtake the world and swallow the *rest* of us up whole, taking no prisoners.

While modern times discourage overt pondering of ethnic-based discussion of whether a group is having *too many* babies, the feint is still used. In one March 2016 article in the *Independent,* Syrian refugees in Jordan refugee camps were accused of the very deed:

> In the Azraq refugee camp in northern Jordan, husbands often discourage their wives from using contraception, partly out of a sense of duty to repopulate the country. On average, 70 babies are born per month in the camp and of the 639,000 Syrian refugees in Jordan, whether in camps or not, 16,000 women and girls are pregnant, according to UNFPA, the UN's Population Fund.

The images of displaced people of a certain ethnicity deciding to overcrowd their camp with newborns still invoked the same images of r-selectionism as it implies that refugees should continue to be displaced and put their lives on indefinite hold, but it also indicates that should it be an accurate assessment, the refugees have been terrorized into rushing to replace their own as their enemy has taken away their own citizens. Like much of propaganda, the same message can be used to different effects on various groups.

But it does not have to be the birth of children: recruiting our own to become enemies – or just more enemies joining the takeover will do in a pinch. Terrorist threats have been growing for decades, even if their levels seem infrequent and consistent. Yet always unnamed *experts* and *officials* keep up their siege of warnings, as the *New York Times* reminded readers in 2004 as the appealed to nebulous authority:

> Some of the militant groups, with roots from Southeast Asia, Central Asia and the Caucasus to North Africa and Europe, are believed to be loosely affiliated with Al Qaeda, the officials say.

But other groups follow their own agenda, merely drawing inspiration from Osama bin Laden's periodic taped messages calling for attacks against the United States and its allies, the officials say.

The smaller groups have shown resilience in resisting the efforts against terrorism led by the United States, officials said, by establishing terrorist training camps in Kashmir, the Philippines and West Africa, filling the void left by the destruction of Al Qaeda's camps in Afghanistan. But what is also worrisome to counterterrorism officials is evidence that like Al Qaeda, some of them are setting their sights beyond the regional causes that inspired them.

Swelling ranks of verminous evil is not the only propaganda icon which appeals to biological drives. The threat to life and deprivation icons also bring us dread and fear of out-groups. They are growing in numbers, and when they arrive, they will do their worst and we can do nothing but duck under our desks and wait for it to happen unless we follow the advice of the authority.

Pain, thirst, and hunger are powerful motivators in both animals and humans. War propaganda uses these icons to reinforce the notion that the enemy will destroy us unless we engage in violence – that we "win" at any cost. Ugliness is sold as beauty, and evil is repurposed as good, and everything is justified. These icons play upon the threat to human preservation. Naturally, humans have to eat to survive, and hunger is a powerful motivator. It is also true that human beings tend to avoid situations that can bring pain to them, such as a hot stove, or broken glass. The potent icon claims that the enemy will starve and hurt us, and it is known that starvation and pain avoidance motivates our behaviour.

When we have hunger pangs, we stop what we are doing, and look for food; when we hurt ourselves, we will avoid that activity, even though it previously brought us pleasure. When we are told we will be starved, it is a threat we take seriously. One such article pondered whether Al-Qaeda would resort to *agroterrorism* in 2004:

> Our nation is bracing for the next punch within our borders.
> Many experts believe that it might just land as a one-two blow
> to our middle...that is, to our Midwest, home of grazing cattle
> and amber waves of grain. The fear has a name: Agroterrorism.
> Our livestock, crops, and soil are vulnerable to attack.

Thus, we are told that our enemy threatens us with pain, suffering, starvation, loss of control, and even hypothermia if we don't rise up and defeat them with brute force before they have a chance to expand. Me must eat to survive and we must avoid pain. It is the basics of survival that are our central motivators. When we are dependent on others, such as the state, to protect us, we have very little room to object when the threat is imminent, as the *New York Times* warned its readers on July 6, 2018:

> From the scheming of lone extremists with no apparent connections to terrorist groups, like the ricin plots, to fighters aligned with the Islamic State or Al Qaeda in more than two dozen countries, terrorist threats are as complex and diverse as ever, American and other Western intelligence officials said in interviews.

The Apocalypse is coming any day. The vague "intelligence officials" said so. Run under your desks.

If it isn't bombs or agroterrorism, the enemy will take away our electricity, as USA Today reminded its readers on November 14, 2012:

> After Hurricane Sandy left millions in the dark, a long-delayed federal study Wednesday says the U.S. power grid is also vulnerable to terrorist attacks that could cause months of blackouts and billions in economic damages.

> The nation's grid is spread out across hundreds of miles, and many key pieces of equipment are either unguarded or so old they lack the sensors to limit outages from cascading, according to the study by the National Research Council (NRC), a private independent agency operating under a congressional charter.

As of this writing, it has not happened anywhere...*yet*.

So why are the threats always so big?

It is the justification for war. We are not likely to risk our lives over middling threats. We will not agree to sacrifice our rights for mere nuisance. How else can a propagandist convince a young audience – especially to those ideal soldiers – young, healthy, and robust – that they must put their lives on the line unless there is no other choice? Propaganda can be used to modify thinking and behaviour as well as create a believable enemy in the bargain.

Potential soldiers are to be exploited for such purposes, after all. These motivators can be exploited by the propagandist as people are disturbed when danger lurks, and those same propagandists can spin conspiracy theories to create threats to rig an outcome with narrative alone. If the masses believe there is a group of people who will harm, starve, and freeze them out of existence, then they will feel irrational hatred toward the enemy, shut down any alternative explanations or skepticism, and attack, regardless if the message is true or not. It is cold terror as our blood freezes at the notion someone wants to kill us slowly when we have merely lived our lives without harming them. We are provoked as the dark clouds of doomsday approach us. Cults fear the ticking clock. So do those who believe their lives could end at any second.

When we are evaluating information from war zones or regions of unrest, we must take many factors in mind: we have an uneven playing field that is rigged to favor those who know how to spread misinformation. We can level that playing field on our own, if we learn how to break down stories and question what information we are receiving:

1. **Does the subtext of the report inspire fear, anger or hatred?:** What are your own personal reactions to the information? Do you feel helpless, scared, or nervous? Are you looking for a saviour? Do feel vulnerable or violent? If the answer is yes to *any* of the emotions above, you are being manipulated, and the best course of action is to begin to look for facts. In this case, your personal subjective emotions are the starting point to finding objective information as you examine each trigger to see its mechanisms and source.

2. **Do the sources parse their words or use qualifiers to describe events?:** Many times, there are hints at darker forces, but on closer inspection, there is no actual proof. When the threats are big, logically, there should be ample tangible and verifiable evidence. When it is speculation, word parsing, and a discussion of possibilities, there is a lack of evidence, indicating there is no real threat to be found, or else it would have been presented prominently.

3. **Do the sources qualify what they claim?:** Whenever there are qualifiers used, such as the word *if,* they are used because there are no hard facts or evidence in play, yet the messenger or the source wish to push a certain policy or course of action regardless. Unless there is hard evidence presented, we need to be skeptical of the information and its context.

4. **Is there threats of an Apocalypse?:** Whenever a sink or swim argument is made, it is used as a false rush in order to prevent a collective from thinking or verifying information. Whether it is an in-group or out-group who is trying to force the hand of a collective, the bigger the threat, the more likely it is an exaggeration used to terror and control mass thought or demands.

Yet it is only the end of our world if we take the bait and rush into violence without considering how real is the threat – or whether we are seen as the ideal marks for a propagandist's scam as the following chapter shows.

Chapter Nineteen
Victimology

Advertisers prefer targeting the young who have yet to find their preferred brands and tastes. They are fresh and prime to be swayed, have access to their own money and that of their older relatives as they spend it on themselves, and it is the real reason why corporations target them – they lack life experience to see how they are to be exploited, and are looking for validation in what is acceptable to like. This is sanctioned social manipulation and persuasion. We have publications that openly discuss what different advertisers are doing to be better persuaders. We discuss effective ad campaigns, and debate how much of our identities are tied to the ideals presented in them.

But advertising panders to wants. If collectives shun the message, they also shun the product as the campaigns do not speak to them or offer them an ideal that they value. Gillette toned down its masculine ads when they discovered that women were the purchasers of their products, while men were shunning a clean-shaven look for beards. Ad campaigns ushered in diversity as they began to use models of more realistic body types. They follow the lead of the collective, not the other way around, and they pander in order to persuade enough members to purchase the product. With social media companies able to target specific groups to advertisers, it is less a focus of persuasion, and more one where advertisers mine for the most sympathetic crowds. Celebrity endorsements have given way to so-called "social media influencers" and ads revealing who on your friend or follow list had positive experiences with them.

It is a form of propaganda, to be certain, but it is still a *me*-centred form of it. We are to be indulged, not made to agree to austerity measures for the greater good.

But when we begin to look at political propaganda, and war propaganda, we have more at stake: our lives will be shaped and altered by the outcomes of those campaigns. We know very little about those political operatives who are trying to game their in-group into a forced choice. The stakes are higher and the consequences will often be lethal.

We take much for granted. We do not think whether an anonymous Twitter user attacking us may be a paid political operative going after opposing voices. We become defensive, not analytical. Few of us will think to ask the person in a public forum who is *paying* them for abusing and shaming opposition. It is Machiavellian, and yet those same methods have been employed in less technological ways over the centuries: hiring instigators to infiltrate demonstrations and then cause damage in a bid to discredit the opposition is a common ruse, yet even now, we rarely have those members ask those disruptors who is footing the bill for their games, or think to follow them to see who is responsible for it.

Even televised "town hall" meetings have planted questions. CNN has been caught using the feint more than once: in 2003, a softball question asked by one university student during a Democratic debate was dismissed and derided as frivolous before the young woman stated that she was told to ask it by producers. It happened again in 2007 and 2016, with one planted questioner being the daughter of a senator.

How well do we understand the process of cultivation? How well do we know the differences between cultivated events and organic ones?

Often, we assume all that is presented is organic. We rarely make that assumption when it comes to consumer advertising, but there have been stunning cases of political interference that had a profound impact on nations. One of the most stunning examples in modern political history came in Serbia in 2008 during their national elections when US Ambassador Cameron Munter took personally a demonstration that took place outside the embassy and went to stunning lengths to alter the outcome.

As he later recounted:

Once evidence surfaced that Serbian Prime Minister Vojislav Kostunica had personally approved the assault, Munter decided that he was "going to ensure the prime minister was gone" and that "the best revenge was making sure this guy lost the next election," which was less than five months away.

Munter determined that the key to weakening Kostunica…was taking away the support of the Socialist Party of Serbia… Its new leader was Ivica Dacic, who Munter admitted "[G]ot him to flip over and join the pro-Europeans."

His plan was a complex one that recruited world leaders to get the job done:

"We didn't pay him off; we just persuaded him. What he really wanted was international legitimacy. So we got [José Luis Rodríguez] Zapatero, the Spanish prime minister at the time, and George Papandreou, the future Greek prime minister, who ran Socialist International at the time, to invite Dacic to visit them abroad, where they wined and dined him. They told him they would let him in [to the Socialist International] if he joined the pro-European forces, and he did. He put a knife in Kostunica's back."

Munter succeeded in ousting Kostunica. Dacic became prime minister four years later, though he did not join Socialist International. The campaign was an unmitigated success and a foreign agent was the silent campaign manager in an election, though he was neither hired or elected to do so. There was no paper trail or registration with a government body, but he knew his target audience, knew how to persuade them, and knew how to impress a target to achieve a desired result. Few will openly admit to machinating in a foreign nation's elections, yet this does give us a rare look into how deep persuasion works.

War propaganda functions in the same way: we do not know who are the instigators or actors. It is not common knowledge and certainly not common knowledge to regular middle-class citizens who are neither schooled and made aware in the ways of psychological combat or have any expertise in the matter. It may not be a world leader, but a civil servant who sees the world as a chess or go game, and works as he or she flies underneath the radar.

In a way, solving the mystery of war propaganda is a game of whodunnit: we need to consider the agent's means, motive, and opportunity. We need to also consider the *whydunnit:* why would someone go through all that trouble and risk to alter massive events without being certain that the final outcome will be profitable and desirable?

We cannot foresee everything or control every variable, but it possible to predict enough factors to alter an outcome. If we slap tariffs on a nation with limited trading partners, they will suffer economic losses, altering their tax base, which will stymie their wealthy, frighten their middle class into tightening their belts, and drive the poor into desperate circumstances, making all three vulnerable in different ways. Should be pit one powerful ally against a smaller target nation, not only is a layer of protection removed, but it turns into a threat, distracting the larger nation's attention as it seeks to punish the smaller former ally, but also distracts the junior partner as it must find ways to stave off an attack. We can then cause further chaos to the smaller partner and isolate it as we take its resources, or forge friendly and preferred ties with the stronger former ally.

Often, it takes very little to create rifts between nations as many have problematic histories that may have taken decades to mend.

But that is political propaganda, and as powerful as it is, it is not the same as war propaganda, though it can bleed into it. Political propaganda courts more than just voters, but also politicians as well, strong arming them into accepting certain positions in public. When it targets voters, it is usually to frighten them with xenophobia stories. In 2016, the foreign enemies to fear were Mexicans who needed a wall to tame them, according to the Right, or Russians who needed to be investigated, according to the Left. Aside from the mutual bigotry, neither party had much of a platform or vision of governance to give to the electorate, nor did their citizens seem to notice as they cowered fearing the bogeymen of their preferred party's decrees and the outcome should the rival candidate win the election.

That is the power of political propaganda: it blinds *millions* from seeing the obvious. Like a stage magician who can manipulate optics right out in the open in front of a live audience, the deft political strategist can do the same to a larger audience. During the 1988 US Presidential elections, Lee Atwater, political strategist for then Republican candidate George W. Bush has painted Democratic rival Michael Dukakis as being an irresponsible governor of Massachusetts by means of a single campaign ad publicizing one African-American criminal named Willie Horton, a convicted killer, who was on a furlough, and used it to commit armed robbery and rape. It is considered to be one of the most effective – racist – examples of political propaganda that hobbled Dukakis and brought Bush a decisive victory. As Atwater quipped, "By the time we're finished, they're going to wonder whether Willie Horton is Dukakis' running mate."

War propaganda exploits the same xenophobic means, but many assume that the xenophobia must be based on physical traits. It is often religious, ideological, economic, or political. As we saw in Chapter 5, Brett Silverstein's experiments showed mere random-based grouping of individuals resulted in each decreeing themselves to be superior on every variable. When we are that vulnerable to rigging our perceptions to game the system to our own advantage, a propagandist can easily take advantage of our own innate chauvinistic and egocentric tendencies.

War propaganda is a more extremist form of political propaganda. It divides and labels people by design. But it need not convince everyone within an in-group to commit violence and discrimination: just those who must do the grunt work as they must be convinced the will get the most rewards for doing so, even though they are taking the biggest risks and must be exposed to the most danger. The propaganda must pick two kinds of victims very carefully: the targeted out-group who has something of value that must be looted or destroyed, and those in the in-group who will be the most successful at achieving the goal. The target audience must be a group that is naïve, idealistic, afraid, and ignorant of their manipulation.

This leaves us with two reliable groups: young, childless men who have yet to pass on their genes to the next generation, and young men and women whose own children are not old enough to have children themselves. Population grow is a concern. When the populace is not growing through the natural means of reproduction, governments tend to make-up the deficit through immigration policy. The human race is often a peculiar pyramid scheme: we must bring in fresh blood to support to the established group. We have a labor pool and a tax base to create a society, but often reality gets in the way. When there is slow or negative growth, nations begin to borrow money as their tax base decreases. The elderly require more funding to subsist. The young may not find employment and will be in debt, and they may frown on the manual labor jobs as they believe their university degrees make the work beneath them. When youth begin to demand more government funding than is available, it is often foreign workers who are brought in to keep the scheme going. Exploitation is rife.

In Canada, for instance, foreign workers have found themselves in dismal conditions where their pay is clawed back by their unethical employers, and yet Canada is thought of as a progressive nation, yet the recent scandals have shown how vulnerable exploited out-groups happen to be even in a progressive nation during peacetime.

When there are threats to reproduction, the propagandist will exploit the fear. The Horton ad could have just as easily been war propaganda as Horton's rapist and murderous past was revealed. Murder ends life prematurely. Rape may prevent a woman from reproducing. The fears both cause are at the heart of war propaganda that equates reproducing with an out-group as a "wasted" chance to keep the in-group functional. These cold calculations may be irrational, but the Horton ad alone decided the election even though Horton was born in the US and is a US citizen. He is not a Them. He is an Us, but what the ultimate goal was had been to ensure enough voters choose Bush.

With war propaganda, the goal is to ensure enough soldiers agree to do battle, meaning that enough youth enlist, or their parents agree that a draft is acceptable when the numbers are low.

But when there have been decades of peace, neither youth nor their parents would willingly agree. They are too me-centred. Propaganda is the means to manipulate their me-centred tendencies where they fear an enemy enough to accept the gamble: it is far more dangerous to refuse to fight as the enemy will capture and harm us, and the threat must be a prolonged one. In the US, despite using the hook of the September 11, 2001 attacks on US soils to recruit new soldiers, there was a modest and temporary increase. As there were no secondary attacks, or ongoing threat, the drive failed to reach its target audience.

The areas targeted did not speak to the target audience, either. These were not hubs for youth, such as the Pentagon or the World Trade Center. There were no young faces of the fallen.

Yet when we have seen youth paraded as part of war propaganda from the first Gulf War, the attitude shifts. Terrorist attacks at music concerts strike more fear than in a government building. Propaganda is an advertising campaign and one cannot expect twenty-year-olds to anxiously wait in line for the latest denture cream to be released, but they can be expected to line up for a new installment of Mortal Kombat.

Effective propaganda is aware of the importance of exploiting the appropriate age by giving the right threats to the things that matter most. There must be a sense of gain and loss. During the First and Second World War, hedonistic desires could not be obtained as there were real threats and protests would be ignored. Other nations who are not in the crosshairs, but are still nearby, begin to wonder about their chances of having to engage in combat: the propaganda will push the narrative, and here, will be successful.

It will rarely be those who have grown children who will sign up for battle. They may be physically fit and cunning, but they will be less easy to control than youth who do not have experience to deal with threats. These people are also the ones most likely to enlist or be drafted to fight – and an extreme situation demands justification, both physical and moral.

But if the war in question does not impact a nation directly, then how does a government encourage these people to agree to go off to a foreign country to fight?

While Americans were more supportive of US interventions in Middle Eastern nations after September 11th, they were not as likely to enlist, but the propaganda campaign had not targeted youth. The first Gulf War was a different matter: there, it was about the alleged murder of infants that had a profoundly different effect.

But when there are times of peace, military recruitment appeals to more *commercial* motives, such as world travel and receiving an education. There hints and promises of adventure, accolades, and hedonism coupled with threats of disaster, but the emphasis is on adventure. War propaganda uses hedonistic methods when there is no reason to fear-monger, as the *Military Times* explained:

> Recruiters said what did attract the Hermans to military service — the opportunity for travel and the ability to pay for school — is far more often what convinces a new recruit to join these days than the memory of Sept. 11.

"The motivation to join has obviously changed a little bit since 9-11," said Adam Wainwright, a Navy recruiter based in Pittsburgh. "For the most part, it's not one of biggest reasons people join."

We often assume propaganda merely appeals to threat. It can also appeal to pragmaticism and ennui. War propaganda appeals to all the instincts of the young, unestablished, and inexperienced, including the dream to be education without debt or see different countries in a more controlled environment. While many travel to dangerous countries on their own or a companion, many have found themselves detained by police, kidnapped and held for random, and some have bene killed in terrorist attacks. These cases will be played up in the press, and the alternative of enlistment seems the wiser risk.

But even then, the element of fear is used. We have safety in numbers and *training.* The fear of university debt looms as no matter what kind of posh school we attend, what in-demand degree we earn – or what our average will be, we are threatened with never crawling out of the hole, but enlistment is presented as a genuine solution.

It is fear that shuts down our reasoning abilities, and forces us to make rash decisions and ones we would not make if we thought we had a second choice. Recruitment into the army is not primarily seen as an independent career choice; it is not sold as such to target in-groups – it is present as a solution to some *other* problem, making it a form of propaganda. It is not presented in the same manner as becoming a police officer. It's methods greatly differ than other professions where physical contact is part of the job. Its message always targets youth: it is predatory by design, making the audience its prey.

But when it is times of violence and unrest, war propaganda takes a different turn. It is about ensuring the audience are perpetually offended and outraged by opposing opinions and scenarios. Political propaganda operates on the same level where two sides are led to believe they are polar opposites and only one of them can be right, and always so. The peculiar rules of one side will always be in reaction to the other side's beliefs, making for often peculiar line of reasoning: someone on the left will demand a CEOs salary be made public, but become enraged if someone on the right wants the consumer to know how much tax money is being taken by the government at the gas pump. Someone on the right will demand salaries of public servants be made public, but will become outraged that CEOs are being pressured to disclose their bonuses in public.

Yet neither side will call for physical harm for those beliefs – they will usually accuse the other side as being stupid, primitive, and mentally unbalanced. They will stoop to name-calling on Twitter and litter their Facebook page with hundreds of meme post tweaking the nose of those on the other side of the line in the sand.

But they are identifying themselves to war propagandists who seem them as prey and victims to sucker, should the need call for it. If either side is not careful, their virtue-signalling and superiority complexes will make them vulnerable to those who will begin to plant seeds of how the other side is an enemy who must be defeated through violent means. Civil wars begin this way and can spread to other nations. With the most vulnerable group being young, naïve, idealistic, and profoundly unaware of their more primitive selves, their hedonistic ways can be exchanged for violent ways where they give up their comforts in order to ensure their designated enemy has none, either.

It is the reason we must ask hard questions to determine what is reality and what is a war propagandist's illusion:

1. **Who is the target audience of the message?:** If it is geared to affect young, childless adults, it is a red flag the message may be a propagandistic one.
2. **Is the story meant to frighten or hint that oppression is upon us?:** The use of fear can stifle debate and stymie critical thinking. The more we are frightened, the more we need to focus on rationality to verify information.
3. **Are we meant to see the in-group as victims with no recourse?:** If we feel as if we are backed into a corner, we will behave differently than if we feel that we have options. It is when we are being asked to react that we must reflect and demand more concrete information.
4. **Does the proposed solution entail violence, or the relinquishing of rights for ourselves or others?:** The more extreme and oppressive the proposed solution, the more evidence we need to demand, especially as there many creative ways to solve problems.

So far, we have looked at the ways a war propagandist tries to force our choice as the perceptions are rigged to seem absolute, but now let us take a look at how to inoculate ourselves from those methods in order to find constructive solutions that are based on fact and reality.

SECTION FOUR
Inoculation

Chapter Twenty
Cold logic

Fear, anger, and hate. Those destructive emotions are what certain religions, such as Buddhism, have tried to address directly with mixed results. Christianity, on the other hand, tried to deal with the negative emotions of envy, greed, and vanity, among others. We still are overwhelmed by all that psychic toxicity on a global scale each and every moment.

War propaganda deliberately creates emotional and intellectual chaos by playing up on those feelings on a subconscious level, but then providing the conscious mind with a moral justification to hide our personal failings from others, and even ourselves. Xenophobia is justified, even if there is no proof that the out-group poses any sort of threat to us, or that we cannot deal with the threat through some more constructive and elegant means that won't result in vendettas and retribution that can last for decades or centuries.

For example, we can look at the bloody history between the Croats and Serbs – it repeatedly occurs every few decades, meaning is ever resolved. Libya fortunes were once seemingly strong, and then intervention resulted in open slavery in a place that never knew of the heinous atrocity before (while its previous regime was accused of various atrocities, many multinational corporations in Western nations propped up the regime through bribery, and once those companies left, the nation fell into an abyss few could have imagined, making a once oppressive nation an anarchistic one of pure horror). Many places seem to patch together their past only to see it explode decades later, often with worse consequences than before. How many nations waded into the complex web of other nation's battles, only to create more chaos and darkness to their own fortunes and the fortunes of others?

How do we prevent old wounds from re-infecting? How do we prevent new wounds from being formed in the first place?

One method is to recognize war propaganda in order to neutralize its effects and stay focussed on facts, not narrative. When our primal drives are being provoked as our minds are being distracted with logical fallacies and sophistry, we must become aware of both the emotional and the intellectual, and not lose sight of our goal of using cold logic to *understand* the background and situation. We do not need moralizing fairy tales to get to the heart of the matter.

For example, when war broke out in the former Yugoslavia, there were many unanswered variables: what are the current boundaries? What are the *proposed* boundaries? How many people of each ethnicity and of mixed ethnicity live in each area? What are their various demands? Are there any foreign countries pushing certain agendas? Who is raising money for arms? How much are they raising? What is happening to the prisons? Are these individuals free to harm? What PR firms are involved? Are there mercenaries being paid to enter the country to harm another side? If a region divides, how do we divide *within* the region if those who voted to stay are given an equal voice for *their* wishes?

Had *any* of these questions been asked, the war could have been entirely prevented. It is interesting to note that the question of regional divisibility, was never raised during that conflict, yet has been repeatedly raised elsewhere for *other* nations. For example, in Canada, Quebec separatism has been an on and off issue, yet both the *Globe and Mail* and the *National Post* have drawn attention to the concept of Quebec being divisible – yet the press in Canada did not offer the same curtesy to any ethnic minority in the warring regions during the civil war: it was considered *heinous* to consider the idea. The *Globe* even went so far as calling it a *gaffe* that one prominent politician wasn't considering partitioning could be a reality – yet when it came to *foreign* nations, the *Globe* never saw their own identical gaffes.

What it means is simple: we are completely equipped with the ability to ask hard questions, but do not do so consistently or justly. What we demand of others, we must do ourselves, and what we expect for ourselves, we must also allow to others as well. Trying to rig our situation to produce a certain outcome must be challenged – and it is far better when we are challenging it than when a party we are threatening rise up and decide to do it for us. When it is Us Versus Us, we have a more empathetic approach than when we always respond with an Us Versus Them mindset. We can talk about placing ourselves in other people's shoes, but unless we see ourselves as being part of the other side, we can always be blind to the wants, needs, and realities of others.

If the Other has prejudices, then so do we. If the Other makes unreasonable demands, then so do we. Once we begin to see the similarities, we can begin to negotiate. We have a plan, and a view of reality, meaning we have found enough facts to diffuse and not ignite.

After all, if we have prejudices, then so do they. If we are being unreasonable, then so are they. For any tyrannical elements on either side of the dividing line, their strength comes from enhancing the sins of their target by downplaying our own, as does the same elements on the opposite side. Once the façades are taken down and acknowledged by both, then any disrupting forces cannot employ propaganda effectively.

When those disruptors point to the sins of the other side, we can merely say, *yes, and here are our own.* When it is Us Versus Us, we begin to remove artificial linear divides. We can keep our individuality and identities, but when both sides see they have the same problems, they are more likely searching for the same solution. War propaganda thrives in fear and division, but collapses in tolerance and common ground.

We can easily break down propagandistic messages in order to separate lies from truths. Real acts of war atrocities can be identified and discerned from the over-the-top hoaxes and lies meant to incite hatred and suppress logical thought. Tensions often take years or even decades to explode. We can usually follow the trail of discontent clearly. Wars do not just break out without cause, justified or not. We could assign blame, or gather information. War propaganda merely wishes to superimpose a narrative over the facts. By following the logic, we can see the landscape as it is and begin to formulate a solution.

As we have seen throughout the book, propagandistic narratives are patriarchal and binary. We are in a science fiction realm where an entire race of aliens are faceless and lockstep evil. We do not have to "negotiate" with evil aliens – we have to wipe them out of existence in order to find our utopia. Of course, this is the path to death and destruction, not utopia. It has repeatedly cost Europe millions of lives. We have seen what propaganda has done to other regions. Al Qaeda and ISIS caused destruction. So have European fascists. When we challenge Us Versus Them and demand the facts, we can find the reality. It is no different than being diagnosed with a cancer: no narrative will save us. Facts will.

How do we break down war narratives to look for factual and logical flaws, lies, and exaggerations?

By learning to ask questions. Skepticism and critical thinking demand cold logic, and the kinds of questions we ask have a goal: to find as many facts we can that can confirm or refute our theories in order to prevent violence and oppression.

Are we do be guided by baser drives or reason? Do we allow jealous and fear to taint our solutions or rationality? Do we wish to dismantle our every step of progress or add more to climb in the right direction?

We are searching for rational *efficiencies*: what is the simplest and most constructive way to a solution?

But without formulating the correct questions, we are vulnerable to propaganda.

What are the kinds of questions to ask?

We need to establish factual *provenance* for one. We are following a trail of information, sorting where did it *originally* come from, and how it was obtained and verified. We are looking for raw *primary* sources, not press releases, PR firms, experts, activists, or journalists. None of these sources are primary ones. They may give information, but we need to focus on where did they obtain their intelligence.

Notice we are not reacting to the content of the anecdotes. We are trying to find the most reliable and credible veins of information. What is the satellite footage? What is the forensic proof? Where is the evidence? The more information we gather and verify, the more accurate picture emerges. We can find reasonable solutions. We are meant to rail and sanction death with war propaganda. If we choose to isolate a threat by ensuring prisoners in jails do not go out during civil unrest, we have found a solution that is more effective than choosing to carpet bomb an area and do nothing to contain a source of the violence.

The more questions we ask, the less leeway a propagandist has to spin a narrative, trying to create heroes and villains. Often, we fail to find the hints of an elaborate ruse a war propagandist sets up in order to justify war. We ignore the beginnings of the narrative, or the set-up, giving too much leeway for that narrative to take root and grow. Propagandists strike *first* and have control of the perceptions of reality. If we ask questions all along, we clarify those perceptions and show how they are *off* from reality, making the *misperceptions.*

The questions need to establish a clear and *concise* picture of reality. By the time the campaign has begun, the forced choice of *you are either for us and morality, or against us and morality* has control of perceptions. When we reply *we are for the truth that is greater than ourselves,* we have taken the argument away as we fill perceptions with factual data and cold logic.

Without truth or logic, there can be no morality. In order to find that truth, our questions must be without rigging perceptions, and looking for proof. We can begin to ask any of the these questions to begin our journey to the truth:

What are the populations of the conflicting sides? How many are young, vulnerable, and inexperienced in the ways of ideological manipulation?

Are there any third parties fanning the flames of discontent? What is their motive?

What is the heart of the problem? Why is there an impasse in the first place?

How are the conflicting sides handling the problem? What is the gain of negotiation? What is the gain for walking away?

What have the conflicting sides down to retaliate against the other? Was it justified?

Has any third party made promises to either side to prolong the conflict?

Is there poverty? Has there been a loss of personal freedoms? Who is behind it and what is their gain?

Have any wealthy third parties paid to support a side in the conflict?

Are any outside parties making headway in the dispute for financial or political gain?

Who has the most to gain by keeping the conflict going?

Has there been any incidents of violence or harm? How will these acts be addressed, acknowledged, and remedied?

Once we begin to focus on facts, and not finding excuses for violence, we move away from dangerous ground. We look for any solution that demands civility and rationality.

For example, during the first Gulf War, then Iraqi leader Saddam Hussein made his intentions to annex Kuwait known, and he was not challenged. Had the proper questions been asked, global focus could have been on why such an invasion had was encouraged. When Kuwait hired firms to call for war, their tactic should have been exposed earlier. When feints and ruses are immediately exposed, we break a narrative spell and prevent ideological or political justification from happening. When we begin to hold *government structures* – ones that have been cultivated and maintained by all political parties – and not ideology accountable, rivals cannot point a finger of blame at the other side. Pull the collective together, and then no party can feign innocence.

What facts are missing? Why? How do we find them?

If war propaganda awakens our primal selves, then it is our primal selves we must educate. We become a hunter of truth and a gatherer of facts. We believe no fairy tale. We verify information and then try to confirm and refute our theories.

What truly caused the First World War? Was it the match we lit, or the flammables that have been poured for many years prior?

How did the Second World War happen? Was it the Nazis – or the other nations who did nothing until their enabled neighbor decided to expand his empire?

How did the second Gulf War happen? Was it a belief that Weapons of Mass Destruction existed – or because journalists spread misinformation to the public, compelling the government to address it?

How did September 11th happen? Was it a terrorist group that just arose – or was it the training they received while practicing their methods in the former Yugoslavia first where their behavior was tolerated by the Western world?

How did Vietnam happen? How did it get out of hand?

When we answer questions, we can formulate solutions. When we see a photograph of mass graves, do we know who is in there and how they got there? When we hear testimony from a source with a vested interest, how to we ensure she has been vetted and her story verified? When we hear of enemy soldiers cannibalizing our youth – what evidence do we have that it is true?

When Serbs were accused of committing atrocities in one rival town, the "evidence" left was a makeshift flag of their people. As we discussed, the flag was flawed in the orientation of the four C's, something Serbian nationals would not do – but it was something someone unfamiliar with the symbolism would have easily missed. It was a Shibboleth and the error pointed at a clumsy attempt at staging, yet no journalist covering the story saw it.

Why not?

The same reason why journalists do not question how cryptography can be secretly monitored by corporations and governments, and then misused by various propagandists to hide their trail or how they do not question how it is possible for an isolated town to have reportedly lose more people than the last census recorded citizens living in the area.

They do not use cold logic.

We must question every sign, symbol, and omen presented to us. We may be in the crosshairs of a pity or greed scam. We may believe false claims of war atrocities, and then disbelieve genuine ones as they are not as over-the-top as the ones that manipulate our biological drives.

Atrocities need not trigger our emotional reactions, and often, the worse ever do. Passing a hidden law in an omnibus bill may seem conniving, if innocuous, but the law may set up the conditions to remove rights and freedoms from a targeted group. A lobbyist may successfully convince a politician that their client is in need of foreign aid – but fail to disclose that none of the aid will go to the poor or vulnerable, but be funnelled into rigging a board to harm a fringe group for financial benefit.

It is at these seemingly benign stages where the worst atrocities begin. War propaganda pushes our attention away from those responsible and forces us to look at physical battlefields, and even then, wants us to merely look at a designated enemy's sins. By then it is too late.

Cold logic works best when we begin to look at the mundane reality of those who have power and control. We can practice it until we can begin to look at more stressful environments.

War propaganda doesn't want us to look where the seeds came from or how they were planted and cultivated, but when we do, we are less vulnerable to chauvinism and xenophobia, and more primed to look for facts, feeling the winds to see if war is coming or if we can stop the games before they ever begin.

Chapter Twenty-One
Hot buttons

Propaganda shuts of reason by overwhelming the collective into reacting, not reflecting. When the US President George Bush declared the end of the second Gulf War, a banner was placed behind him declaring *Mission Accomplished.* The message was clear: our nation *won,* and there is no more need to quibble about it. The call was right and just, the heroes won and saved the day, and the victors control the narrative as they earned the right.

The fact the idea to enter the war was based on inaccurate information about the Iraq's alleged WMDs was to be forgotten. The ends justify the lack of evidence, let alone the means. The Fox News Channel enthusiastically played into this narrative and repeatedly so. John Moody, then Fox News Chief, issued memos to staff on how to cover the war, as he did in this April 4, 2004 missive:

From: John Moody

Date: 4/4/2004

MONDAY UPDATE: Into Fallujah: It's called Operation Vigilant Resolve and it began Monday morning (NY time) with the US and Iraqi military surrounding Fallujah. We will cover this hour by hour today, explaining repeatedly why it is happening. It won't be long before some people start to decry the use of "excessive force." We won't be among that group.

The continuing carnage in Iraq – mostly the deaths of seven US troops in Sadr City – is leaving the American military little choice but to punish perpetrators. When this happens, we should be ready to put in context the events that led to it. More than 600 US military dead, attacks on the UN headquarters last year, assassination of Irai [sic] officials who work with the coalition, the deaths of Spanish troops last fall, the outrage in Fallujah: whatever happens, it is richly deserved.

The message is clear: whatever the facts, the channel will not consider whether what has happened to be "excessive force", and whatever happens to the Iraqis, it is *richly deserved.* This is not the language of a news producer. *Whatever happens* means the facts are not counted toward a pre-set narrative as another memo shortly thereafter implies:

> From: John Moody
>
> Date: 4/6/2004
>
> The events in Iraq Tuesday are going to be the top story, unless and until something else (or worse) happens. Err on the side of doing too much Iraq rather than not enough. Do not fall into the easy trap of mourning the loss of US lives and asking out loud why are we there? The US is in Iraq to help a country brutalized for 30 years protect the gains made by Operation Iraqi Freedom and set it on the path to democracy. Some people in Iraq don't want that to happen. That is why American GIs are dying. And what we should remind our viewers.

Moody instructs his journalists to *not fall into the easy trap of mourning the loss of US lives and asking out loud why are we there,* and to *remind viewers* of what the narrative is in this story. There is no suggestion of looking for facts, verifying information, challenging authority, interviewing the other side, or asking questions. In other words, all the intellectual tools used to find the truth are taken off the table *before information has even been gathered.*

That is not news, but war propaganda.

In order not to stray from this strict narrative, the coverage will have to focus on certain elements, while others, if not distorted, must be ignored. There must be sleight of hand and misdirection to keep news consumers distracted enough not to ask the questions or challenge the narrative.

Many times, a propagandistic approach will try to hide the facts with trigger words that are meant to incite instead of ponder. For example, during the civil war in the former Yugoslavia, BBC's Jeremy Bowen's August 4, 1992 report from Sarajevo referred to a group of Bosnian Muslim children as "orphans"; however, even within the report, Bowen clearly states that the *mothers* of these children were with them – and that their very-much alive *fathers* were soldiers fighting on the front line, meaning these children were not orphans by any sense of the definition, including a legal one:

> *An orphan generally is a person without living parents to care for them. The legal definition of an orphan is important for various legal issues, such as adoption and immigration, child welfare, and others.*

There is no wiggle room for interpretation, yet Bowen clearly misrepresented his report. ABC News also made the same use of the word "orphan", even though their reporting admitted the children met up with their parents in Germany. If the children weren't orphans, then why mislabel a group of children in the first place? Why mischaracterize a group of people and deliberately bring inaccuracy in a news report?

Because the word is a manipulative one meant to trigger certain emotions and shade beliefs – never mind their own fathers were also doing the same military fighting as the Serb soldiers who were also were engaged in combat during the war. But the point was to make it seem as if the Serbs were orphan-makers, even if Bowen failed on his end to find them.

But the emotional trigger of the word *orphan* is a powerful one. Vulnerable children in wartime conjures up absolute horror in a public and compels people to protect the youngest at all costs without thinking whether the situation may not be what the facts suggest.

The First World War saw its share of uncorroborated stories of horror. On May 10, 1915, the *Times of London* recounted a harrowing tale of a soldier who allegedly been "pinned to a wall by bayonets thrust through his hands and feet," a deliberate piece of propaganda meant to draw comparisons to the crucifixion of Christ. The phantom soldier's death is meant to *trigger* emotions and enrage more young men to enlist for a divine cause.

What key emotional triggers are likely to be found in war propaganda? As we have seen throughout the book, our most basic primal instincts – the ones we take for granted, are vulnerable to manipulation, but we can delve even deeper to find the weakest and most neglected parts of our psyche that are prime for a mind siege. Our instincts to protect children have been abused for war purposes for centuries. The first Gulf War was signed off by the public on the false testimony of a single teenaged girl.

The First World War also produced countless propaganda tales of children in peril with a September 25, 1914 article in the *Washington Post* claiming German soldiers in the Belgium city of Liege were killing and *feasting* on infants in full view of horrified onlookers. There was no proof of this over-the-top claim, yet it did not matter to the public: the *possibility* of infant cannibalism was too frightening, and it was wholly believed.

It is not just our desire to protect the young that propagandists bank on – the threats to young female adults of child-bearing years is another common propagandistic ploy, and the threats are not always of the savage variety. The Nazis employed "Axis Sally" – an American woman named Mildred Gillars – for radio propaganda aimed at demoralizing US soldiers with suggestions that their wives and girlfriends back home were living it up and cheating on them. Our deepest fears and terrors bring insecurity that propagandists exploit as they fill in the gaps by deliberately keeping people uninformed. Wherever we have fears and no information, propaganda can thrive.

Sensory overload is a real phenomenon. Those with Post Traumatic Stress Disorder and refugees have their own documented issues with their natural anxiety preventing rational thought as studies looking at both groups have documented, with one 2017 showing those with PTSD negatively correlating with prefrontal cortex connectivity, the area of the brain that regulates everything from personality to decision-making to social behaviour. Propaganda may take advantage of those vulnerable groups – or at least try to simulate those conditions with its psychological siege. When we cannot deal with extreme stimuli barging in our own minds, we begin to shut down in order to cope. War propaganda willfully adds to the stimuli as it seeks to shut down independent and individual thought to provide a rigged escape through its violent demands. The more overwhelmed we become, the less control of our thoughts we retain.

The advantage in times of upheaval is clearly in the propagandist's camp, but how can we spot theses triggers to prevent our judgement from being manipulated and our outcomes rigged?

There are several solutions, but we can learn to overcome by learning to shut out the extreme elements, and focus on specific information. When we shift our focus and search for information by changing our filters, we behave contrary to what a manipulator banks on.

We scour for our own facts in reports, and then begin to seek clarity. Are we told to believe an Us Versus Them dichotomy? Are we given primary evidence? Are there any contradictions in the visuals or eyewitness testimony? Is there reliance on second-hand or anonymous sources?

If there are eyewitness accounts, are they too much alike? Do they sound rehearsed?

We do not believe. We demand legitimate verification that places the onus on the information disseminator to be specific, and define their terms. They cannot merely use the phrase "independently verify"; they must *define* the phrase in precise terms. Hot buttons are used to damper rationality. The sense of urgency – whether it is genuine or manufactured – must be secondary to finding the facts to arrive at the conclusion that will the least destructive. To be asked to give up freedoms, rights, and lives is not a minor request: to be asked to demonize an entire group of people has profound and permanent consequences.

The more serious and grimmer the accusation, the more facts we must demand, yet propaganda thrives by insinuating we must go along with the conclusions on faith alone. The word of an authority is not fact. We need a full account of facts in order to see the full picture. A propaganda will often make excuses for not having the data: from privacy to classified designations, to endangering others – yet, will in the same breath, ask citizens to give up their privacy, be exposed to danger, and risk their own lives. When we see authorities as being equal, we can begin to orient ourselves without becoming trapped in sensory overload.

War propaganda seeks lies over facts. Real stories of atrocities are specific on details, while lies are not, and propaganda will rely on vaguely-sourced anecdotes over documented evidence. Why? With documented cases of atrocities, they may not provoke citizens in the same way. There is also a risk that our in-group has done something to provoke or contribute to the act of violence, negating the myth of our own flawlessness. It is safer to incubate and control a narrative from beginning to end rather than risk a wayward fact from nullifying the story's potency.

How colour and emotional triggers affect our perceptions? How do we avoid falling for those flowery and emotional misdirection in the first place? Each question can be answered in turn.

With many propaganda stories being barren in fact, they must not only hide the deficits, but also draw attention. Colour and emotional pull are common. Using the word "orphan" to describe children with parents is a prime example of such a feint. Cannibalism is another example – we are not given the names of the victims nor of the perpetrators, let alone put a name and face to witnesses: we are merely told this happened in front of a crowd in a particular city, and we are shamed and frightened into believing it.

When we are given any sort of anecdote, we begin to break down the narrative by literally counting the number of facts and the number of emotional triggers and colour. We look for specific information. Where did this alleged cannibalism take place? Which street? Where? When? Is there video or photographic evidence? Is there forensic evidence? Who are the witnesses? Who are the accused?

We then look at visual evidence to see what makes sense and what is out of place. With the CBC's Syrian war coverage, we were witness to a journalist and her crew shine bright lights at night while shushing each other – if the point is to be inconspicuous because danger is imminent, they failed, yet were safe from harm. They were obviously not in a dangerous area, and it is surprising that such an oversight could happen from experienced journalists at all.

When there is possible financial gain from the coverage, we also must take a skeptical look. When 60 Minutes' Lara Logan's debunked Benghazi piece aired, the dishonest source who was revealed to have fabricated his account also happened to have a book deal with Simon and Schuster – a publisher owned by CBS that also owns 60 Minutes. He was not a source unearthed via investigative journalism: the network had a book to sell and chose a newsmagazine to do it.

When the elderly in one Bosnian nursing home were said to be without heat in below-freezing temperatures, we expect to see their breaths, buttoned-up and bundles in coats and blankets, and see no plants surviving, but when people are relaxed in unbuttoned sweaters with succulent plants in the background, the visuals are misaligned with the narrative.

Once we begin to break down narratives and visuals, we can see what information is missing – from the "enemy's" side, but more importantly, our own from all ideological and political stripes. No one narrative is given a pass from scrutiny. We look to confirm or refute, and then we revise the stories based on the information given.

Colour and emotional misdirection can be easily spotted – those are the places where the hot buttons are nested. They are meant to take attention away from the facts. If, for example, an accusation of a mass slaughter is reported, and a specific number and location is given, we begin to look for census data first: is it even possible for that many people to perish in a given region? Does the enemy have the manpower to do it? Often, one or both numbers are off. Conversely, many people attempt to hide or downplay atrocities by revising numbers downward. Holocaust deniers are such a case. They minimize the number of Jews murdered, often to less than six figures, even though the size of concentration camps – and the overall number of losses in Europe totalled *millions* of civilians, make their downgraded estimates dubious. If millions of Europeans perished, it stands to reason some of those millions were Jewish. With the Nazis cataloguing and photographing their own atrocities, denial is more than just propaganda: it is an act of violence – a hot button meant to *provoke*. War propaganda is not always about deceiving by commission, but also *omission*.

Propaganda's effects can be nullified and contained by simple means of factual cataloging. We hear a claim, and we begin to examine the basic facts, not unlike a police investigation. False accusations are common in criminal matters, after all, and we expect law enforcement to follow the evidence rationally, not emotionally. We do not fear facts, nor the possibility of our own prejudices being proven wrong. We look to liberate ourselves, not enslave ourselves to deceptions meant to control our behaviour.

For those who misuse morality as the reason not to verify, they should remember that morality comes from truth, not deception. Skepticism allows us to find the stories that stand up to scrutiny, while credulity taints our perceptions. Once we are primed to verify every aspect of a claim, we can begin to see the truth – and the solution should there be unrest and imploding violence. It is far easier to create an accurate public record than try to correct it once it has been proven false. By then, there will be bloodshed and prolonged vendettas with deceivers gaining the most of their lies.

Chapter Twenty-Two
The statistics behind deviation

War is deception, as Sun Tzu warned us, and when the battleground is made from lies, all information is subject to careful inspection.

Particularly when Mark Twain once quipped, "There are three kinds of lies: lies, damned lies, and statistics." While Twain was musing comically, the points collide: war is often planted in the seeds of statistics as numbers are used to "prove" lies. We can easily manipulate figures, being careful what we define in order to include or exclude what we need in order to gain compliance.

Propaganda thrives in exploiting the world of numbers.

In the war in Yugoslavia, Bosnian Muslims claimed their army had 200, 000 soldiers, yet British intelligence sources, such as the February 4, 1994 edition of *Intelligence Digest* at the time had reliable sources place the figure much *lower* – about *65, 000*, less than half of the official report. So why inflate the numbers, particularly as the Bosnian government would absolutely know the actually total?

It is not only an attempt to frighten enemy forces into thinking they were a bigger threat than they were (as one of the thirty-six stratagems of war decreed, *deck the tree with false blossoms*), but it is then a simple affair to claim *higher* losses to account for the phantom deficits, and then make their targeted enemy seem more dangerous, making the case for foreign intervention easier to make.

Or downplay other numbers to hide the extent of the dead or of true military strength. Civic protests often have their true numbers downplayed in the press, though it is difficult to make an accurate guess: activists may inflate the numbers, while the police or government downplay it. Conversely, conservative media outlets also downplay numbers while liberal ones overestimate them, but in any case, it should be clear that far from being empirical and objective quantities of fact, numbers are a narrative.

War propaganda thrives on demographic illiteracy of the public. We do not know the psychographic make-up of our own nation. In 2017 Landy, Guay, and Marghetis showed that xenophobic tendencies resulted in people overestimating the percentage of certain marginalized groups and minorities (thinking these groups had a bigger population than they did, believing they were a "threat"), while underestimating "mainstream" group percentages (believing they were in decline or in peril). We do not know our own citizenry. We do not know who we are.

Nor do we know who we were. In 2018, Zaromb, Liu, Páez, Hanke, Putnam, and Roediger surveyed 6185 students from 35 countries asking, "What contribution do you think the country you are living in has made to world history?" The subjects vastly overestimated their own nation's importance and influence, causing the authors of the study to ponder on their subjects' own narcissism.

But the age of the subjects is a war propagandist's prime audience, as we have seen throughout this book. We may not know who we are or what we have actually contributed to the world, but we are extremely confident that there is an Us and it is not only different, but superior to Them.

If we are to break free of the shackles of war propaganda, we must acknowledge our ignorance of our own identity. We must be aware of our demographic information, and learn how to use it to determine a war story's truthfulness and veracity. We have no business assuming we know who is Us, let alone who is Them. Our own inner circle is not representative of the whole collective, and for us to expand our knowledge of how propaganda works, we must understand who we are as an in-group.

When we fill out a census form, for instance, do we think about our neighbors or colleagues filling the forms as well? When we are people watching in a mall, concert, or park, do we see who is there? When we are fretting in a hospital's emergency room or listening to a university lecture, is the demographics similar between the two, or *different?*

We do not notice during times of peace, but during times of unrest, we see even less. The war propagandist will always claim our numbers are in peril, while the enemy's numbers are flourishing. As we have seen in earlier chapters, r-selectionist and k-selectionist traits are superimposed on both groups in order to make a nonexistent case for war.

But we have ways of verifying numbers though various means, such as the census, and professional data and intelligence gatherers, such as Jane's. For example, how large is our military, and the designated villain's army? Are either likely to be able to inflict large scale damage? How? A nation's military vessels are well-known, for instance – the number they have, their age, make, and abilities. We can be given false information about the military capabilities during times of discontent, but it is not difficult to *verify* what was said about those capabilities before the conflict. Often, we are given conjecture and rumour, as the *New York Times* repeatedly did with their grim proclamation's of Iraq's WMDs. Even in the late 1990s, Pakistan has been repeatedly portrayed as an imminent threat with stories of their nuclear capabilities, and yet those stories never translated into reality. When we are given rumour instead of verified information, it is a sign that our ignorance is being exploited.

And what we do not know can destroy us, unless we begin to look for what don't know.

What is the population of a region? How many people are part of our in-group? How many in the out-group? Like a Venn diagram, it would also be of use to ask which can be of *both* groups, such as those in mixed marriages or have familial ties to each. During the Yugoslav conflict, Western media repeatedly ignored the crucial fact that there were millions of people with relatives on *all* of the warring sides. The Western press made much ado of the "Romeo and Juliet of Sarajevo": Admira Ismic and Bosko Brkic, who were killed by a sniper in May 1993 as if their inter-ethnic relationship (she was a Bosnian Muslim, and he a Serb) were some anomaly, rather than a mundane part of life before the war. Had the press done their due diligence, they would have presented a more nuanced and painful portrait of families who were torn apart, picked sides, or became refugees rather than become divided by the conflict. Very few outlets at the time noticed the banality, save for the *Alberta Report* three years after their deaths as Canadian churches has sponsored mixed-marriage refugees from the region. As one refugee aptly explained:

"Of the 22 millions in the former Yugoslavia, four millions of us were in mixed marriages, and we had a wonderful life," says Danica ("Danka") Uzelac, a Croatian Catholic married to an Orthodox Serb. "Most of the time, you didn't even know what nationality somebody was. Then one day, nationality became the only thing. It was a shock. I was a teacher, and suddenly all my problem students had guns. It was their chance to be important."

War propaganda can erase four million people to push an agenda and hide the nuances that show how Us Versus Them is truly Us Versus Us. Interestingly enough, while Western press continues to see the factions as separate, distinct, and parallel entities with no common interactions, it is a very different landscape today where Serbian singers are consistent and popular picks on Croatian YouTube and intermixed relationships have resumed and thrive. Once war propaganda was removed from the region's equations, so too were the frenzied hate and skewed narratives.

In fact, one of the most popular young singers in 2019 is Anastasia Ražnatović, whose mother is Serbian singer Ceca – and father was Željko Ražnatović, otherwise known as Arkan – the commander of the paramilitary Serbian Volunteer Guard whom Hague tribunal indicted in 1999, though he was assassinated. When there is no war propaganda fanning the flames, ethnicity, history, and lineage are entirely ignored, and citizens are free to choose to enjoy whomever speaks to their souls.

That freedom was stimied in the 1990s, however. If war propaganda can disguise the former ethnic union of almost twenty percent of a nation, then what else does it hide from us? For example, do we know whether as many people die as were claimed? How many bodies were found? By whom? How were they identified? If less than expected, has someone claimed that the bodies were conveniently "destroyed" by the enemy (more likely, the numbers of dead were vastly inflated)? Who is the source of the information? What is the provenance of those figures? Do other groups keep an account? What and who are their sources? Do they use different methods and sources – or do they all rely on the same unreliable authority figure or PR firm to conjure those figures for them?

We need to know many factors before we can begin to assess a story's truthfulness. For instance, what is the birth rate in a certain region? Has it been rising or falling? How likely is it that there were mass killings of infants or children? Would an enemy waste resources in such as manner? What is the motive? When we begin to pair demographic-based questions with ones of motive and gain, we can begin to orient ourselves. In the case of the Romeo and Juliet – why was it so important to make it seem as if there weren't mixed unions and offspring from the area? Because if the ultimate campaign is to ensure a region is not made to be divisible, them a high percentage of mixed unions calls the very demand into question: how can any region expect the right not to be divisible when a sizable percentage do not identify themselves in the same way?

More importantly, if there is a high degree of multi-ethnicity, then the ideas of Us Versus Them lose their potency. It is Them Versus Them. We do not seek to punish with intervention, we seek to mediate as we remind the warring sides that their hatred is likely have been instigated by other parties who have vested interests in fanning the flames as a form of misdirection.

We also need to ask questions that will show the likelihood of criminal instigation of war crimes. For instance, what is the criminal population? Were they released during wartime? Could their actions account for the more brutal cases? During wartime, prisons and psychiatric institutions are abandoned, meaning the region or nation's most violent predators are out roaming free, knowing they can cause whatever harm they wish with impunity. Serial killers and rapists who were predatory during peace now have the cloak of war to act out their most heinous fantasies, and can pin their crimes on either or both sides of the battleground. A war propagandist will take full advantage of the most treacherous demographic, but if we are to find an antidote to war propaganda, it is one of the *first* considerations we must make for many reasons. One reason is to know that the violence is one of opportunity, not nationality or government sanction. Organized cartels who already smuggle arms in peace will take advantage of war. We must face that reality of war.

But if we understand how dangerous offenders use propaganda as a cloak, we can uncover their disguise and ensure they are the ones apprehended and made accountable not as crimes of nationalism, but crimes of extreme *convenience*. When factions believe the most heinous of crimes was committed by their designated enemy, their wounds never heal for generations. If they are shown that the crime was one of opportunity that had nothing to do with the war, they can begin to see their enemy as human – and in being in the same perilous situation as they are. The battleground turns into a common ground, and war propaganda loses its power to divide by fear and hate.

We must focus on finding hard numbers in order to determine a more accurate number and realistic account of the fate of victims, soldiers, and casualties. Statistics should never tell a story: they should tell the truth. We are not looking for blame. We are looking for facts. Once we are focussed on facts over narrative, the deceptive power of statistics dissipates. We must compare and contrast figures in a matrix: what was the situation before? Who is involved? How different are the sides? We begin to create Venn diagrams looking for overlap. It in these areas where we begin to see the common ground. We look for similarities, not differences. War propaganda does not want any of the similarities to be seen, or else the Us Versus Them feint cannot work. The warring sides must see themselves as diametric, clashing, a without a single trait in common. They wish to distance themselves: when the delusion is debunked, the enemy is no longer a faceless being, but a mirror image.

But then it is the propagandist's distorting mirror that shatters in the bargain, and that is our goal to finding truth and cultivating both freedom and peace.

Chapter Twenty-Three
Breaking narrative shackles

Propaganda is a form of communications that is entirely dependent on *narrative*. Specifically, a patriarchal narrative where they can be one heroic group who are superior, and the rest are inferior: if they side with the hero, they are allies, but if they disagree, they are *villains*. While the in-group all share numerous positive traits, such as morality and bravery, they have *faces* and personality, while the enemy is faceless and all behave alike.

As we have seen throughout the book, enemies are to be seen as unintelligent yet cunning, evil, insane, racist, sexist, unenlightened, hateful, dangerous, and of inferior stock to be point that ridding the world of them is seen as the natural and most moral solution. The web of undesirable out-groups rises exponentially. With the Nazis, it began with the Jews and then to most of Europe and North America. With ISIS, their targets were more than just the US, but any who did not conform to their rules for behaviour. Saddam Hussein was *the bad man*. The Serbs were *ethnic cleansers*.

With so much *political propaganda* mimicking war propaganda, we can see how the narratives begin to divide and destroy. In the 2016 US presidential election, Donald Trump mantras of *Lock Her Up, Build a Wall,* and *Make America Great Again* implied dark forces that were holding the nation back, yet his rival Hillary Clinton likened those who wouldn't be casting their vote for her as *deplorables*. When we have two sides fight to creating a false pecking order by means of virtue-signalling and demonization, we are on dangerous ground as there will be those who cannot get off the wheel and wish to prove their in-group to be superior to the other on every variable. There can never be peace when the script calls for an antagonist to make our in-group protagonists look better in comparison.

In the former Yugoslavia, there were well over one million ethnically mixed marriages prior to the war with millions more who were of mixed heritage, and were fully aware of what war and destruction did to their various ethnicities. By all logic, the idea of a civil war should have been laughable. It wasn't, especially after foreign mercenaries, such as the Mujahidin enter the fray, paving the way for Al Qaeda to strengthen and take their campaigns of violence elsewhere.

So how did narrative override an entire nation's humanity, violent history, and common sense?

Once Tito died and the Cold War was over, Yugoslavia no longer remained a strategic country for either the US nor the USSR to court, forcing the nation to borrow heavily from the IMF. When no economic salvation was forthcoming, panic made a fertile ground for nationalism and the belief that other provinces were holding them back. Then the propagandistic narratives of fairy tales seemed real, and the various groups began to turn on one another before they broke away, imagining that removing one another would solve all of their problems. The narrative was preferable to the reality of the situation and the various provinces gambled for the narrative.

They are hardly the only ones. The Syrian Civil War has been so difficult to decipher, that the Stockholm International Peace Research Institute (SIPRI) noted the extent of narrative trumping any reliable information:

> After three years of conflict in Syria, many remain sceptical that a viable way to bring peace will be found. Any attempt to mediate in the conflict requires an understanding of the conflict's dynamics, an area to which the discipline of peace and conflict research can contribute. However, as shown in 2013 by divisions in the United Nations Security Council and among states in the region, discussions of the evidence for chemical weapon use and disputes over which groups represent the anti-government forces, there is no unified, reliable, evidence-based narrative of the conflict.

In other words, there is so much conflicting propaganda that we no longer know how to find facts, or perhaps more accurately, we have been relying on propagandistic narratives for so long and took them for granted that we do not even know where to begin to find reality.

In a pre-Internet world accepting patriarchal and authoritative narratives was an easy choice. Those who would be offended by the prejudicial smears had no means of expressing their outrage in a public forum, other than a protest that could be perceived as disloyalty to the in-group. Social media blurred many of those lines. We may be shamed if we believed propaganda based on race or ethnicity, but then find *ideological* reasons to condemn entire groups. Propaganda still endures as serves as a barrier to confronting truths. Two narratives is an impediment to finding solutions as is wholly believing one.

At its most basic level, propaganda is the exploitation of perceptions and misinterpretations of reality. Finding facts about reality to bring us a clear picture of the truth is a simple mandate, but often a near-impossible task. Social media has muddied the waters greatly, as mainstream outlets lament the lack of narrative cohesion, as the BBC did with regards to the Syrian war in an April 19, 2018 online piece:

> As the investigation continues into another alleged chemical attack in Syria, one group of influential online activists is busy spreading their version of events.
>
> Inspectors from the Organisation for the Prohibition of Chemical Weapons (OPCW) are attempting to access the previously rebel-held town of Douma, where medical organisations and rescue workers say President Bashar al-Assad's forces dropped bombs filled with toxic chemicals in an attack on 7 April, killing more than 40 people.
>
> The Syrian government and its key ally, Russia, say the incident was staged. But the US, UK and France - who support the opposition to Mr Assad - say they are confident that chlorine and possibly a nerve agent were used.
>
> Despite the uncertainty about what happened in Douma, a cluster of influential social media activists is certain that it knows what occurred on 7 April.
>
> They've seized on a theory being floated by Russian officials and state-owned media outlets that the attacks were "staged" or were a "false flag" operation, carried out by jihadist groups or spies in order to put the blame on the Assad government and provide a justification for Western intervention.
>
> The group includes activists and people who call themselves "independent journalists", and several have Twitter followings reaching into the tens or hundreds of thousands.

We have conflicting narratives in an age of social media. We lack facts to give perspective. We have legacy journalists jealously trying to cut their social media competition by placing them beneath them, rather than provide facts and evidence, which is in itself another layer of narrative.

With so much narrative being used, how do they reinforce the feints and ruses of war propaganda? We need to look no further than *The 36 Stratagems of War,* a manual of how to win wars through deceptions. A sampling of the rules of this ancient text are well-known, but some of them are based in narrative sleight of hand:

Make a sound in the east, then strike in the west
Create something from nothing
Hide a knife behind a smile
Stomp the grass to scare the snake
Borrow a corpse to resurrect the soul
Lure the tiger off its mountain lair
Tossing out a brick to get a jade gem
Point at the mulberry tree while cursing the locust tree
Feign madness but keep your balance
Deck the tree with false blossoms
Inflict injury on oneself to win the enemy's trust

Narratives are about confining thought in order to prevent critical thinking and skepticism. *Tossing a brick to get a jade* means to make your arrogant target feel superior and *correct* you, thereby giving you valuable information as paint yourself in the role of the vulnerable fool. Inflicting injury on oneself disarms others as you paint a narrative of being a weaker rival. When one feigns weaknesses, for instance, they wish to be seen as in need of intervention by others as their rivals become overconfident. Appealing to narrative hides facts as it rigs perceptions to be blind to pertinent information. We do not look for facts that refute our theories or present the positive *and* negatives of bickering sides, and hence, look to prove that the side we chose is absolutely right in every way while the "opposite side" must be wrong in every way by default.

But narrative is not reality. It is a way we explain a series of events. We add judgement and value by downplaying, enhancing, ignoring, or manufacturing events to suit our purposes. When *Time* magazine displayed Serbian mass graves as they painted a narrative of Serbian villainy, they did not correct their error or clarify the image. They did not consider who was in those graves, how they got there, or by whose hands. When the identity of Nayirah was exposed, media outlets did not self-evaluate or come up with protocols to label narratives manufactured by public relations firms to the public. They changed nothing because narrative has far more value to the communications industries than facts.

And often we have actors who create divides as they benefit from the rifts, as Hassan noted in 2014:

> In the case of post-9/11 Pakistan, a similar propaganda war was fought. Many private television channels in the country provided a platform to the Taliban/jihadi groups and the radical Islamic political parties between 2002 and 2007 by selling anti-American- ism. Simultaneously, a large section of the same private media made financial arrangements with the US, offering to assist the American cause after 9/11 while covering the Afghan war. By advancing the cause of these two non-state actors, the Pakistani private media considerably aided its own self-serving agenda. Politically, the private media extracted considerable advantage from this situation, by playing the role of bargainers, offering either to sell stories or to shape or suppress critical information regarding the Afghan war. This wheeling and dealing helped the private media to form relationships with the two critically important non-state actors in post-9/11 Pakistan, and to emerge as an informal power player in Pakistan's domestic politics.

The divide is an illusion. We often believe the façade without looking at whether another agent wants the division, and should we follow the trail of information as we established their provenance, we discover the game requires deliberate manufactured friction to deflect attention away for the true motives of creating those divides. Skepticism is often the only defence we have against being lured into these deadly distractions.

In order to inoculate ourselves from the manipulative forces of war propaganda, we must be able to recognize when narratives have been mistaken for facts and logic. Fortunately, we can create a checklist to remind ourselves of how simple it is to create webs of deceit:

1. Does the narrative rely on fairy tale structures and assumptions? Are we to assume there is a single hero and villain?
2. Does the narrative rely on racist or sexist stereotypes?
3. How much information are we given? How has it been verified? By how many independent sources? What are their qualifications?
4. How many public relations firms have been hired by the source? How many social media influencers?
5. Are multiple media outlets reporting the same information in the same manner? If they are allegedly in different places with different sources, and have various degrees of expertise and experience, why are they reporting the same narrative in the same way?
6. What are the unspoken conclusions from a given report? Is it a violence-based solution?
7. How rehearsed is the source in media relations? How flawless is their behavior? What are the chances they have received media training or have a publicist?
8. What is there to gain by believing the narrative?
9. What is being asked of the audience? Support for war? Demonizing another group of people? Relinquishing freedoms and liberties?
10. Does the narrative make you angry or afraid? Why?
11. Is the narrative logical? If you were to re-enact the scenario, would there be inconsistencies? How so?
12. Does the source ask for donations or imply that they are the only ones who can shed light or deliver information?
13. How many anonymous sources is the news producer using? How many authorities? Where is this person getting their information?
14. Does the news producer rely on translators? How well-versed are they in the culture?
15. Does the narrative rely on cultural assumptions of a particular source?
16. Does the narrative fit in with a current trending social cause? What are the chances of all the issues to notice, that would be the most salient one?
17. How many sources have been interviewed? What are their qualifications? Are the sources implying superiority over other sources?

18. Does the source attempt to demonize or negate conflicting information?
19. Does the source explain away flaws in their narratives?
20. Does the narrative suffer from a confirmation bias?
21. Does the narrative appeal to authority?
22. Does the narrative have a sink or swim assumption?
23. If there is video, audio, or photographic supplements, are there any logical flaws? Could these supplements be doctored or staged (i.e., the reporter is wearing a bulletproof vest, but no one else in the video is wearing protective gear)?
24. What voices are missing?
25. What information is missing?
26. Does the narrative tie up loose ends too easily?
27. Have you heard similar narratives before recently, such as a movie or a book?
28. Are skeptics painted as immoral or unintelligent? Are believers painted the same way by another side?
29. Are evolutionary fears invoked?
30. How well-versed in cultural Shibboleths are the news producers?

We can break free of narratives to have a better understanding of truth and reality as well as spotting when our own lofty self-image turn us into marks for a propagandist's games. We can see where we need facts and when we have too much narrative. What are the numbers? Who is providing information and why? How has the information been verified? How qualified are those who give us information? Are they merely giving us facts, or have they already come up with a list of demands from us as they pressure us to act in destructive ways?

Once we grasp how we are being manipulated, we can begin to demand answers by learning to form the right questions. We reflect before we react. We seek voices from all corners, as we look for proof. Warring regimes are placed on notice that they cannot dictate to us how we will feel or what we will think. We ignore the meme posters and the bullying headlines as we ask for proof, and then look to verify that information before devising peaceable solutions.

A war monger seeks anger, fear, hatred, and compliance. They create chaos and cold terror in order to rig our thinking. They employ virtue-signaling and shaming, wasting time in moral arguments that are not based in the facts, but on assumptions. When lives are at stake, we cannot afford to be so cavalier with the truth as it too often requires us to also be too cavalier with our lives and the lives of others. To break narrative shackles, we must examine every link in its chain by asking questions to clarify as well as verify. If what we are presented is the truth, then the facts can withhold scrutiny, but should the messengers become offended and use misdirection, we know there is more to the narrative than meets the eye, and we must break the shackles in order to liberate truth from lies, and find solutions that create and not destroy.

Chapter Twenty-Four
Burden of proof

War propaganda seems as if it is the real enemy we must fight as much as any physical threat: its persuasive messages compel us to abandon ourselves and everything we have ever toiled to earn and cherish in order to destroy in the name of survival. We place ourselves in mortal danger. We turn on neighbours and even family and friends and are primed to question their motives and find reasons to demonize them should they deviate from the script. Millions of people have perished believing propaganda over the centuries. It defies logic, morals, and every human instinct for betterment, and yet when left unquestioned, trumps our most benevolent drives as it disguises our darkest impulses as our saving graces.

As we have seen throughout the book, war propaganda is not based on intellectual arguments. It is not based on cunning. It is a grifter's con used to lure pigeons into giving up their liberties, virtues, and even *lives* to kill others even at the expense of their own lives and the lives of their children. It goes against every evolutionary instinct by exploiting each one, triggering our hatred and our fears to force us to comply as we relinquish our free will and independent thought.

Like Thomas Hardy's classic poem *The Man He Killed,* we allow others to guide us into ridiculous and maddening realities without question:

"I shot him dead because —
   Because he was my foe,
Just so: my foe of course he was;
   That's clear enough...

"You shoot a fellow down
You'd treat if met where any bar is,
   Or help to half-a-crown."

We do, and repeatedly, without so much as a shred of proof that we are in the right to do so.

Of course, there are real cases of atrocities during war; however, blindly taking sides can, in fact, harm and hinder us later on with lifelong ramifications. We destroy our own families, homes, livelihoods, and future without thinking about the burden of proof we need – or determine whether war is the best answer to the dilemma.

As we have seen throughout the book, it is critical to know how to actively think about missing and hateful information in order to make more information decisions during chaotic and turbulent times – but also during times of order and peace. How do we fight against propaganda during chaos – or order?

Reflection and reaction are two ways of thought: war propaganda demands that we react without so much as demanding confirming and *refuting* evidence, banking on the speed of decisions to hide the fact the misinformation has a severe confirmation bias and appeals to authority with its sink or swim logic and personal attacks. Of all of the combinations of flaws, war propaganda is one of the most illogical, and yet its own logic prevents individuals or the collective from questioning its structure, premises, and content. With reflection, we begin to unravel the ludicrous nature of the stories and begin to demand *evidence* and *logic.*

It is the demand for *freedom of skepticism* that is war propaganda's greatest weakness. The freedom to question *all sides* of potential and real conflicts tears down façades and reveals the deceits festering within. The freedom to scrutinize both in-groups and out-groups gives us the time and space we need to question, verify, and analyze, and judge even the most incendiary story used to manipulate the masses.

Diversity of thought brings us multiple checks and balances: monolithic thought prevents it, and it is the reason various authorities fight for political and ideological unity: if all think alike, no one is thinking at all, and it suits a propagandist's purposes perfectly.

To question emotional narratives takes courage: are those mass graves really of one group? Did soldiers really murder newborns? Did they cannibalize civilians? Is that country holding weapons of mass destruction?

What is really happening? How do we know? What are the motives for inciting us? What is there to gain? What is the reality? What is the truth?

Propaganda preys on our competitive tendencies: it is a greed scam and a pity scam that banks on us believing in pecking orders and narratives where we must prove our superiority or perish. We want to be seen as heroes at all costs, and we must justify our actions by turning others into villains with no redeeming qualities.

That is the cruel nature of propaganda. It confines us and restricts us – but the shackles begin in our own minds. Facts liberate us as we consider alternative interpretations of the reality we see in front of us. Are both sides unequal in morals? Perhaps, or perhaps they are the same, both recruiting primed and groomed citizens on to their chess and go boards to be used and discarded as pawns.

Propaganda is its own religion where the flock must *believe:* break the spell, and propaganda is no longer effective. It becomes a farce. To bring peace, we must reject the notion that war is a viable option. We will be cornered by such a bold declaration, but tear down the wall, and there is no corner for a predator to use to marginalize those who see a better solution that negotiates without exploitation or manipulation.

Propaganda thrives of manipulative lies. It starves with logic and facts. We refuse to fall for narratives or the confirmation bias as we challenge authorities and look for alternate explanations. We make alliances with out-groups as we begin to move away from finding comfort within in-groups. We look to create, not destroy. We challenge our own fears and prejudices. We abandon our scripts and masks, daring to find information and not justifications for blood shed.

When we see that propaganda is deception, we begin to look away from its misdirection, and start looking for the feints and ruses used to force our own thoughts. We see the *36 Stratagems* as they become the visible trick wires used to create false illusions.

We stop propaganda by asking questions, such as how and why. We see ourselves as no better or worse than anyone else. The more we question our own assumptions, the easier we can spot the assumptions of propagandists.

We reject narrative as the burden of proof determines our reactions. A weeping teenaged girl's testimony means very little without corroborating evidence, or at least verifying that she has not been trained by a public relations firm and her family foot the bill. We allow ourselves to be impudent, and downright *rude,* but once we have the facts, we can make decisions that are based in rationality and pragmatism, not fear, hatred, greed, or jealousy.

It all comes down to looking for *facts,* not narratives. We look at the motives and gains of those who demand war and even question those who proclaim to provide peace through treacherous means. We look for facts as we reject attempts at manipulation or the threat of demonizing us when we question the lies being sold as facts.

We learn to look inward to our own evolutionary drives as we see how they can be exploited. We learn not to take sophistry as logic, and we learn to question ourselves as we question authority. It is a process of liberation of thought and emotion, learning to roam out in the wild as we shun the cages predators use to lure us into their games. Propaganda is the bait, and once we learn to recognize all its forms, we can begin to inoculate ourselves from its exploitative methods as we then bring the antidote to those who cannot spot the same ruses.

When we make the decision not to move in the direction the winds of war push us, we begin to become the foundation for rational and constructive ideology, as we build more peaceful futures where we build alliances and with them, opportunities for healthier lives that thrive in balance, independence, cooperation, and diversity.

References

ABC News. (1992). "Sarajevo Under Siege." July 10, transcript.

Ackerman, S. and Judis, J.B. (2003). "The First Casualty: The selling of the Iraq war." *The New Republic,* June 30, newrepublic.com.

Agbiboa, D., and Maiangwa, B. (2014). Why Boko Haram kidnaps women and young girls in north-eastern Nigeria. *Conflict Trends,* 2014(3), 51-56.

Airey, J. L. (2012). The Politics of Rape: Sexual Atrocity, Propaganda Wars, and the Restoration Stage. University of Delaware.

Alabaster, O. (2016). "Birth rate soars in Jordan refugee camp as husbands discourage wives from using contraception: While Syrian men are keen to repopulate their homeland, women are facing difficult decisions on family planning." *The Independent,* March 13, independent.co.uk.

Albright, M. (1998). The fight against terrorism. *Vital Speeches of the Day,* 64(23), 707.

Alcock, J., and Rubenstein, D. R. (2019). *Animal behavior.* Sunderland: Sinauer.

Alexander, A. (2016). Cruel intentions: Female jihadists in America. Washington, DC: Program on Extremism, The George Washington University.

Ali, M. (2015). ISIS and propaganda: How ISIS exploits women. Reuters Institute for the Study of Journalism, 10-11.

Alinksy, S. (1971). *Rules for Radicals: A Practical Primer for Realistic Radicals.* New York: Random House.

Allen, E. (2016). "Chilcot Inquiry: What is it and what did the Iraq War report say?" *The Telegraph,* July 16, telegraph.co.uk.

All Things Considered. (2004). "Analysis: Former Justice Department lawyer says the agency is smearing her name because of issues she raised about the prosecution of John Walker Lindh." *NPR,* January 20, broadcast.

Almosawa, S. and Hubbard, B. (2018). "Saudi Coalition Bombs a Bus in Yemen, Killing Dozens of Children." *New York Times,* August 10, nytimes.com.

Alter, J. (2003). "In bed with the Pentagon." *Newsweek,* March 10, 141 (10), 45.

Alterman, E. (1992). Operation Pundit Storm. *World Policy Journal,* 9(4), 599-616.

Al-Yasin, Y. and Dashti, A.A. (2008). "Foreign Countries and U.S. Public Relations Firms: The Case of Three Persian Gulf States." *Journal of Promotion Management,* Vol. 14, No. 3-4, pages 355-374.

American Psychiatric Association. (2013). *Diagnostic and statistical manual of mental disorders (5th ed.).* Arlington, VA: Author.

Anderson, K. G., Kaplan, H., and Lancaster, J. B. (2007). Confidence of paternity, divorce, and investment in children by Albuquerque men. Evolution and Human Behavior, 28(1), 1-10.

Anonymous (undated). "Orphan Law and Legal Definition." *US Legal,* uslegal.com.

Anonymous. (1972). *"Rep. Ichord Requests Laws Covering Jane Fonda Trip." New York Times,* August 15, nytimes.com.

Anonymous. (1990). Editorial, *San Antonio Express,* December 23, mysanantonio.com.

Anonymous. (1996). "Only a bullet' could separate them: Bodies of Sarajevo's 'Romeo and Juliet' come home." CNN, April 10, cnn.com.

Anonymous. (2001). "Bush: 'You Are Either With Us, Or With the Terrorists'." *Voice of America,* October 27, voanews.com.

Anonymous. (2003). "Marine shot in head four times and lives." *The Times,* March 27, thetimes.co.uk.

Anonymous. (2004). "New 'bin Laden' tape aired on eve of 9/11." *CBC,* September 11, cbc.ca.

Anonymous. (2003). "Marine's 'miracle escape' rumbled." *BBC,* April 15, bbc.co.uk.

Anonymous. (2004). "Editor of British newspaper fired after fake abuse photos published." *Newshour (PBS),* May 14, pbs.org.

Anonymous. (2004). "The Times and Iraq." *New York Times,* May 26, nytimes.com.

Anonymous. (2005). "CBS ousts four over Bush Guard story". *CNN,* January 11, cnn.com.

Anonymous. (2006). "Al-Qaeda's terror game for kids." *Sydney Daily Telegraph,* September 21, suntelgraph.com.

Anonymous. (2011). "Canada faces risky world." *Toronto Star,* January 11, thestar.com.

Anonymous. (2014). Taliban kill vaccination workers. *Lateline,* November 27, abc.net.au.

Anonymous. (2015). "PKP's gaffe: If Canada is divisible, why isn't Quebec?" *The Globe and Mail,* November 26, globeandmail.com.

Anonymous. (2016). "The dangerous chill of Chilcot". *The Economist,* July 9, economist.com.

Anonymous. (2017). "Fury as Channel 4 News brand 'Serb fascists'." *Britić,* January 27, ebritic.com.

Anonymous. (2018). "Syria war: The online activists pushing conspiracy theories." BBC, April 19, bbc.co.uk.

Anonymous. (2018). Video Games as War Propaganda. (2018). Reason, 50(1), 5.

Anonymous. (2019). "Serbian singers rule Croatian YouTube." *Total Croatia News,* April 11, total-croatia-news.com.

Apicella, C. L., and Marlowe, F. W. (2004). Perceived mate fidelity and paternal resemblance predict men's investment in children. *Evolution and Human behavior, 25*(6), 371-378.

Archer, J. (2004). Sex differences in aggression in real-world settings: A meta-analytic review. *Review of general Psychology, 8*(4), 291-322.

Arraf, J. (2017). "Children Orphaned By Battle Against ISIS Remain Vulnerable Amid Conflict." *All Things Considered (NPR),* October 24, npr.org.

Asch, S.E. (1956). "Studies of independence and conformity: 1. A minority of one against a unanimous majority". *Psychological Monographs,* Vol. 70, No. 9, Whole No. 416.

Ashford, M. W., and Huet-Vaughn, Y. (1997). The impact of war on women. War and public health, 186-197.

Ashton-James, C. E., Kushlev, K., and Dunn, E. W. (2013). Parents reap what they sow: Child-centrism and parental well-being. *Social Psychological and Personality Science, 4*(6), 635-642.

Associated Press. (1990). "Kuwaiti refugees tell tales of murder, rape by Iraqis." November 28, journaltimes.com.

Associated Press. (1990). "STANDOFF IN THE GULF; Amnesty Report Says Iraqis Tortured and Killed Hundreds." *New York Times,* December 20, nytimes.com.

Associated Press. (2002). "Pentagon debates propaganda role U.S. wants to woo anti-Americans Considers using military for job." *Toronto Star,* December 17, A27.

Associated Press. (2019). "Russian court grants early release to would-be Islamic State bride." *Japan Times,* April 17, japantimes.co.jp.

Baddeley, A. (1992). Working memory. *Science, 255*(5044), 556-559.

Baker, P. (2018). *"Bush Made Willie Horton an Issue in 1988, and the Racial Scars Are Still Fresh." New York Times,* December 3, nytimes.com.

Baliki, G. (2014). "Measuring conflict incidence in Syria." *SIPRI Yearbook 2014,* sirpriyearbook.org.

Barlovac, B. (2010). "Key Parties in Serbia." *Balkan Insight,* September 27, balkaninsight.com.

Barsamian, D. and Chomsky, N. (2001). *Propaganda and the Public Mind: Conversations with Noam Chomsky.* London: Pluto Press.

Bates, S. (1987). *If No News, Send Rumors: Anecdotes of American Journalism.* New York: St. Martin's Press.

Baum, M.A. (2011). *Soft News Goes to War: Public Opinion and American Foreign Policy in the New Media Age.* Princeton: Princeton University Press.

Bennhold, K. (2015). *"For Woman Dead in French Police Raid, Unlikely Path to Terror." New York Times,* November 20, nytimes.com.

Berger, P.L. and Luckman, T. (1966). The Social Construction of Reality: A treatise in the Sociology of Knowledge. New York: Anchor Books.

Berthiaume, L. (2019). "15 Canadian Forces members died by suicide last year, despite new prevention strategy." *Global News,* January 19, globalnews.ca.

Bilski, A. (1990). "Witness to Terror: Refugees accuse Iraq of savagery." *Maclean's,* October 22, page 22.

Bingham, J.B. and Bingham, A.M. (1970). *Violence and Democracy.* New York: Excalibur Books.

Blake, M. (2013). "A bizarre and telling book excerpt from *60 Minutes'* bogus Benghazi source". *Mother Jones,* November 8, motherjones.com.

Bilewicz, M., and Vollhardt, J. R. (2012). Evil transformations: Social-psychological processes underlying genocide and mass killing. *Social psychology of social problems: The intergroup context, 280.*

Black, C. (2018). *Personal Interview,* November 6.

Blatchford, C. (2019). "Journalists may be hacks, but they are better than hackers." *National Post,* April 12, nationalpost.com.

Bloom, H. (1997). *The Lucifer Principle: A scientific expedition into the forces of history.* New York: Atlantic Monthly Press.

Bloom, M., and Matfess, H. (2016). Women as symbols and swords in Boko Haram's terror. *Prism, 6*(1), 104-121.

Bolinger, D. (2014). *Language-the loaded weapon: The use and abuse of language today.* Routledge.

Bonner, R. and Van Natta Jr., D. (2004). "Regional Terrorist Groups Pose Growing Threat, Experts Warn." *New York Times,* February 8, nytimes.com.

Bowen, J. (1992). Report from Sarajevo: War orphans. *BBC World Service,* August 4, bbc.co.uk.

Breuninger, K. (2019). "US charges WikiLeaks co-founder Julian Assange with conspiracy to commit computer hacking." *CNBC,* April 11, cnbc.com.

Burn, S. M., and Oskamp, S. (1989). Ingroup biases and the US-Soviet conflict. *Journal of Social Issues, 45*(2), 73-89.

Buss, D., and Schmitt, D. (2011). Evolutionary Psychology and Feminism. Sex Roles, 64(9–10), 768.

Buunk, B. P., Angleitner, A., Oubaid, V., and Buss, D. M. (1996). Sex differences in jealousy in evolutionary and cultural perspective: Tests from the Netherlands, Germany, and the United States. *Psychological Science, 7*(6), 359-363.

Byrne, D., and Nelson, D. (1965). The effect of topic importance and attitude similarity-dissimilarity on attraction in a multistranger design. *Psychonomic Science, 3*(1-12), 449-450.

Cameron, O. G., Lee, M. A., Curtis, G. C., and McCann, D. S. (1987). Endocrine and physiological changes during "spontaneous" panic attacks. *Psychoneuroendocrinology, 12*(5), 321-331.

Campbell, M. (2001). "Taliban forced orphanage girls to become married sex slaves." *Sunday Times,* December 23, 2001, thetimes.co.uk.

Carlsen, A., Salam, M, Cain Miller, C., Lu, D., Ngu, A., Patel, J.K., and Wichter, Z. (2018). "#MeToo brought down 201 powerful men. Nearly half of their their replacements are women." *New York Times,* October 23, nytimes.com.

Carter, B. (2013). "CBS News Defends Its '60 Minutes' Benghazi Report". *New York Times,* November 6, nytimes.com.

Carter, B. (2013). "CBS Report on Benghazi Is Called Into Question". *New York Times,* November 8, nytimes.com.

Carver Jr, G. A. (1965). The Faceless Viet Cong. *Foreign Aff., 44,* 347.

Castells, M. (1975). Immigrant workers and class struggles in advanced capitalism: The Western European experience. *Politics and Society, 5*(1), 33-66.

Chalk, F. and Jonassohn, K. (1990). *The History and Sociology of Genocide: Analyses and Case Studies.* New Haven: Yale University Press.

Chandrashekhar, V. (2019). "India's Media Is War-Crazy." *Foreign Policy,* March 1, foreignpolicy.com.

Chapelle, D. (1962). *What's a Woman Doing Here?: A Reporter's Report on Herself.* New York: Morrow.

Chesler, P. (2011). "France is brave and right to ban the burka." *Fox News Channel,* April 18, foxnews.com.

Chen, D., Katdare, A., and Lucas, N. (2006). Chemosignals of fear enhance cognitive performance in humans. *Chemical senses, 31*(5), 415-423.

Chilcot, J. (2016). *The Report of the Iraq Inquiry: Report of a Committee of Privy Counsellors.* London: Government Publications, His Majesty's Stationery Office.

Chinlund, C. (2004). "A series of errors on lewd images." *Boston Globe,* May 4, bostonglobe.com.

Chomsky, N. (1987). *Power and Ideology.* Montreal: Black Rose Books.

Chomsky, N. (1987). Propaganda, American-style. *Propaganda Review Winter, 1988.*

Chomsky, N. (1989). *Necessary Illusions: Thought Control in Democratic Societies.* Boston: South End Press.

Christian, S.E. (1990). "Witnesses tell of Iraqi atrocities in Kuwait Congress: Members are shaken by what they hear, Kuwait's ambassador warns that 'time is running out.'" *Los Angeles Times,* October 11, page 6.

Christenson S. (2005). Truth and Trust: In Iraq War Coverage, They've Become Casualties. Nieman Reports. 59(2):6.

Cialdini, R.B. (2009). *Influence: The psychology of persuasion.* New York: Harper.

Cockburn, A. (2004). NYT: "Maybe We Did Screw Up a Little." *Nation,* 278(23), 13.

Collingham, L. (2011). *The Taste of War: World War Two and the Battle for Food.* London: Allen Lane.

Collins. R. (1982). *Sociological Insight: An introduction to non-obvious sociology.* New York: Oxford University Press.

Collins, D. (2003). "CNN planted Dem debate question." CBS News, November 11, cbsnews.com.

Colombo, M. (2013). Discourse and politics of migration in Italy: The production and reproduction of ethnic dominance and exclusion. *Journal of Language and Politics, 12*(2), 157-179.

Cummins, E. (2018). "We created a frankenhouse of the most common phobias."

Popular Science, October 31, popsci.com.

Conners, J. L. (1998). "Hussein as Enemy: The Persian Gulf War in Political Cartoons." *Harvard International Journal of Press/Politics, 3*(3), 96–114.

Copp, T. (2017). "Recruiting a generation with no memory of Sept. 11." *Military Times,* September 11, militarytimes.com.

Corcione, D. (2018). The Shitty Media Men List is the# MeToo of toxic newsrooms: a failure to protect non-male freelance workers. Feminist Media Studies, 18(3), 500-502.

Cotton, J. L. (1981). A review of research on Schachter's theory of emotion and the misattribution of arousal. *European Journal of Social Psychology, 11*(4), 365-397.

Cutlip, S. M. (1966). "The Nation's First Public Relations Firm." *Journalism Quarterly, 43*(2), 269–280.

D'Aliesio, R. (2017). "Veterans face much higher suicide rate than civilians." *Globe and Mail,* December 7, globeandmail.com.

Daly, M. and Wilson, M. (1983). *Sex, Evolution, and Behavior.* Belmont: Wadsworth Publishing Company.

Danso, R., and McDonald, D. A. (2001). Writing xenophobia: Immigration and the print media in post-apartheid South Africa. *Africa today,* 115-137.

Darwin, C. (2004). *On the origin of species, 1859.* London: Routledge.

Davidson, A. (2013). "'60 Minutes' and the Benghazi Trap". *New Yorker,* November 12, newyorker.com.

Davidov, D. et al. (1990). *Jasenovac.* Belgrade: The Holy Synod of Bishops of the Serbian Orthodox Church.

Davies, N. (2006). *Europe at War 1939-1945: No easy victory.* London: Macmillan.

Davis, A. (2000). "Public relations, business news and the reproduction of corporate elite power". *Journalism,* Vol. 1 (3), pages 282-304.

Davis, A. (2003). *Public Relations Democracy: Public Relations, Politics, and the Mass Media in Britain.* Manchester: Manchester University Press.

Davis, A. (2007). "Investigating Journalist Influences on Political Issue Agendas at Westminster". *Political Communication,* May 18, 24:2, pages 181-199.

Davis, A. (2017). Personal Interview.

Davis, N. (2008). *Flat Earth News: An Award-winning Reporter Exposes Falsehood, Distortion and Propaganda in the Global Media.* London: Chatto and Windus.

Dearden, L. (2017). "How Isis attracts women and girls from Europe with false offer of 'empowerment'." *The Independent,* August 5, independent.co.uk.

De Becker, G. (1998). *The Gift of Fear: And Other Survival Signals That Protect Us from Violence.* New York: Dell.

de Courcy, J. (1993). "Manipulating the Media". *Intelligence Digest,* February 4, 1-2.

de Courcy, J. (1993). "Briefings". *Intelligence Digest,* February 4, 2.

della Cava, M., and Knox, N. (2003). "British opinion appears to shift in favor of war." *USA Today,* March 24, usatoday.com.

Deichmann, T. (1997). "The Picture that Fooled the World." *Living Marxism,* February, 97.

Del-Teso-Craviotto, M. (2009). Racism and xenophobia in immigrants' discourse: The case of Argentines in Spain. *Discourse and Society, 20*(5), 571-592.

Deluga, R. J. (2001). American presidential Machiavellianism: Implications for charismatic leadership and rated performance. *The Leadership Quarterly, 12*(3), 339-363.

DePaolo, J. (2019). "Glenn Greenwald Rages Against Assange Arrest, Battles Journos: 'It's the Criminalization of Journalism'." *Mediaite,* April 11, mediaite.com.

Desbarats, P. (1997). *Somalia Cover-up: A Commissioner's Journal.* Toronto: McClelland and Stewart.

De Vries, G. J. (1990). Sex differences in neurotransmitter systems. *Journal of neuroendocrinology, 2*(1), 1-13.

DeYoung, K. (2013). "60 Minutes' broadcast helps propel new round of back-and-forth on Benghazi". *Washington Post,* October 31, washington post.com.

Dittmer, L. (2006). Pitfalls of charisma. *The China Journal,* (55), 119-128.

Doornbos, H. (2014). "Saudi photographer tells me: This is not Syria, its not a grave and the boys parents are not dead." January 17, harolddoornbos. com.

Douglas, J., Burgess, A. W., Burgess, A. G., and Ressler, R. K. (2013). *Crime classification manual: A standard system for investigating and classifying violent crime.* John Wiley & Sons.

Douglas, M. (1975). *Implicit Meanings: Essays in Anthropology.* London: Routledge.

Duodo, C. (2006). The "hoax-masters" who have seized America. (cover story). New African, (449), 50.

Durkin, E. (2018). "'A national emergency': suicide rate spikes among young US veterans." *The Guardian,* September 26, theguardian.com.

Dutta, S., Kanungo, R. N., and Freibergs, V. (1972). Retention of affective material: effects of intensity of affect on retrieval. *Journal of personality and social psychology, 23*(1), 64.

Dutton, D. G., and Aron, A. P. (1974). Some evidence for heightened sexual attraction under conditions of high anxiety. *Journal of personality and social psychology, 30*(4), 510.

Eaglesham, B. (2004). A GROWING FEAR: Will Agriculture Be the Next Terrorist Target? Odyssey, 13(3), page 38.

Ehntholt, K. A., and Yule, W. (2006). Practitioner Review: Assessment and treatment of refugee children and adolescents who have experienced war-related trauma. *Journal of Child Psychology and Psychiatry*, *47*(12), 1197-1210.

Eichelberger, E. (2013). "Violence on the home front." *Mother Jones,* April 25, motherjones.com.

Eisen, M. L., Quas, J. A., and Goodman, G. S. (Eds.). (2001). *Memory and suggestibility in the forensic interview*. Routledge.

Ekman, P. and Friesen, W.V. (2003). *Unmasking the Face: A guide to recognizing emotions from facial expressions*. Los Altos: Malor.

Ellul, J. (1965). *Propaganda: The Formation of Men's Attitudes*. New York: Vintage.

Epatko, L. (2017). "These Soviet propaganda posters once evoked heroism, pride and anxiety." *PBS News Hour*, July 11, pbs.org.

Ernsberger Jr., R. (2019). The Fog Factory. MHQ: Quarterly Journal of Military History, 31(3), 66.

Fager. J. Ortiz, A. (2013). *Memo regarding 60 Minutes' Benghazi report.*

Farrow, R. (2017). "From aggressive overtures to sexual assault: Harvey Weinstein's accusers tell their stories." *New Yorker,* October 10, newyorker.com.

Festinger, L. (1957). *A theory of cognitive dissonance* (Vol. 2). Redwood City: Stanford university press.

Fisher, L. (2019). "Bethnal Green trio fled Britain with help from Isis's best female recruiter." *The Times,* February 13, thetimes.co.uk.

Fiske, S. and Taylor, S. (1984). *Social Cognition.* Boston: Addison-Wesley Publishers.

Fluckiger, K. M. (2006). Xenophobia, Media Stereotyping, and Their Role in Global Insecurity. *Policy Briefs on the Transcultural Aspects of Security and Stability*, 21.

Fontenrose, J. (1968). "The hero as athlete." *California Studies in Classical Antiquity*, 1, 73-104.

Fox, R. (1986). "Contras only interested in self-aggrandizement." *Toronto Star*, July 9.

Frankel, G. (1990). "Amnesty International accuses Iraq of atrocities in Kuwait." *Washington Post,* December 19, washingtonpost.com.

Ferenc, L. (2004). "Truth is war's first casualty, journalist says." *Toronto Star*, April 1, A15.

Folkenflik, D. (2004). "USA Today documents reporter's fabrications." *Baltimore Sun,* March 20, baltimoresun.com.

Fox, E., Griggs, L., and Mouchlianitis, E. (2007). The detection of fear-relevant stimuli: are guns noticed as quickly as snakes? *Emotion, 7*(4), 691–696.

Frenda, S. J., Knowles, E. D., Saletan, W., and Loftus, E. F. (2013). False memories of fabricated political events. *Journal of Experimental Social Psychology*, *49*(2), 280-286.

Friedman, H. S., Riggio, R. E., and Casella, D. F. (1988). Nonverbal skill, personal charisma, and initial attraction. Personality and Social Psychology Bulletin, 14(1), 203-211.

Furedi, F. (2019). "The crusade against masculinity." *Spiked,* January 21, spiked-online.com.

Fyne, R. (1997). *The Hollywood Propaganda of World War II.* Lanham: Scarecrow Press.

Gangarosa, E., Galazka, A., Wolfe, C.R., Phillips, O.L., and Gangarosa, R. (1998). Impact of anti-vaccine movements on pertussis control: the untold story. *The Lancet, 351,* 356-361.

Garofolo, J. (2015). *Dickey Chapelle under fire: photographs by the first American female war correspondent killed in action.* Madison: Wisconsin Historical Society Press.

Garry, M., and Gerrie, M. P. (2005). When photographs create false memories. Current Directions in Psychological Science, 14(6), 321-325.

Garry, M., and Wade, K. A. (2005). Actually, a picture is worth less than 45 words: Narratives produce more false memories than photographs do. *Psychonomic bulletin and review, 12*(2), 359-366.

Gentzkow, M. and Shapiro, J. M. (2008). "Competition and Truth in the Market for News". *Journal of Economic Perspectives,* Spring, Vol. 22, No. 2, pages 133-154.

Gessen, M. (2018). "The Undoing of Bill Clinton and Boris Yeltsin's Friendship, and How It Changed Both of Their Countries." *New Yorker,* September 5, newyorker.com.

Gettleman, J. (2017). "Rohingya Recount Atrocities: 'They Threw My Baby Into a Fire'." *New York Times,* October 11, nytimes.com.

Goffman, E. (1963). *Stigma: Notes on the management of spoiled identity.* New York: Penguin.

Goldenberg, Suzanne. (1998). "Fear of the Muslim bomb." *The Guardian,* June 3, page 19.

Gorham, M. S. (1996). From Charisma to Cant: Models of Public Speaking in Early Soviet Russia. *Canadian Slavonic Papers,* 38(3-4), 331-355.

Gorman, G. (2019). "Internet trolls are not who I thought – they're even scarier." ABC, February 1, abc.au.net.

Gorman, G. (2019). *Troll Hunting: Inside the world of online hate and its human fallout.* Victoria: Hardie Grant Publishing.

Gove, M. (2001). "Bombing Saddam is not enough to oust him." *The Times,* February 20, thetimes.co.uk.

Gozzi, M., Zamboni, G., Krueger, F., and Grafman, J. (2010). Interest in politics modulates neural activity in the amygdala and ventral striatum. *Human Brain Mapping, 31*(11), 1763-1771.

Gradus, J. L. (2018). Posttraumatic stress disorder and death from suicide. *Current psychiatry reports, 20*(11), 98.

Graf, P., and Komatsu, S. I. (1994). Process dissociation procedure: Handle with caution! *European Journal of Cognitive Psychology,* 6(2), 113-129.

Graham, B. (2003). "He lived as a king but was snared like a sewer rat - CAPTURE OF A TYRANT." *Sydney Daily Telegraph,* December 17, dailytelegraph.com.au.

Grant, L. K. (2007). The veils of Clio: Dimensions of a behavioral narratology. *The Analysis of verbal behavior, 23*(1), 57-69.

Greene, R. (1998). *The 48 Laws of Power.* New York: Penguin.

Greene, R. (2006). *The 33 Strategies of War.* New York: Penguin.

Grice, H.P. (1989). *Studies in the Way of Words.* Cambridge: Harvard University Press.

Griffin, R., Recht, H., and Green, J. (2018). "#MeToo one year later." *Bloomberg,* October 5, Bloomberg.com.

Gross, M. R. (2005). The evolution of parental care. *The Quarterly review of biology, 80*(1), 37-45.

Gullace, N. F. (2002). The Rape of Belgium and Wartime Imagination. In *"The Blood of Our Sons"* (pp. 17-33). Palgrave Macmillan, New York.

Hagan, J. (2014). "Benghazi and the Bombshell". *New York,* May 4, nymag.com.

Halimi, S., and Rimbert, P. (2019). "Le plus gros bobard de la fin du XXe siècle." *Le Monde Diplomatique,* April, page 5.

Hamilton, D. L. (2015). *Cognitive processes in stereotyping and intergroup behavior.* Psychology Press.

Handley, P. (2019). "WikiLeaks set 21st century model for cyber-leak journalism." *Agence France-Presse,* April 12, news.yahoo.com.

Haney, C., Banks, W. C., and Zimbardo, P. G. (1973). Interpersonal dynamics in a simulated prison. International Journal of Criminology and Penology, 1, 69-97.

Hanley, C.J. (2003). "AP Enterprise: Former Iraqi detainees tell of riots, punishment in the sun, good Americans and pitiless ones." *Associated Press,* November 1, ap.org.

Haq, L. (2018). "Bruce MacKinnon's Viral Kavanaugh Cartoon Depicts Graphic Assault Of Lady Justice." *Huffington Post,* September 30, huffington post.com.

Harricharan, S., Nicholson, A. A., Densmore, M., Théberge, J., McKinnon, M. C., Neufeld, R. W., and Lanius, R. A. (2017). Sensory overload and imbalance: Resting-state vestibular connectivity in PTSD and its dissociative subtype. *Neuropsychologia, 106*, 169-178.

Harris, G. T., Hilton, N. Z., Rice, M. E., and Eke, A. W. (2007). Children killed by genetic parents versus stepparents. Evolution and Human Behavior, 28(2), 85-95.

Hassan K. (2014). "The Role of Private Electronic Media in Radicalising Pakistan." *Round Table,* 103(1):65.

Hebb, D.O. (1949). *The Organization of Behavior.* New York: Wiley and Sons.

Herman, E.S. and Chomsky, N. (1988). *Manufacturing Consent: The Political Economy of the Mass Media.* New York: Pantheon Books.

Hersey, J. (1946). *Hiroshima.* New York: Knopf.

Hersh, S.M. (2004). "Torture at Abu Ghraib." *New Yorker,* April 30, newyorker. com.

Hiebert, R. E. (2003). Public relations and propaganda in framing the Iraq war: A preliminary review. Public Relations Review, 29(3), 243-255.

Hill, C.R. (2013). "When to talk to monsters." *New York Times,* May 15, nytimes.com.

Hinkle, L. E. (1961). The physiological state of the interrogation subject as it affects brain function. *The manipulation of human behavior.*

Hinckley, D. (2013). "Lara Logan, producer ordered to take leave in aftermath of '60 Minutes' Benghazi reporting scandal". *New York Daily News,* November 26, nydailynews.com.

Hinton, D., Chau, H., Nguyen, L., Nguyen, M., Pham, T., Quinn, S., and Tran, M. (2001). Panic disorder among Vietnamese refugees attending a psychiatric clinic: Prevalence and subtypes. *General Hospital Psychiatry, 23*(6), 337-344.

Holiday, R. (2012). *Trust Me, I'm Lying: Confessions of a media manipulator.* New York: Portfolio/Penguin.

Holt, R.R. and Silverstein, B. (1989). "On the Psychology of Enemy Images: Introduction and Overview". *Journal of Social Issues,* Vol. 45, No. 2, pages 1-11.

Holt, R. R. (1989). College students' definitions and images of enemies. *Journal of Social Issues, 45*(2), 33-50.

Holsti, O.R., Hopmann, P.T., and Sullivan, J.D. (1973). *Unity and Disintegration in International Alliances: Comparative Studies.* New York: John Wiley and Sons.

Hopper, T. (2014). "Everyone line up: Canada's tradition of orderly queuing 'foreign and strange' to many newcomers." *National Post,* July 25, nationalpost.com.

Howard, R. E. (1986). *Human Rights in Commonwealth South Africa.* Towota: Roman and Littlefield.

Howell, T. (1997). "The Witers' War Board: US Domestic Propaganda in World War II". *The Historian,* Summer, Vol. 59, No. 4, pages 795-813.

Hugdahl, K., and Öhman, A. (1977). Effects of instruction on acquisition and extinction of electrodermal responses to fear-relevant stimuli. *Journal of Experimental Psychology: Human Learning and Memory, 3*(5), 608.

Hugdahl, K., and Johnsen, B. H. (1989). Preparedness and electrodermal fear-conditioning: Ontogenetic vs phylogenetic explanations. *Behaviour Research and Therapy, 27*(3), 269-278.

Hull. M. (2000). "The Allies achieved victory in North Africa by choking off the German supply lines." *World War II,* 15(3), 62.

Hunt, C.L., and Walker, L. (1974). *Ethnic Dynamics: Patterns of intergroup relations in various societies.* Homewood: The Dorsey Press.

Hunter, S. T., Shortland, N. D., Crayne, M. P., and Ligon, G. S. (2017). Recruitment and selection in violent extremist organizations: Exploring what industrial and organizational psychology might contribute. American Psychologist, 72(3), 242.

Hussein, S. (2019). *From Victims to Suspects: Muslim Women Since 9/11.* New Haven: Yale University Press.

Hussey, K. and Robbins, L. (2018). "A Ban on Parents in the School Lunchroom? Everyone Seems to Have an Opinion." *New York Times,* December 6, nytimes.com.

Iacoboni, M., Freedom, J., and Kaplan, J. (2007). "This is your brain on politics." *New York Times,* November 11, nytimes.com.

Jackson, S. (1978). The social context of rape: Sexual scripts and motivation. Women's Studies International Quarterly, 1(1), 27-38.

Jacoby, L. L. (1991). A process dissociation framework: Separating automatic from intentional uses of memory. *Journal of memory and language, 30*(5), 513-541.

Jiménez, M., Aguilar, R., and Alvero-Cruz, J. R. (2012). Effects of victory and defeat on testosterone and cortisol response to competition: evidence for same response patterns in men and women. *Psychoneuroendocrinology, 37*(9), 1577-1581.

Johnstone, V. (2002). *Fools' Crusade: Yugoslavia, NATO and Western Delusions.* New York: Monthly Review Press.

Jones, C. (1981). "In the land of the Khmer Rouge." *New York Times magazine,* December 20, nytimes.com.

Jowett, G.S. (1987). "Propaganda and Communication: The Re-emergence of a Research Tradition". *Journal of Communication,* Winter, pages 97-114.

Jowett, G.S. and O'Donnell, V. (2012). *Propaganda and Persuasion,* 5th edition. Los Angeles: Sage.

Kabir, N. A. (2019). Can Islamophobia in the Media Serve Islamic State Propaganda? The Australian Case, 2014–2015. In *Islamophobia and Radicalization* (pp. 97-116). Palgrave Macmillan, Cham.

Kampfer, J. (2003). "The Truth about Jessica". *The Guardian,* May 15, the guardian.co.uk.

Kassebaum, N. J., Barber, R. M., Bhutta, Z. A., Dandona, L., Gething, P. W., Hay, S. I., ... and Lopez, A. D. (2016). Global, regional, and national levels of maternal mortality, 1990–2015: a systematic analysis for the Global Burden of Disease Study 2015. *The Lancet, 388*(10053), 1775-1812.

Kay, J. (2014). "If Quebec separates, we keep Montreal." *National Post,* March 5, nationalpost.com.

Keen, S. (1988). *Faces of the Enemy: Reflections of the hostile imagination.* San Francisco: Harper and Row.

Keigher, S. M. (1997). America's most cruel xenophobia. *Health and Social Work, 22*(3), 232.

Kelley, J. (2001). "Explosion, then arms and legs rain down." *USA Today,* August 9, usatoday.com.

Kellman B. (2008). "Bioviolence: A Growing Threat." *Futurist.* 42(3):25-30.

Kieh Jr, G. K. (1990). Propaganda and United States foreign policy: The case of Panama. *Political Communication, 7*(2), 61-72.

Kincaid, V. (2017). Islamic state, child soldiers, and intolerable Islamic schools. *Quadrant, 61*(1/2), 56.

Kitty, A. (1998). "Objectivity in Journalism: Should we be skeptical?" *Skeptic,*

Vol. 6, No. 1, pages 54-61.

Kitty, A. (2002). "Dangerous Liaisons." *Elle Canada,* November, 90-92.

Kitty, A. (2003). "Appeals to Authority in Journalism". *Critical Review,* 15, 3-4, pages 347-357.

Kitty, A. (2005). *Don't Believe It!: How lies become news.* New York: The Disinformation Company.

Kitty, A. (2005). *OutFoxed: Rupert Murdoch's war on journalism.* New York: The Disinformation Company.

Kitty, A. (2018). *When Journalism was a Thing.* London: Zer0 Books.

Koch, W. (2012). "Study: U.S. power grid vulnerable to terrorist attack." *USA Today,* November 14, usatoday.com.

Kopelson, G. (2018). "Trump's Baltic summit echoes Reagan's first proclamation for Eastern European freedom 50 years ago." *Washington Examiner,* April 2, washingtonexaminer.com.

Koppes, C. R., and Black, G. D. (1977). What to show the world: The Office of War Information and Hollywood, 1942-1945. *The Journal of American History,* 64(1), 87-105.

Koppes, C. R., and Black, G. D. (1990). *Hollywood goes to war: How politics, profits and propaganda shaped World War II movies.* Univ of California Press.

Kracauer, S. (1943). The Conquest of Europe on the Screen-The Nazi Newsreel, 1939-40. *Social research, 10*(1), 337.

Kralev, N. (2012). "America's Other Army: Interviews with diplomats in the line of fire – an exclusive excerpt from the new book America's Other Army: The U.S. Foreign Service and 21st Century Diplomacy." *Foreign Policy,* September 13, foreignpolicy.com.

Kuehn, B. M. (2009). Soldier suicide rates continue to rise. *Jama, 301*(11), 1111-1113.

Kumar, D. (2004). War propaganda and the (ab) uses of women: Media constructions of the Jessica Lynch story. *Feminist media studies,* 4(3), 297-313.

Kurtz, H. (1998). *Spin Cycle: Inside the Clinton Propaganda Machine.* New York: The Free Press.

Lakoff, R. (1975). *Language and Woman's Place.* New York: Harper and Row.

Landy, D., Guay, B., and Marghetis, T. (2017). Bias and ignorance in demographic perception. *Psychonomic bulletin and review,* 1-13.

Lane, J. M., Millar, J. D., and Neff, J. M. (1971). Smallpox and smallpox vaccination policy. Annual review of medicine, 22(1), 251-272.

Laney, C., and Loftus, E. F. (2005). Traumatic memories are not necessarily accurate memories. *The Canadian Journal of Psychiatry, 50*(13), 823-828.

Lembcke, J. (2010). *Hanoi Jane: War, Sex, and Fantasies of Betrayal.* Univ of Massachusetts Press.

Leff, L. (2006). *Buried by the Times: The Holocaust and America's Most Important Newspaper.* Cambridge: Cambridge University Press.

Lees, M. (1990). *The Rape of Serbia: The British role in Tito's grab for power 1943-1944.* San Diego: Harcourt Brace Jovanovich.

Lenz, R. (2005). "U.S. soldiers struggle with a faceless enemy on second tour of Iraq." *Canadian Press,* December 14.

Leung, J. T., and Shek, D. T. (2011). "All I can do for my child"–development of the Chinese Parental Sacrifice for Child's Education Scale. *International journal on disability and human development, 10*(3), 201-208.

Levitin, D. J. (2014). *The organized mind: Thinking straight in the age of information overload.* Penguin.

Lieberman, A. V. (2017). Terrorism, the internet, and propaganda: A deadly combination. J. Nat'l Sec. L. and Pol'y, 9, 95.

Liesen, L. (2011). Feminists, Fear Not Evolutionary Theory, but Remain Very Cautious of Evolutionary Psychology. Sex Roles, 64(9–10), 748.

Lifton, R.J. and Markusenm E. (1990). *The Genocidal Mentality: Nazi Holocaust and Nuclear Threat.* New York: Basic Books.

Lindenmuth, J. E., Breu, C. S., and Malooley, J. A. (1980). Sensory overload. *AJN The American Journal of Nursing, 80*(08), 1456-1458.

Lindsay, D.S. and Johnson, M.K. (1989). "The eyewitness suggestibility effect and memory for source." Memory and Cognition, 17: 349

Lipowski, Z. J. (1975). Sensory and information inputs overload: Behavioral effects. *Comprehensive Psychiatry, 16*(3), 199-221.

Loftus, E.F. and Palmer, J.C. (1974). "Reconstruction of auto-mobile destruction: An example of the interaction between language and memory". *Journal of Verbal Learning and Verbal Behavior*, 13, 585-589.

Loftus, E. F., and Pickrell, J. E. (1995). "The formation of false memories." *Psychiatric annals, 25*(12), 720-725.

Loftus, E. F. (1997). Creating false memories. *Scientific American, 277*(3), 70-75.

Loyn, D. (1992). Report from Bosnia. *BBC World Service,* September 6, bbc.co.uk.

Lucas, R. (2013). *Axis Sally: The American Voice of Nazi Germany.* Havertown: CaseMate.

Machiavelli, N. (1966). *The Prince.* New York: Bantam Books.

MacArthur, J.R. (1992). "Remember Nayirah, Witness for Kuwait?" *New York Times,* January 6, page A17.

MacArthur, J.R. (1993). *Second Front: Censorship and Propaganda in the Gulf War.* New York: Hill and Wang.

Macksoud, M. S. (1992). Assessing war trauma in children: A case study of Lebanese children. *Journal of refugee studies, 5*(1), 1-15.

Maloy, S. (2014). "CBS' Lara Logan problem: Why is disgraced reporter returning to '60 Minutes'?" *Salon,* June 5, salon.com.

Manhattan, A. (1986). *The Vatican's Holocaust: The sensational account of the most horrifying religious massacre of the 20th century.* Springfield: Ozark Books.

Manheim, K. (1936). *Ideology and Utopia.* San Diego: Harvest.

Mann, L. (1974). Counting the crowd: Effects of editorial policy on estimates. *Journalism Quarterly, 51*(2), 278-285.

Markham, J.M. (1982). "Writer admits he fabricated an article in Times magazine." *New York Times,* February 22, nytimes.com.

Marshall, J. P. (2013). "The Mess of Information and the Order of Doubt". *Global Media Journal, Australian Edition,* Vol. 7, Issue 1.

Martin, D. (1990). *The Web of Disinformation: Churchill's Yugoslav blunder.* San Diego: Harcourt Brace Jovanovich.

Maslow, A. H. (1943). A theory of human motivation. *Psychological Review, 50*(4), 370.

Masters, C. (2010). "We heard the blast that killed our boys – Australians at war." *Sydney Daily Telegraph,* June 10, 2.

Matsumoto, D. (1996). *Culture and Psychology.* Pacific Grove: Brooks/Cole.

Maurer, D. (1985). Infants' Perception of Facedness. In T. M. Field and N. A. Fox (Eds.), *Social Perception in Infants* (pp. 73-100). Norwood, NJ: Ablex Publishing Corporation.

Maurer, D., and Maurer, C. (1988). *The world of the newborn.* New York: Basic Books.

Mcallister, J.F.O. (1992). "Must it go on?" *Time,* August 17, time.com.

McLaughlin, A. (2018). "WAR! Wikileaks Rages Against *The Guardian*: We'll Bet a Million Dollars and 'Editor's Head' Manafort Meeting Never Happened." *Mediaite,* November 27, mediaite.com.

McLuhan, M. (1964). *Understanding Media: The Extensions of Man.* New York: Pantheon.

McNally, R. J. (1987). Preparedness and phobias: a review. *Psychological bulletin, 101*(2), 283.

Mehta, P. H., Jones, A. C., and Josephs, R. A. (2008). "The social endocrinology of dominance: basal testosterone predicts cortisol changes and behavior following victory and defeat." *Journal of personality and social psychology, 94*(6), 1078.

Merckelbach, H., Arntz, A., and de Jong, P. (1991). Conditioning experiences in spider phobics. *Behaviour Research and Therapy, 29*(4), 333-335.

Meredith, E. T. (2010). *Jane Fonda: Repercussions of Her 1972 Visit to North Vietnam.* AIR COMMAND AND STAFF COLLEGE, AIR UNIVERSITY MAXWELL AIR FORCE BASE United States.

Merlino, J. (1993). *Les Verites Ne Sont Pas Toutes Bonnes A Dire.* Paris: Albin Michel Paris.

Merskin, D. (2004). "The construction of Arabs as enemies: Post-September 11 discourse of George W. Bush." *Mass Communication and Society, 7*(2), 157-175.

Melton, H.K. and Wallace, R. (2009). *The Official CIA Manual of Trickery and Deception.* New York: William Morrow.

Meteran, H., Vindbjerg, E., Uldall, S. W., Glenthøj, B., Carlsson, J., and Oranje, B. (2019). Startle habituation, sensory, and sensorimotor gating in trauma-affected refugees with posttraumatic stress disorder. *Psychological medicine, 49*(4), 581-589.

Milgram, S. (1974). *Obedience to Authority; An Experimental View.* New York: Harper and Row.

Miller, J. (2003). "THREATS AND RESPONSES: INTELLIGENCE; Defectors Bolster U.S. Case Against Iraq, Officials Say." *New York Times,* January 24, nytimes.com.

Miller, J. (2003). *"THREATS AND RESPONSES: DISARMING SADDAM HUSSEIN; TEAMS OF EXPERTS TO HUNT IRAQ ARMS." New York Times,* March 19, nytimes.com.

Miller, J. (2003). "A NATION AT WAR: IN THE FIELD, WEAPONS SEARCH; Hunt Finds Hint of How Iraqis Fill Power Void." New York Times, April 10, nytimes.com.

Miller, J. (2003) "A Battle of Words Over War Intelligence." New York Times, November 22, nytimes.com.

Milton, D. and Dodwell, B. (2018). "Jihadi Brides? Examining a Female Guesthouse Registry from the Islamic State's Caliphate." *CTC Sentinel,* Vol 11 (5), ctc.usma.edu.

Missal, M.J. and Coe Lanpher, L. (2005). Report of the Independent Review Panel Dick Thornburgh and Louis D. Boccardi on the September 8, 2004 60 Minutes Wednesday Segment 'For the Record' Concerning President Bush's Texas Air National Guard Service. January 5.

Mlodinow, L. (2008). *The Drunkard's Walk: How randomness rules our lives.* New York: Vintage.

Modlin J. and Brown K. (2002). Enemy Agent. *People,* 58(22):105.

Mohan, B. (1997). "The Professional Quest for Truth: Paradigm, Paradox, and Praxis". *International Journal of Contemporary Sociology,* Vol. 34, No. 1, pages 51-63.

Montoya, R. M., Horton, R. S., and Kirchner, J. (2008). Is actual similarity necessary for attraction? A meta-analysis of actual and perceived similarity. *Journal of Social and Personal Relationships, 25*(6), 889-922.

Moody, J. (2004). *Memo from April 4,* Fox News Channel.

Moody, J. (2004). *Memo from April 6,* Fox News Channel.

Moore, H. F. (2010). Immigration in Denmark and Norway: Protecting Culture or Protecting Rights?. *Scandinavian studies, 82*(3), 355.

Morewedge, C. K., Gilbert, D. T., and Wilson, T. D. (2005). The least likely of times: How remembering the past biases forecasts of the future. *Psychological Science, 16*(8), 626-630.

Morford, M. (2003). "The Big Lie Of Jessica Lynch". *Common Dreams,* September 5, commondreams.org.

Morris, D. (1977). *Manwatching: A field guide to human behavior.* New York: Abrams.

Morrison, B. (2004). "Ex-USA TODAY reporter faked major stories." *USA Today,* March 19, usatoday.com.

Moyer, K. E. (1976). *The psychobiology of aggression*. New York: Harper and Row.

Moynihan, C., and Meier, B. (2019). "Clare Bronfman Pleads Guilty in Nxivm 'Sex Cult' Case, Leaving Leader to Stand Trial Alone." *New York Times*, April 19, nytimes.com.

Nacos, B. L. (2000). Accomplice or witness? The Media's Role in Terrorism. *Current History*, 99(636), 174.

Naidoo, M. (2014). "80% of victims know their killers." *IOL*, November 16, iol.ca.za.

Naifeh, J. A., Ursano, R. J., Kessler, R. C., Gonzalez, O. I., Fullerton, C. S., Mash, H. B. H., ... and Kao, T. C. (2019). Suicide attempts among activated soldiers in the US Army reserve components. *BMC psychiatry*, 19(1), 31.

Neander, J., and Marlin, R. (2010). "Media and Propaganda: The Northcliffe Press and the Corpse Factory Story of World War I." *Global Media Journal*, 3(2), 67.

Nelson, J. (1989). *The Sultan's of Sleaze: Public Relations and the Media.* Toronto: Between the Lines.

O'Donnell, D. (2018). "CNN's Long History of Planting Town Hall Questions." *News Talk 1130 WISN,* February 22, newstalk1130.iheart.com.

Ogun, M. N. (2012). Terrorist Use of Internet: Possible Suggestions to Prevent the Usage for Terrorist Purposes. *Journal of Applied Security Research*, 7(2), 203.

Öhman, A., and Mineka, S. (2001). Fears, phobias, and preparedness: toward an evolved module of fear and fear learning. *Psychological Review*, 108(3), 483.

Öhman, A. (2009). Of snakes and faces: An evolutionary perspective on the psychology of fear. *Scandinavian journal of psychology*, 50(6), 543-552.

Olsen, M.E. (ed.) (1970). *Power in Societies.* London: Macmillan.

Paquette, V., Lévesque, J., Mensour, B., Leroux, J. M., Beaudoin, G., Bourgouin, P., and Beauregard, M. (2003). "Change the mind and you change the brain": effects of cognitive-behavioral therapy on the neural correlates of spider phobia. *Neuroimage*, 18(2), 401-409.

Paris, E. (1961). *Genocide in Satellite Croatia, 1941-1945: A record of racial and religious persecutions and massacres.* Chicago: The American Institute for Balkan Affairs.

Parker-Pope, T. (1997). "Hill and Knowlton Will Polish Its Own Controversial Image". *Wall Street Journal,* February 19, wsj.com.

Patil, A. (2018). "'You can't ... look away': Halifax cartoonist on his image of Lady Justice with a hand over her mouth." *CBC News,* September 30, cbc.ca.

Pearl, D. and Block, R. (1999). "War in Kosovo was cruel, bitter, savage: genocide it wasn't – tales of mass atrocity arose and were passed along, often with little proof – no corpses in the mine shaft." *Wall Street Journal,* December 3.

Pearson, B. (2008). Insurgency via Internet. *Variety*, 409(9), 8.

Perreaux, L. (2006). "Seeking a Faceless Enemy; Canadian Troops in Afghanistan's Rugged South Patrol for Taliban." *The Kitchener-Waterloo Record*, March 31, A1.

Peterson, D. and Herman, E.S. (2010). "The Oliver Kamm School of Falsification: Imperial Truth-Enforcement, British Branch." *Monthly Review,* January 22, mronline.com.

Pico-Alfonso, M. A., Garcia-Linares, M. I., Celda-Navarro, N., Herbert, J., and Martinez, M. (2004). Changes in cortisol and dehydroepiandrosterone in women victims of physical and psychological intimate partner violence. *Biological psychiatry*, 56(4), 233-240.

Picotte, M. S., and Campbell, C. G. (2010). The Effects of War on Iraq's Food System: A Historical Analysis and Proposal for Future Direction. *Journal of Hunger and Environmental Nutrition*, 5(2), 234-253.

Pilger, J. (2005). We Need to Be Told. *New Statesman*, 134(4762), 30.

Platek, S. M., Raines, D. M., Gallup Jr, G. G., Mohamed, F. B., Thomson, J. W., Myers, T. E., ... and Arigo, D. R. (2004). Reactions to children's faces: Males are more affected by resemblance than females are, and so are their brains. *Evolution and Human behavior*, 25(6), 394-405.

Plotkin, H. (2002). The Imagined World Made Real: Towards a natural science of culture. London: Penguin.

Poniewozik, J. (2013). "CBS's Benghazi Apology: Sorry Is the Hardest, or At Least Slowest, Word". *Time,* November 15, time.com.

Qui, L. (2017). *"Fingerprints of Russian Disinformation: From AIDS to Fake News." New York Times,* December 12, nytimes.com.

Rachman, S. (1977). The conditioning theory of fear acquisition: A critical examination. *Behaviour research and therapy*, 15(5), 375-387.

Rampton, S., and Stauber, J. C. (2003). *Weapons of Mass Deception: The Uses of Propaganda in Bush's War on Iraq*. New York: TarcherPerigee.

Randal, J. (2007). "Edward Behr: Foreign correspondent with a flair for reporting conflicts." The Guardian, August 6, theguardian.com.

Richter, N., Over, H., and Dunham, Y. (2016). The effects of minimal group membership on young preschoolers' social preferences, estimates of similarity, and behavioral attribution. *Collabra*.

Roberts, C. (1992). Broadcast report, *ABC News,* August 5, abcnews.go.com.

Roberts, P.W. (2004). *A War Against Truth: An Intimate Account of the Invasion of Iraq.* Vancouver: Raincoast Books.

Rogan, T. (2015). "Jihadi John's Destruction Would Be a Great Blow to ISIS's Morale." *National Review,* November 13, nationalreview.com.

Roholl, M. (2012). Preparing for Victory. The US Office of War Information Overseas Branch's illustrated magazines in the Netherlands and the foundations for the American Century, 1944-1945. European journal of American studies, 7(7-2).

Romero, D., and Lavanga, C. (2018). "Multiple deaths reported after panicked stampede at Italian nightclub: Among the dead were five minors, police said." *NBC News,* December 8, nbcnews.com.

Rohrer, J., Mugo, M., Joubert-Ceci, B., Khan, S., Eisenstein, Z., Nusair, I., ... and Carty, L. (2013). *Feminism and war: Confronting US imperialism.* Zed Books Ltd..

Roskill, M. (1989). *The Interpretations of Pictures.* Amherst: The University of Massachusetts Press.

Roth, W. T. (2005). Physiological markers for anxiety: panic disorder and phobias. *International Journal of Psychophysiology, 58*(2-3), 190-198.

Sack, W. H., Him, C., and Dickason, D. A. N. (1999). Twelve-year follow-up study of Khmer youths who suffered massive war trauma as children. *Journal of the American Academy of Child and Adolescent Psychiatry, 38*(9), 1173-1179.

Salzman, J. (2003). *Making the News: A guide for activists and nonprofits.* Boulder: Westview.

Sande, G.N, Goethals, G.R., Ferrari, L., and Worth, L.T. (1989). "Value-Guided Attributions: Maintaining the Moral Self-Image and the Diabolical Enemy-Image". *Journal of Social Issues,* Vol. 45, No. 2, pages 903-913.

Sargent, C., and Cordell, D. (2003). Polygamy, disrupted reproduction, and the state: Malian migrants in Paris, France. *Social science and medicine, 56*(9), 1961-1972.

Saunders, A. (2004). *Jane: A Pin-Up at War.* Barnsley: Pen and Sword.

Saunders, Stephen. (2009). *Jane's Fighting Ships 2009-2010.* Surrey: HIS Jane's.

Sawer, P. (2015). Who is Jihadi John? How did Mohammed Emwazi, a quiet football fan, become the symbol of Isil. *The Telegraph.*

Sawyer, C. B., and Márquez, J. (2017). Senseless violence against Central American unaccompanied minors: historical background and call for help. *The Journal of psychology, 151*(1), 69-75.

Schachter, S. and Singer, J.E. (1962). "Cognitive, social and physiological determinants of emotional state." *Psychological Review,* 69,379-399.

Schachter, S. and Wheeler, L. (1962). "Epinephrine, chlorpromazin and amusement." *Journal of Abnormal and Social Psychology,* 65,121-128.

Scheflin, A.W. and Opton, E.M. (1978). *The Mind Manipulators.* New York: Paddington Press.

Schindehette, S. (1991). "As Bombs Fell on Baghdad, Three CNN Reporters Scored a Coup". *People,* February 4, people.com.

Schmit, J. and Morrison, B. (2004). "Unbelievable timing, incredible account." *USA Today,* March 19, usatoday.com.

Schmidt, S. and Loeb, V. (2003). "She was fighting to the death." *Washington Post,* April 3, washingtonpost.com.

Schmitt, E. (2018). "ISIS May Be Waning, but Global Threats of Terrorism Continue to Spread." *New York Times,* July 6, nytimes.com.

Schultheiss, O. C., Wirth, M. M., Torges, C. M., Pang, J. S., Villacorta, M. A., and Welsh, K. M. (2005). Effects of implicit power motivation on men's and women's implicit learning and testosterone changes after social victory or defeat. *Journal of personality and social psychology, 88*(1), 174.

Searcy, D. (2016). "Victims of Boko Haram, and now shunned by their communities." *New York Times,* May 18, nytimes.com.

Seligman, M. E. (1971). Phobias and preparedness. *Behavior therapy, 2*(3), 307-320.

Seligman, M. E. P. (1972). "Learned helplessness." *Annual Review of Medicine.* 23 (1), 407–412.

Semple, K. (2006). "Baghdad erupts in mob violence by gun and bomb." *New York Times,* July 10, nytimes.com.

Sengupta, K. (2015). "Hasna Aitboulahcen: Tracking the final moments of Europe's first female suicide bomber: Europe's first woman suicide bomber may yet provide further clues which could lead to the capture or killing of more of her jihadist comrades." *The Independent,* November 19, independent.co.uk.

Sereny, G. (2011). *Into that darkness: An examination of conscience.* New York: Vintage.

Shabad, R. (2013). "Publisher halts books by Benghazi witness". *The Hill,* November 8, thehill.com.

Shaw, J., and Porter, S. (2015). Constructing rich false memories of committing crime. *Psychological science, 26*(3), 291-301.

Shields, W. M., and Shields, L. M. (1983). Forcible rape: An evolutionary perspective. Ethology and sociobiology, 4(3), 115-136.

Shumer, S. M. (1979). Machiavelli Republican Politics and its Corruption. *Political Theory, 7*(1), 5–34, doi.org.

Sideris, T. (2003). War, gender and culture: Mozambican women refugees. *Social science and medicine,* 56(4), 713-724.

Sifakis, C. (1993). *Hoaxes and Scams: A compendium of deceptions, ruses, and swindles.* London: Michael O'Mara Books.

Silverstein, B. (1987). "Toward a Science of Propaganda". *Political Psychology,* Vol. 8, No. 1, March, pages 49-59.

Silverstein, B. (1989). "Enemy Images: The Psychology of US Attitudes and Cognitions Regarding the Soviet Union". *American Psychologist,* 44, June, pages 903-913.

Silverstein, B. and Flamenbaum, C. (1989). "Biases in the Perception and Cognition of the Actions of Enemies". *Journal of Social Issues,* Vol. 45, No. 2, pages 51-72.

Simkus, K., VanTil, L., and Pedlar, D. (2017). Veteran Suicide Mortality Study: 1976 to 2012. *Charlottetown, PE: Veterans Affairs Canada.*

Singer, P. W. (2003). Fighting child soldiers. *Military Review, 83*(3), 26.

"60 Minutes". (1992). "Nayirah". CBS Television, September 6, broadcast.

"60 Minutes". (2013). "Benghazi". CBS Television, October 27, broadcast.

Sjoberg, L. (2018). Jihadi brides and female volunteers: Reading the Islamic State's war to see gender and agency in conflict dynamics. *Conflict management and peace science, 35*(3), 296-311.

Speckhard, A. (2015). The hypnotic power of ISIS imagery in recruiting Western youth. *International Center for the Study of Violent Extremism: Research Report.*

Sprecher, S. (1989). The importance to males and females of physical attractiveness, earning potential, and expressiveness in initial attraction. Sex Roles, 21(9-10), 591-607.

Sproule, J.M. (1998). "Propaganda, History, and Orthodoxy". *SSMC Review and Criticism*, December, 457-459.

Stark, R., Wolf, O. T., Tabbert, K., Kagerer, S., Zimmermann, M., Kirsch, P., ... and Vaitl, D. (2006). "Influence of the stress hormone cortisol on fear conditioning in humans: evidence for sex differences in the response of the prefrontal cortex." *Neuroimage, 32*(3), 1290-1298.

Starr, M. (2019). "Dozens of Neolithic 'Human Sacrifice' Victims Have Been Found in England." *Science Alert*, April 16, sciencelaert.com.

Staub, E. (2006). The cultural and psychological origins of war with notes on prevention. In Stout, C.E. and Fitzduff, M. (eds.). *The psychology of war*. Praeger.

Stauber, J. and Rampton, S. (1995). *Toxic Sludge Is Good For You: Lies, Damn Lies and the Public Relations Industry.* Monroe: Common Courage Press.

Stein, J. (2013). "Lara Logan's Mystery Man". *Newsweek,* November 22, newsweek.com.

Stone, A. (2002). "US: Iraq nuclear threat is growing." *USA Today,* September 9, usatoday.com.

Stone, G. R. (2004). *Perilous Times: Free speech in wartime.* New York: Norton.

Strangert, E., and Gustafson, J. (2008). What makes a good speaker? subject ratings, acoustic measurements and perceptual evaluations. In *Ninth Annual Conference of the International Speech Communication Association.*

Straziuso, J. (2013). "US family in South Sudan refugee camp desperate to save their 10 adopted orphans from war." *Canadian Press,* December 31.

Summers, D. (1992). Editorial cartoon. *Orlando Sentinel, USA Today,* August 7, usatoday.com.

Sun-tzu, and Griffith, S.B. (1964). *The art of war.* Oxford: Clarendon Press.

Tamarkin, B. (1993). *Rumor Has it: A curio of lies, hoaxes, and hearsay.* New York: Prentice Hall.

Tate, C. (2013). Addressing Conceptual Confusions About Evolutionary Theorizing: How and Why Evolutionary Psychology and Feminism Do Not Oppose Each Other. Sex Roles, 69(9–10), 491.

Taub, B. (2018). Iraq's Post-ISIS Campaign of Revenge. *The New Yorker*, December 17, newyorker.com.

Temrin, H., Buchmayer, S., and Enquist, M. (2000). Step–parents and infanticide: new data contradict evolutionary predictions. Proceedings of the Royal Society of London. Series B: Biological Sciences, 267(1446), 943-945.

Thiessen, M.A. (2016). "Thanks to Obama, the terrorist cancer is growing." Washington Post, May 23, washingtonpost.com.

Thompson, R. R., Jones, N. M., Holman, E. A., and Silver, R. C. (2019). Media exposure to mass violence events can fuel a cycle of distress. Science Advances, 5(4), eaav3502.

Tilly, C. (2006). Why: What happens when people give reasons... and why. Princeton: Princeton University Press.

Tompkins, A. (2017). Aim for the heart: Write, shoot, report and produce for TV and multimedia. Cq Press.

Traywick, C.A. (2014). "Whoops: Tragic Photo of Orphaned 'Syrian' Boy is Fake." Foreign Policy, January 17, foreignpolicy.com.

Turshen, M. (2001). The political economy of rape: An analysis of systematic rape and sexual abuse of women during armed conflict in Africa, 55-68.

Turvey, B. E. (2013). Forensic victimology: Examining violent crime victims in investigative and legal contexts. Academic Press.

Turvey, B.E., Savino, J.O., and Coronado Mares, A. (eds.) (2018). False Allegations: Investigative and forensic reports of crime. London: Academic Press.

Usborne, S. (2015)."Jihadi John: Why do we give notorious criminals nicknames?" The Independent, March 3, independent.co.uk.

Van Veen, V., Krug, M. K., Schooler, J. W., and Carter, C. S. (2009). Neural activity predicts attitude change in cognitive dissonance. Nature neuroscience, 12(11), 1469.

Van Vugt, M. (2009). Sex differences in intergroup competition, aggression, and warfare. Annals of the New York Academy of Sciences, 1167(1), 124-134.

Veissière, S. P. L. (2018). "Toxic Masculinity" in the age of# MeToo: ritual, morality and gender archetypes across cultures. Society and Business Review, 13(3), 274-286.

Verkaik, R. (2016). Jihadi John: The making of a terrorist. Oneworld publications.

Volkan, V. D. (1985). The need to have enemies and allies: A developmental approach. Political Psychology, 219-247.

Vrij, A., and Granhag, P. A. (2012). Eliciting cues to deception and truth: What matters are the questions asked. Journal of Applied Research in Memory and Cognition, 1(2), 110-117.

Wade, K. A., Garry, M., Read, J. D., and Lindsay, D. S. (2002). A picture is worth a thousand lies: Using false photographs to create false childhood memories. Psychonomic bulletin and review, 9(3), 597-603.

Waldron, K. (1992). "Spin doctors of war". New Statesman and Society, July, 5 (215), pages 12-13.

The United States Attorney's Office for the Eastern District of Virginia. (2019). "WikiLeaks Founder Charged in Computer Hacking Conspiracy." Press

Release, April 11, justice.gov.

Weinbaum, M. G. (1980). Food and political stability in the middle east. *Studies in Comparative International Development, 15*(2), 3-26.

Weiner, J. (2013). "Dylan Davies, the Benghazi security officer who tricked *60 Minutes,* forgot to also trick the FBI". *Vanity Fair,* November 8, vanityfair.com.

Weinberg, S. (1996). *The Reporter's Handbook: an investigator's guide to documents and techniques.* New York: St. Martin's Press.

Weiner, R. (1992). *Live from Baghdad: Making journalism history behind the lines.* New York: St. Martins Griffin.

Wemple, E. (2014). "The disaster of the '60 Minutes' Benghazi story." *The Washington Post,* May 5, washingtonpost.com.

Wertheimer, L. (2001). Profile: US briefs NATO defense ministers on status of US military and economic plans after terrorist attacks. *All Things Considered* (NPR) September 26, npr.org.

White, S. H. (1999). What is a hero? An exploratory study of students' conceptions of heroes. *Journal of Moral Education, 28*(1), 81-95.

Willsher, K. (2015). "Hasna Aitboulahcen: police examine remains of 'cowgirl' turned suicide bomber: Details emerge of the life of Hasna Aitboulahcen, the woman who blew herself up during a police shootout after the Paris terrorist attacks." *The Guardian,* November 20, theguardian.com.

Woodard, J. (1996). "Four million Romeos and Juliets."*Alberta Report / Newsmagazine, 23* (14), 37.

Woodward, B. (1996). *The Choice.* New York: Simon and Schuster.

Woodward, B. (2008). *The War Within: A Secret White House History 2006-2008.* New York: Simon and Schuster.

Wouters, R., and Van Camp, K. (2017). Less than expected? How media cover demonstration turnout. *The international journal of press/politics, 22*(4), 450-470.

Yanagizawa-Drott, D. (2014). Propaganda and conflict: Evidence from the Rwandan genocide. *The Quarterly Journal of Economics, 129*(4), 1947-1994.

Youseef, M. (2009). "Bin Laden threatens Americans in new tape as Obama begins Mideast tour." *Canadian Press,* June 3, thecanadianpress.com.

Youssef, N.A. (2013). "Questions about '60 Minutes' Benghazi story go beyond Dylan Davies interview; CBS conducting 'journalistic review'". *McClatchy DC,* November 13, mcclatchydc.com.

Zajonc, R. B., Heingartner, A., and Herman, E. M. (1969). Social enhancement and impairment of performance in the cockroach. *Journal of Personality and Social Psychology, 13*(2), 83.

Zajonc, R. B. (2001). Mere exposure: A gateway to the subliminal. *Current directions in psychological science, 10*(6), 224-228.

Zaromb, F. M., Liu, J. H., Páez, D., Hanke, K., Putnam, A. L., and Roediger III, H. L. (2018). We Made History: Citizens of 35 Countries Overestimate

Their Nation's Role in World History. *Journal of Applied Research in Memory and Cognition, 7*(4), 521-528.

Zenn, J., and Pearson, E. (2014). Women, Gender and the evolving tactics of Boko Haram. *Journal of terrorism research.*

Zimbardo, P. G. (1975). On transforming experimental research into advocacy for social change. *Applying social psychology: Implications for research, practice, and training*, 33-66.

Zonis, M. (1990). "The Bad Man of Baghdad." *The New York Times,* November 11, nytimes.com.

Zorawski, M., Blanding, N. Q., Kuhn, C. M., and LaBar, K. S. (2006). Effects of stress and sex on acquisition and consolidation of human fear conditioning. *Learning and memory, 13*(4), 441-450.

Zur, O. (1991). "The Love of Hating: The Psychology of Enmity." *History of European Ideas,* Vol. 13, No. 4, pages 345-369.

Index

www.ingramcontent.com/pod-product-compliance
Lightning Source LLC
LaVergne TN
LVHW010829130825
818496LV00011B/79